COMPANION
to Visible Learning
for Literacy

Teaching Literacy
IN THE
VISIBLE LEARNING CLASSROOM

DOUGLAS FISHER
NANCY FREY
JOHN HATTIE

https://resources.corwin.com/VL-LiteracyK-5

CL CORWIN
LITERACY

A SAGE Publishing Company

FOR INFORMATION:

Corwin

A SAGE Company

2455 Teller Road

Thousand Oaks, California 91320

(800) 233-9936

www.corwin.com

SAGE Publications Ltd.

1 Oliver's Yard

55 City Road

London, EC1Y 1SP

United Kingdom

SAGE Publications India Pvt. Ltd.

B 1/I 1 Mohan Cooperative Industrial Area

Mathura Road, New Delhi 110 044

India

SAGE Publications Asia-Pacific Pte. Ltd.

3 Church Street

#10-04 Samsung Hub

Singapore 049483

Senior Program Director and Publisher:
    Lisa Luedeke

Editorial Development Manager: Julie Nemer

Editorial Assistant: Nicole Shade

Production Editor: Melanie Birdsall

Copy Editor: Cate Huisman

Typesetter: Hurix Systems Pvt. Ltd.

Proofreader: Sally Jaskold

Indexer: Karen Wiley

Cover Designer: Rose Storey

Marketing Manager: Rebecca Eaton

Printed in the United States of America

Library of Congress Cataloging-in-Publication Data

Names: Fisher, Douglas | Frey, Nancy | Hattie, John.

Title: Teaching literacy in the visible learning classroom, grades K-5 / Douglas Fisher, Nancy Frey, John Hattie.

Description: Thousand Oaks, California : Corwin, 2017. | Includes bibliographical references and index.

Identifiers: LCCN 2016044623 | ISBN 9781506332369 (pbk. : alk. paper)

Subjects: LCSH: Language arts (Elementary) | Student-centered learning.

Classification: LCC LB1576 .F446 2017 | DDC 372.6—dc23 LC record available at https://lccn.loc.gov/2016044623

This book is printed on acid-free paper.

Certified Chain of Custody
Promoting Sustainable Forestry
www.sfiprogram.org
SFI-01268

SFI label applies to text stock

18 19 20 21 10 9 8 7 6 5 4

CONTENTS

Chapter 3. Direct Instruction   50

Chapter 4. Teacher-Led Dialogic Instruction   74

Chapter 5. Student-Led Dialogic Learning   103

Chapter 6. Independent Learning   133

Chapter 7. Tools to Use in Determining Literacy Impact   166

Visit the companion website at
https://resources.corwin.com/VL-LiteracyK-5
to access videos and downloadable resources.

LIST OF VIDEOS

Note From the Publisher: The authors have provided video and web content throughout the book that is available to you through QR codes. To read a QR code, you must have a smartphone or tablet with a camera. We recommend that you download a QR code reader app that is made specifically for your phone or tablet brand.

Videos may also be accessed at
https://resources.corwin.com/VL-LiteracyK-5

ACKNOWLEDGMENTS

The ideas in this book come from a wide range of researchers and teachers who have individually and collectively helped us refine our ideas. We appreciate all of the interactions we have had with literacy experts around the world. Having said that, we are indebted to two individuals who have significantly shaped the ideas in this book.

Kristen Anderson is Senior Director of Global Consulting and Evaluation at Corwin. Her knowledge of visible learning and her commitment to high-quality learning for all students is unparalleled. She has been a significant source of support for our work and has greatly assisted us with the translation of complex ideas into classroom practice. Kristen also facilitated the original meeting between the three of us, which resulted in the Visible Literacy Learning initiative. Beyond her knowledge of visible learning, Kristen is a brilliant presenter of ideas and a deeply caring colleague. We are honored to have her leading our work. She is a wonderful friend and advocate.

Lisa Luedeke is another ally and friend from Corwin who has shaped the Visible Literacy Learning experience, from books to professional learning. As an author herself, she understands the power of the written word. She is an amazing thinker who has an uncanny ability to forecast teachers' needs. She has skillfully guided our thinking, asking critical questions that have allowed us to integrate our ideas. She is passionate and committed and we are lucky to have her support for our efforts.

PUBLISHER'S ACKNOWLEDGMENTS

Corwin gratefully acknowledges the contributions of the following reviewers:

Leslie Blauman
Author, Consultant, and Teacher
Cherry Creek School District
Centennial, CO

Michael Rafferty
Director of Teaching and Learning
Region 14 Schools
Woodbury, CT

Melanie Spence
K–12 Curriculum Coordinator, Assistant Principal
Sloan-Hendrix School District
Imboden, AR

INTRODUCTION

We'd like to introduce you to the Danish philosopher Søren Kierkegaard, the father of existentialist philosophy, who wrote

> If we wish to succeed in helping someone to reach a particular goal we must first find out where he is now and start from there.
>
> If we cannot do this, we merely delude ourselves into believing that we can help others.
>
> Before we can help someone, we must know more than he does, but most of all, we must understand what he understands. If we cannot do that, our knowing more will not help.
>
> If we nonetheless wish to show how much we know, it is only because we are vain and arrogant, and our true goal is to be admired, not to help others.
>
> All genuine helpfulness starts with humility before those we wish to help, so we must understand that helping is not a wish to dominate but a wish to serve.
>
> If we cannot do this, neither can we help anyone.

Kierkegaard died in 1855, long before *visible learning* or *visible learning for literacy* had been conceptualized, much less published. But look at how much he understood about the work teachers do every day. Here are some key takeaways from this philosopher:

- There has to be a goal.

- Attaining that goal requires an understanding of current performance.

- Teachers have to know stuff, but even more important, they need to understand what their learners understand.

- If we just try to show how much we know (rather than impact students' learning), we do so to be admired rather than to be helpful.

- Teachers should strive to serve others and ensure that goals (learning) are reached.

These are among the key points from *Visible Learning* (Hattie, 2009) that guide the lessons described in this book. There is no one way to teach, or one best instructional strategy that works in all situations for all students, but there is compelling evidence for tools that can help students reach their goals. In this book, we use the effect size information that John Hattie has collected over many years to make the case that some things are more likely to be effective than others. Before delving into the lessons themselves, we will explore the ways in which John created his effect size lists.

For readers unfamiliar with visible learning, we'd like to take a moment to explain. The visible learning database is composed of over 1,200 meta-analyses of studies that include over 70,000 studies and 500 million students. That's big data when it comes to education. In fact, some have argued that it is the largest educational research database amassed to date. To make sense of so much data, John focused his work on meta-analyses.

A meta-analysis is a statistical tool for combining findings from different studies with the goal of identifying patterns that can inform practice. In other words, it is a study of studies. The tool that is used to aggregate the information is an effect size, represented by *d*. An effect size is the magnitude, or size, of a given effect. Effect size information helps readers understand the impact in more measurable terms.

For example, imagine a study in which teaching students to write while having them chew gum resulted in statistically significant findings ($p < 0.01$ for example). People might buy stock in gum companies, and a new teaching fad would be born. But then suppose, upon deeper reading, you learn that the gum-chewing students had a 0.03 month gain in reading ability over the control group, an effect size pretty close to zero. You realize that the sample size was so large that the results were statistically significant, but they might not be very powerful. Would you still buy gum and have students chew away? Probably not (and we made this example up, anyway).

Understanding the effect size lets us know how powerful a given influence is in changing achievement, the impact for the effort, in other words. Some things are hard to implement and have very little impact. Other things are easy to implement and still have limited impact. We search for things that have a greater impact, some of which will be harder to implement and some of which will be easier to implement. When you're deciding what to implement to impact students' learning, wouldn't you like to know what the effect size is? Then you can decide if it's worth the effort. John was able to demonstrate that influences, strategies, actions, and so on with an effect size greater than 0.40 allow students to learn at an appropriate rate, meaning at least a year of growth for a year in school. Before this level was established, teachers and researchers did not have a way to determine an acceptable threshold, and thus weak practices, often supported by studies with statistically significant findings, continued.

Let's take two real examples. First, let's consider class size. There have been many efforts to reduce the number of students enrolled in a given teacher's classroom. To help people understand effect sizes, John created a barometer so that information could be presented visually. The barometer for class size can be found in Figure i.1. As you can see, the effect size is 0.21, well below the zone of desired effects of 0.40. This is based on three meta-analyses that included 96 studies and a total population of 550,339 students. We don't know a teacher who wouldn't enjoy smaller class sizes, but the evidence suggests that there are more effective ways to increase learning.

Second, let's consider increasing classroom discourse (synonymous with classroom discussion or dialogue). Students would be invited to talk with their peers in collaborative groups, working to solve complex and rich tasks. The students would not be ability grouped, but rather grouped by the teacher intentionally to ensure that there is academic diversity in each group as well as language support and varying degrees of interest and motivation. As can be seen in the barometer in Figure i.2, the effect size of classroom discourse is 0.82, well above our threshold, and likely to result in two years of learning gains for a year of schooling.

Figure i.1   The Barometer for the Influence of Class Size

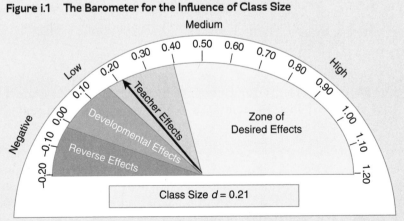

Source: Adapted from Hattie, J. (2012). *Visible learning for teachers: Maximizing impact on learning*. New York: Routledge.

Figure i.2   The Barometer for the Influence of Classroom Discussion

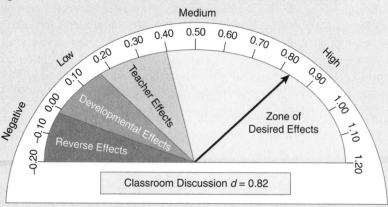

Source: Adapted from Hattie, J. (2012). *Visible learning for teachers: Maximizing impact on learning.* New York: Routledge.

STRUCTURE OF THIS BOOK

As authors, we assume you have read *Visible Learning* and *Visible Learning for Literacy* (Fisher, Frey, & Hattie, 2016), so we are not going to recount all of the information contained in those resources. Rather, we're going to focus on aspects of literacy instruction that are critical for students' success. In each chapter, we profile three teachers who have worked to make learning visible for their students and have impacted learning in significant ways. In addition, all chapters have a few things in common:

- Effect size information when available

- Specific teaching tips

- A boxed feature that shows how learning can look when it is visible for students

The characteristics of visible learners are addressed in Chapter 1, but for now know that students should know what they are learning and should have evidence of their learning. Each chapter helps develop this visible learner in literacy.

In the first chapter, we focus on the aspects of literacy instruction that must be included in lessons. We review evidence about the components of effective literacy instruction and note that there is a need to recognize that student learning has to occur at the surface, deep, and transfer levels. These concepts served as the organizing feature of *Visible Learning for Literacy*, and we will briefly review them and their value in learning. This book focuses on the ways in which teachers can develop students' surface, deep, and transfer learning, specifically by providing students with direct instruction, engaging students in dialogic instruction, and facilitating their independent learning. Chapter 1 also provides an overview of literacy development during the elementary school years. Finally, Chapter 1 contains information about the use of instructional minutes during the literacy block. We understand that we run the risk of focusing more on the teaching and less on the learning, which is counter to the message in this book, but we decided that it was important to discuss the use of time so that readers don't believe that a given instructional approach can and should consume all of students' learning time.

For example, we are confident that repeated reading is a useful approach, but we wouldn't want that to consume the bulk of the literacy block. Importantly, there are numerous approaches that can be used within the literacy block to accomplish a given aspect of learning. When we suggest an average amount of time for teacher direct instruction, through think-alouds and the like, we recognize that there are many, many ways to provide students with this aspect of instruction. Again, there isn't one right way to do this, but there are several wrong ways, which we will explore further in the chapter on direct instruction. Having said that, we add that it is important for teachers to determine the impact of the experiences students have on their learning (and by *their*, we mean both teachers and students). If learning isn't happening, then change the approach by all means!

Following this introductory chapter, we turn our attention to teacher clarity. In Chapter 2 we focus our attention on what students need to know. This requires that teachers understand the grade-level expectations and communicate those learning intentions to students. It also requires that teachers and students understand what success looks like. Teacher clarity is an important aspect of literacy learning, as it sets the stage for challenging tasks, which students appreciate, and provides teachers with actionable information that they can use to make adjustments in the learning environment.

In Chapter 3, we focus on direct instruction in literacy, because there is considerable evidence that direct instruction works. This does not mean simply telling students what to think or do. We recognize that there are a lot of educators who have negative reactions to the phrase *direct instruction,* so we hope you'll allow us to explain why we have included it in this book. When people first hear the phrase *direct instruction,* many of them think of scripted programs for reading instruction that rely on transmission of information, especially basic skills. They often think of prepackaged curricula that do not take into account the current performance of students or their responses to individual lessons.

We don't think of direct instruction in this way. Rather, as John has noted, the essence of direct instruction is actually very common. In his words (2009), "The teacher decides on the learning intentions and success criteria, makes them transparent to students, demonstrates them by modeling, evaluates if they understand what they have been told by checking for understanding, and re-tells them what they have been told by tying it all together with closure" (p. 206). We hope you'll read Chapter 3 with an eye toward these aspects of learning.

In Chapters 4 and 5, we turn our attention to dialogic approaches to learning. Chapter 4 focuses on teacher-led dialogic instruction whereas Chapter 5 focuses on peer-led dialogic learning. In general, these approaches are more effective for deep and transfer learning than for surface learning. That's not to say that direct instruction is only useful for surface learning. We've seen direct instruction lessons on analyzing multiple texts, writing critiques, and public speaking that had demonstrable impacts on students' learning. Dialogic approaches can be teacher-led or peer-mediated, but all require students to interact with their peers and teacher to reach a better understanding. Some of the ideas and examples will likely be familiar to literacy educators while others may be new, as some are drawn from research conducted decades ago. Irrespective of the time frame from which they came, each of these approaches allows teachers and students to

- Explain their ideas and understanding

- Clarify their thinking through examples, nonexamples, and anecdotes

- Reflect on the thinking of others, revising their perspectives along the way

- Use technical language

In Chapter 6, we turn our attention to independent learning. Although we recognize that much of what students learn, they learn with and through others, there are some things that are best learned independently. Importantly, this does not mean assigning students a pile of worksheets to do on their own, but rather inviting students to direct some of their own learning, which is a central tenant of *Visible Learning*. Independent tasks can be used to develop students' surface, deep, or transfer learning. Reading the book *Voice of Freedom* (Weatherford, 2015) might contribute to students' surface knowledge about the civil rights movement. As surface knowledge is developed, students move into deeper learning by engaging in more formal discussions and viewing video clips from that period in history. Transfer may occur when students read across multiple texts or when they are asked to analyze a present-day situation, tracing it to the civil rights movement. Teachers use a combination of direct, dialogic, and independent tasks to ensure that learning occurs. And that's the important message here—that learning occurs. If teachers are not having an impact, they should change their approach!

In the final chapter of this book, we focus on literacy assessments that teachers can use to plan instruction and to determine the impact that they have on learning. As part of this chapter, we note the value of feedback and explore the ways in which teachers can provide feedback to students that is growth producing.

In sum, this book contains information on critical aspects of literacy instruction that have evidence for their ability to impact student learning. We're not suggesting that these be implemented in isolation but rather that they be combined into a series of linked learning experiences that result in students reading, writing, speaking, and listening more and better than they did before.

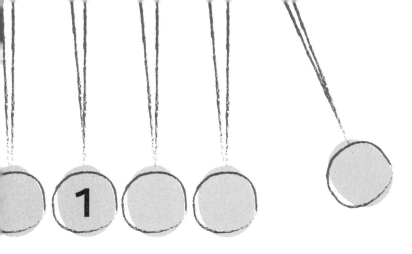

MOBILIZING VISIBLE
LEARNING FOR LITERACY

California is thirsty, and the fourth graders in Alice Nguyen's class know it. They have been reading, writing, and investigating the topic for two weeks. On this morning, she will be conducting a close reading of an informational article on a local water reclamation project in their community. After the close reading lesson, five students will join her for guided instruction, using the article to compose letters to their city council representative. Ms. Nguyen identified these students as being in need of additional instruction through a preassessment of their ability to craft written opinions with evidence.

Other children will use the research materials in the classroom, including web pages she bookmarked, and several digital information articles and videos on the water crisis in the western United States that she has loaded into the learning management system. One collaborative group is using an informational brochure from the local water agency to develop interview questions for a guest speaker who will visit next week. The guest speaker, a local farmer who uses environmentally sound irrigation practices, will answer questions about water use.

Later in the morning, all the students will independently read either *A Drop of Water* (Wick, 1997) or *The Water Cycle* (Harman, 2005) and compare it to the graphic organizer of the water cycle in their science journals. "I chose these two books because they provide a range of complexity for my students without compromising the content," says Ms. Nguyen. She sometimes uses part of her language arts instruction to support her science and social studies content. "We're accomplishing our reading and writing goals, but also acquiring knowledge about content," she remarks.

VISIBLE LEARNING FOR LITERACY

This fourth-grade teacher is mobilizing the principles of visible learning for literacy in each component of the morning's lessons. She holds high expectations for her students ($d = 0.43$) both in terms of the complexity of the content as well as their ability to deepen their knowledge through investigation. She engages in comprehension instruction ($d = 0.60$) using close reading of a complex text and deepening their knowledge through investigation by presenting a problem for them to address ($d = 0.61$). Ms. Nguyen regularly assesses her students for formative purposes such that she can create both teacher-directed and collaborative learning small groups in her classroom ($d = 0.49$). The measures she uses for assessment are generated by the students themselves, and are used to inform their goals ($d = 1.44$). She is mobilizing principles of visible learning such that she is consciously aware of her impact and her students are consciously aware of their learning. In other words, she sees the relationship between visible teaching and visible learning (see Figure 1.1).

The literacy practices discussed in *Visible Learning for Literacy* (Fisher, Frey, & Hattie, 2016) highlight effective practices, and importantly, *when* those practices are best leveraged to maximize their impact on student learning. However, we would be remiss if we did not further contextualize their role in quality reading and language arts instruction for elementary-aged learners. Understanding how components of such programs interface with the developmental progressions of children is vital for accelerating students' literacy learning.

EFFECT SIZE FOR
EXPECTATIONS = **0.43**

EFFECT SIZE FOR
COMPREHENSION
PROGRAMS = **0.60**

EFFECT SIZE FOR
PROBLEM-SOLVING
TEACHING = **0.61**

EFFECT SIZE FOR
SMALL GROUP
LEARNING = **0.49**

EFFECT SIZE
FOR STUDENT
EXPECTATIONS = **1.44**

Figure 1.1   The Relationship Between Visible Teaching and Visible Learning

Highly effective teachers . . .	Such that students . . .
Communicate clear learning intentions	Understand the learning intentions
Have challenging success criteria	Are challenged by the success criteria
Teach a range of learning strategies	Develop a range of learning strategies
Know when students are not progressing	Know when they are not progressing
Provide feedback	Seek feedback
Visibly learn themselves	Visibly teach themselves

Available for download at **https://resources.corwin.com/VL-LiteracyK-5**

COMPONENTS OF EFFECTIVE LITERACY LEARNING

Many are familiar with the work of the U.S. National Reading Panel (NRP) and its influence on elementary reading programs. In 2000, this team of researchers, educators, and parents reported their findings on a review of thousands of research studies conducted since 1966. Their goal was to identify the necessary instructional components key to learning to read. This group named five strategies as evidence based, meaning that a significant number of studies supported their use in effective literacy teaching. The components included developing an awareness of the sounds of the language (*phonemic awareness*) and the relationship between letters and the sounds they represent (*phonics*). In addition, the NRP identified *fluency development* and *vocabulary development* as essential components of comprehension. Finally, intentional instruction in *comprehension* strategies must occur from the beginning of a child's entry into school.

Teaching Takeaway

Effective teaching requires knowing which approaches work and when they work.

But literacy requires more than reading—it is further expressed through speaking, listening, writing, and viewing. Together these compose the language arts, which are furthered through the use of the reading, discussion, and composition of literary and informational texts. Effective literacy programs foster student growth through oral language development, composition, investigation, and performance. More specifically, they address three major areas (Connor et al., 2014):

- **Linguistic processes,** including language, word knowledge, and academic knowledge

- **Cognitive processes,** including comprehension monitoring, inferencing, and sense making for self and others

- **Text-specific processes,** that is, how narrative and informational texts are understood and composed

The indicators for effective literacy programs are not narrow and prescriptive, but rather can be accomplished using a number of different scheduling structures. However they are organized, the emphasis should be on sustained periods of instruction, including time each day when students read independently, talk about their learning with others, and write about their reading. There is a focus on assessment for the purpose of informing instructional decisions and providing feedback to learners. In addition, skills and strategies at the letter, word, and text level are taught, and all of this is accomplished through making connections between reading, writing, and spoken language. The following assumptions inform our collective understanding about teaching and learning:

- **Assessment occurs throughout the academic year and the results are used to inform the teacher and the learner.** Time each day is set aside to understand students' literacy progress and provide feedback to learners.

- **A meaningful amount of time is dedicated to developing literacy.** Every day children engage in sustained, organized, and comprehensive experiences with all of the components of the language arts.

- **Literacy instruction is balanced between part-to-whole and whole-to-part approaches.** Children experience instruction in sounds, letters, and words, reading connected text, authentic writing, oral language development, and comprehension instruction.

- **There is a reading-writing-speaking connection.** Development of reading and writing proficiency occurs when students have rich reading experiences, opportunities for purposeful writing, and occasions for meaningful interactions with peers and the teacher.

- **Reading and writing occur daily.** These events occur with the teacher, with peers, and independently.

Ultimately, an elementary literacy program is intended to work across the day. This curriculum includes science, mathematics, and social studies content as well as the visual and performing arts. Because literacy learning enhances these other curricular areas, it is essential that content area reading and writing are incorporated into these literacy experiences.

KNOWLEDGE OF HOW CHILDREN LEARN

As you can imagine, there is no shortage of ideas, theories, and anecdotes to answer the question about how children learn. The research fields of educational psychology and literacy are dedicated to understanding how learning occurs. Our thinking has been influenced by a number of significant principles, including a developmental view of literacy and the importance of meaningful experiences. These principles help us to answer the question of how students learn.

Developmental View of Learning

Perspectives on learning have moved far from the predominant theories of behaviorism and psychoanalysis of the early 20th century. The influence of the developmental work of Vygotsky, Piaget, Montessori, and others has shaped our approach to learning and the educational systems that support it. Clay (2003) asks,

> How do developmental theories influence teachers' assumptions about children? These explanations, particularly in language and cognitive areas, have created for teachers vocabulary and knowledge structures that allow them to think beyond what the child does to what may be occurring in children's heads. (p. 49)

A developmental perspective in learning means that the teacher understands that a child's response is not merely "correct" or "incorrect" but rather a reflection of what the child understands at that moment. Therefore, the teacher's role is not simply to evaluate what is correct or incorrect, but instead to recognize that children's responses are an opportunity to hypothesize how they are using their knowledge to arrive at an answer. This requires the classroom teacher to understand how children learn as they grow, especially how they develop literacy knowledge. But adopting a developmental view of learning does not mean that we lock children into rigid stages of development. Their cognitive development is either enhanced or inhibited by the context we create for them. A learning environment should support their explorations, errors, and successes, and provide interactions with more capable peers. They need access to challenging, but not defeating, topics of study set within a culturally responsive milieu (American Psychological Association, 2015).

> The teacher's role is not simply to evaluate what is correct or incorrect, but instead to recognize that children's responses are an opportunity to hypothesize how they are using their knowledge to arrive at an answer.

Meaningful Experiences and Social Interaction

A basic premise of learning is that when experiences are meaningful to the learner, the ability to learn increases. For example, your ability to learn the concepts discussed in this book are directly related to the relevancy of learning about literacy teaching in your life. If you were studying to be an engineer, your ability to learn these principles would be somewhat diminished because the content would not be as useful in an engineering degree program. In the same regard, student learning is driven by the questions formulated with and by the learner (Harste, 1994). Furthermore, learning is social in nature and springs from the interactions we have with others (Halliday, 1975). Therefore, an important role of the teacher is to foster questions and dialogue among students and create meaningful experiences that allow them to interact with one another.

Surface, Deep, and Transfer of Learning

The progression of literacy learning through the elementary years follows a spiral as students move from understanding the surface contours of a skill or concept toward an ever-deepening exploration of what lies beneath. But understanding these progressions requires that teachers consider the levels of learning they can expect from students. How, then, should we define learning, since that is our goal? As John suggested in his 2014 Vernon Wall Lecture (see also Hattie & Donoghue, 2016), learning can be defined as

> [t]he process of developing sufficient surface knowledge to then move to deeper understanding such that one can appropriately transfer this learning to new tasks and situations.

Learning is a process, not an event. The movement from surface learning—the facts, concepts, and principles associated with a topic of study—to deep learning, which is the ability to make relationships and leverage knowledge across domains, in increasingly novel situations, requires careful planning. If students are to deepen their knowledge, they must also regularly encounter situations that foster the transfer and generalization of their learning. The American Psychological Association (2015) notes that "student transfer or generalization of their knowledge and skills is not spontaneous or automatic" (p. 10) and requires intentionally created events on the part of the teacher.

And there is a scale for learning. Some things students understand only at the surface level. Some teachers only assign work that students can complete using only surface knowing! While surface learning is often not valued (it is misconstrued as superficial learning), it should be. You have to know something to be able to do something with it. We've never met a student who could synthesize information from multiple sources who didn't have an understanding of each of the texts. With appropriate instruction about how to relate and extend ideas, surface learning becomes deep understanding. Deep understanding is important if students are going to set their own expectations and monitor their own achievement. But schooling should not stop there. Learning demands that students be able to apply—transfer—their knowledge, skills, and strategies to new tasks and new situations. Transfer is very difficult to attain, and it remains one of our closely kept professional secrets. When was the last time you and your colleagues talked about transfer? Therefore, we often pronounce that students can transfer, but the process of teaching them at this level with the expectation of transfer is too often not discussed.

John uses the SOLO (structure of observed learning outcomes) method developed by Biggs and Collis (1982) to explain the movement from surface to deep learning as a process of first branching out and then strengthening connections between *ideas*:

> An important role of the teacher is to foster questions and dialogue among students and create meaningful experiences that allow them to interact with one another.

- One idea

- Many ideas

- Related ideas

- Extended ideas

We'll offer an example from kindergarten to illustrate. Young children are introduced to naming the letters of the alphabet initially through song (*one idea*) that soon morphs into *many ideas*: that a letter has a certain shape, and one or more sounds are associated with that letter. But in order to apply it, the child needs lots of opportunities to begin to *relate* an increasing number of ideas to one another. Therefore, she learns to recognize the letter within words, across an ever-broadening range of print, and to use her knowledge of the letters and sounds to decode familiar and then new words. In time, these ideas are *extended*, as she composes using her knowledge of letters, sounds, decoding, and meaning in order to represent her message in a way others can understand. Transfer is occurring throughout, as she moves from one idea deeper to an extension of ideas. But the transfer of knowledge is not seamless and linear. You see it in children's developmental spelling as they use but sometimes confuse their growing knowledge.

The ultimate goal, and one that can be hard to realize, is transfer. When students reach this level, learning has been accomplished. Transfer occurs throughout surface and deep learning. In fact, *all* learning is really transfer, provided understanding is involved (Bransford, Brown, & Cocking, 2000). By this, we mean that transfer is more than memorization; it also involves recognition on the part of the learner about what has occurred. The kindergartener who *knows* she is reading and writing is bearing witness to her own transfer of learning. At each phase of learning, specific instructional and curricular methods rise to the top. In other words, it isn't just knowing what works, but rather, what works *best*. Figure 1.2 captures some literacy learning approaches that are especially effective at the surface, deep, and transfer phases of learning.

PHASES OF READING DEVELOPMENT

As children learn to read, they move through a series of phases of development. Classroom instruction must be responsive to these phases of development in order for students to acquire the skills necessary to read and the tools necessary to understand what they are reading. Anyone who has spent time with children knows that the expectations for a six-year-old differ from those for a twelve-year-old. This is because these two

---

Deep understanding is important if students are going to set their own expectations and monitor their own achievement. But schooling should not stop there. Learning demands that students be able to apply—transfer—their knowledge, skills, and strategies to new tasks and new situations.

Figure 1.2   High-Impact Literacy Approaches at Each Phase of Learning

Surface Learning		Deep Learning		Transfer Learning	
Strategy	ES	Strategy	ES	Strategy	ES
Wide reading (exposure to reading)	0.42	Questioning	0.48	Extended writing/ writing programs	0.44
Phonics instruction	0.54	Concept mapping	0.60	Peer tutoring	0.55
Direct instruction	0.59	Close reading (study skills)	0.63	Problem-solving teaching	0.61
Note-taking	0.59	Self-questioning	0.64	Synthesizing information across texts	0.63
Comprehension programs	0.60	Metacognitive strategy instruction	0.69	Formal discussions (e.g., debates)/classroom discussion	0.82
Annotation (study skills)	0.63	Reciprocal teaching	0.74	Transforming conceptual knowledge	0.85
Summarizing	0.63	Class discussion	0.82	Organizing conceptual knowledge	0.85
Leveraging prior knowledge/ prior achievement	0.65	Organizing and transforming notes	0.85	Identifying similarities and differences	1.32
Vocabulary instruction	0.67	Cooperative learning 0.59			
Repeated reading	0.67				
Spaced practice	0.71				
Expectations of teacher 0.43					
Teacher clarity 0.75					
Feedback 0.75					
Student expectations of self 1.44					

children differ from one another physically, emotionally, and socially. As well, we view literacy learning through the lens of developmental phases. As we noted earlier, these phases are not rigid and stagebound, for little in human development (except perhaps puberty) is marked by an irreversible advancement from one condition to another. Instead, we look at phases of literacy development as markers of progression that many learners pass through. Not every learner will exhibit all the behaviors, nor will any learner be solely in one phase at a given time. Typical phases of reading can be described as the following:

- **Emergent readers** are experimenting with reading. During this phase they are learning that print carries a message and how books work, and they are beginning to recognize letters and words.

- **Early readers** are reading simple texts and have a larger bank of words they can read and write. They utilize a variety of basic strategies to figure out known and unknown words.

- **Transitional readers** are reading a variety of texts and understand that each has its own unique text structure. When seeking information, they consult more than one source. They are also becoming more aware of the strategies they are using.

- **Self-extending readers** read a wide range of texts and apply critical literacy skills to analyze the authenticity and value of the information. They continue to acquire increasingly more sophisticated literacy skills through extensive reading and discussion.

All readers in every phase of reading utilize a number of clues to figure out the print on the page. These clues are collectively called *cueing systems*. Emergent and early readers rely on a set of cueing systems in order to read a text. These can be thought of as clues readers extract from their knowledge of how print works to determine what the squiggly black lines on the page represent. Over time, these cues become more consolidated and their reading becomes more fluent. Fluency refers to a reader's ability to read smoothly, accurately, and with appropriate pace and expression.

- **Graphophonic cues** are those associated with the relationship between the symbols (letters) and their sounds. As learners develop these sound/symbol relationships, they recognize the patterns in clusters of letters (e.g., *pan, man,* and *fan*).

- **Syntactic cues** are governed by the grammatical rules of the language. This does not mean that the reader can name the rule, but rather that the reader recognizes that words occur in a particular order.

- **Semantic cues** are connected to the meaning of the words. A reader using semantic cues reads, "The house was small and blue" not "The horse was small and blue."

Teaching Takeaway

The goal of schooling is for students to apply what they have been taught—to transfer their learning to new situations, tasks, and problems.

- **Pragmatic cues** are related to the social use of language in a culture. For instance, readers use these cues to recognize that *Mother, Mom, Mommy,* and *Ma* are names for the same person.

Young children learn to activate these cueing systems through reading connected text. Readers are not encouraged to use one cueing system at a time, but rather to utilize all the cueing systems as they read. When students read connected text, they apply comprehension strategies to support their understanding of the meaning of the words.

As children advance through phases of reading development, they acquire an increasingly larger bank of cues, now termed comprehension strategies. The reading comprehension strategies utilized by transitional and self-extending readers include previewing text, identifying main ideas, making inferences, rereading, and utilizing metacognition to monitor their understanding and reflect on the learning (Paris, Wasik, & Turner, 1991). These comprehension and associated vocabulary strategies are collectively referred to as *unconstrained skills,* in that they continue to strengthen and deepen throughout one's lifetime (Paris, 2005). In contrast, *constrained skills* in reading include phonemic awareness, alphabetics, phonics, and fluency. Constrained skills have boundaries and limits (e.g., there are 26 letters in the English alphabet; fluent silent reading norms are finite). Therefore, elementary reading instruction covers a combination of the constrained foundational skills and unconstrained comprehension skills. The relative emphasis on each shifts between kindergarten and fifth grade as students master foundational skills and therefore need less instructional time devoted to them.

PHASES OF WRITING DEVELOPMENT

The development of a writer begins even before a child can compose in a manner that is understood by others. By the age of two or three, many toddlers are scribbling messages on paper and then "reading" their message to a delighted adult. Young children also visually represent ideas and concepts through drawing, an important literacy skill. Students entering kindergarten are exhibiting these very early writing skills. As with reading, they move through a series of phases, often displaying traits in more than one phase at a time.

- **Emergent writers** are learning how print works, especially in seeing the permanence of writing. They can recount events in sequence, such as giving directions or telling a story, and are using known letters and words in their writing.

- **Early writers** possess a larger bank of known letters and words and are able to use them more quickly in their writing, although the writing is sometimes constrained by the limits of their written vocabulary. An early writer's work is characterized by conventions of storytelling, especially formulaic writing such as *Once upon a time.*

- **Transitional writers** apply more sophisticated text structures to their work and can utilize structures used by other authors to create original text, such as using their growing knowledge of a writer's craft and text types to organize the message. Their sentences are more complex and they are beginning to use transitional phrases.

- **Self-extending writers** write for a variety of purposes and audiences. Their word choices are sophisticated and flexible and they engage in all aspects of editing to refine their work.

At every phase of writing development, the act of writing must be promoted. Students need opportunities to write and to receive intentional instruction on the aspects of writing. Like cueing systems in reading, these aspects of writing instruction foster acquisition of skills and strategies necessary for writing. These include conventions of language, purposes and related structures for writing, and instruction in the craft of writing and the processes writers use to revise. It is most important to help students realize that writing is nearly always for a purpose—and the form of writing may differ depending on the purpose—whether it is to persuade, instruct, narrate, describe, explain, or relate.

It probably won't surprise you to hear that writing is an incredibly complex skill. Anyone who has faced a blank page without a clue as to how to begin knows this. Any complex skill is going to require an equally sophisticated set of instructional techniques to teach students to write well. The challenge, of course, is that the act of writing leads writers in directions they may not have expected. Writer Anne Lamott said that "very few writers know what they are doing until they've done it" (1995, p. 22). And she was talking about professional writers!

The goal is to get students writing frequently and fluently using a growing repertoire of skills regarding the conventions of the language such as spelling, punctuation, and word choice. These skills are developed through

- Intentional instruction

- Exposure to other good writers through reading experiences with rich narrative and expository text

> It probably won't surprise you to hear that writing is an incredibly complex skill. Anyone who has faced a blank page without a clue as to how to begin knows this. Any complex skill is going to require an equally sophisticated set of instructional techniques.

- Time to experiment with the craft of writing by creating original texts that serve many purposes, including conveying experiences, informing or explaining, and persuading others using opinions with evidence

We know this:

- Good writing does not occur only because of instruction on conventions.

- Good writing does not occur only after students read good literary and informational texts.

- Good writing does not occur only through writing a lot using lots of different formats.

- Good writing occurs when all of these things are interwoven, in intentional ways that allow students to witness their increasing writing prowess.

Although learners move through developmental phases of reading and writing acquisition, no student will move neatly and conveniently from one phase to the next. This is especially true of students with diverse learning needs in our classrooms, including English language learners and students with disabilities. These learners require more specialized approaches to instruction that support growth in reading and writing.

FORMATS AND SCHEDULING

The purpose of this book is to explore what teaching literacy looks like in a visible learning classroom at the K–5 level. Logistics are a big part of that. Organization of an elementary literacy program should allow for students to participate in a model of instruction that allows them to acquire, consolidate, and deepen their literacy skills and strategies on a daily basis. In addition, students read and write every day, collaborate with peers, and work independently. The teacher meets with students as a whole group, in small groups, and individually. While not every student meets with the teacher every day, these meetings occur several times a week. In most districts, a two-hour block of time is devoted to literacy instruction. Therefore, the following section describes how time is used across a 120-minute time period. The language arts workshop diagram in Figure 1.3 provides an example of instructional phases within this block.

> **Teaching Takeaway**
>
> Learning does not occur in neat, linear stages. Learning is more staccato than flow. Try to adjust your approaches to meet the needs of students where they are.

> The learning intentions and success criteria are reinforced during the literacy block, so that students remain focused on what they are learning, why they are learning, and where they are in their learning.

Figure 1.3   Sample Time Distribution in a Two-Hour Block

Time Period	Purpose	Features	Who?	Purpose	Features	Who?
20 minutes	*Focused Instruction*	Establish learning intentions and success criteria Provide direct instruction for surface level acquisition and consolidation Set goals with students	Whole class			
20 minutes	*Needs-Based Instruction I*	Needs-based skills and strategies development with teacher	Small group	*Collaborative Learning*	Deep acquisition and consolidation of knowledge with peers	Balance of the class
20 minutes	*Needs-Based Instruction II*	Needs-based skills and strategies development with teacher	Small group	*Collaborative Learning*	Deep acquisition and consolidation of knowledge with peers	Balance of the class

Time Period	Purpose	Features	Who?	Purpose	Features	Who?
10 minutes	Focused Instruction	Check-in with class and reteach as needed	Whole class			
40 minutes	Conferring and Assessing	Provide and receive feedback, assess progress, and reteach as needed	Individual students	Independent Reading and Writing	Transfer of skills and concepts	Balance of the class
10 minutes	Focused Instruction	Revisit learning intentions and success criteria Closure Students self-assess and reflect on goals	Whole class			

Available for download at **https://resources.corwin.com/VL-LiteracyK-5**

Video 1

Lesson Elements, Grades K–5

*https://resources.corwin.com/
VL-LiteracyK-5*

*To read a QR code, you must have a
smartphone or tablet with a camera.
We recommend that you download
a QR code reader app that is made
specifically for your phone or tablet
brand.*

Time Organization

Up to about the first 20 minutes is devoted to focused instruction, which consists of time devoted to sharing the learning intentions and success criteria with students. This isn't simply posting them on the board and giving them cursory attention. Instead, students and the teacher engage in dialogue to parse and clarify. The learning intentions and success criteria are reinforced during the literacy block, so that students remain focused on what they are learning, why they are learning, and where they are in their learning. This is a crucial step in making learning visible to students. We discuss learning intentions and success criteria in depth in Chapter 2.

The teacher also uses these first 20 minutes to model and think aloud, and to provide any necessary direct instruction that is needed. Before transitioning to the next phase, the teacher returns to the learning intentions and success criteria, and students name or write the goals they have for themselves for the day.

Next, the teacher meets with small groups of students for 20 minutes for needs-based instruction in reading or writing. Students in these groups have been selected based on formative use of assessment information, and are often (but not always) clustered due to similar needs. While the teacher meets for guided instruction, the rest of the class is engaged in collaborative learning.

Collaborative learning may occur in pairs or in slightly larger groups, but all students are working with at least one other person. Depending on the purposes, students may be consolidating previously learned, but still new, knowledge. Conversely, they may be deepening their knowledge of a skill or concept with peers. For example, students may be involved in word study with a partner as they sort words conceptually and then morphologically.

After two rotations, students independently read. This is an opportunity for them to apply what they have been learning to new text, thus further fostering transfer. While students read independently, the teacher meets with individual students to confer, assess, and provide feedback about reading, working with students toward self-reported goals.

Later in the literacy block, students work on their independent writing for another 25 minutes while the teacher again confers and assesses, this time for writing.

Of course, not all instruction necessary for effective practice can be offered in one lesson. This requires a perspective across the week to see how instruction unfolds. There is flexibility, of course, in how this is implemented on a daily basis. Some days use less time for conferring, as additional time may be devoted to phonics, vocabulary instruction, handwriting, or oral language development.

Across a Week

Figure 1.4, on the next page, features a sample weekly schedule for language arts instruction. This suggested schedule is not meant to be a rigid structure that follows the same pattern day after day. Notice that on some days the teacher is collecting assessment information, while at other times he or she meets with individual students to confer about reading and writing. In addition, while small group, needs-based instruction occurs each day, it is not always with the same students. It is critical not only to assess student learning but to plan time for reteaching concepts students may not have mastered the first time. (In Chapter 7 we will discuss in more detail ways to assess your impact on student learning.) In our experience, well-intentioned teachers do not ever get to reteaching because they do not set aside time to do so. We suggest that time for reteaching is planned each week. If you don't need to reteach anyone during a particular week, you can move on with your curriculum.

> In our experience, well-intentioned teachers do not ever get to reteaching because they do not set aside time to do so.

A note about sample schedules—they are only intended to give a broad guide to the structure of a literacy block of instruction. We believe that the best teaching is responsive teaching that has an impact on student learning. Good teachers watch their students closely to see how the lesson is going and what students are learning. When teachable moments occur, when a student asks a profound question, when a puzzled look on a child's face suggests the child is confused, it's appropriate to follow the child's lead. This undoubtedly messes up the carefully crafted schedule. So be it. After all, who's the schedule for? If something has to give on a particular day in order to accommodate these important events, be flexible about it. Don't let the occasional deviations from the schedule discourage you. But it is equally important to remember that expected lapses in schedules do not mean there should be no schedule at all. Children thrive on knowing what to expect, and teachers find they accomplish far more when a thoughtful schedule is planned and implemented.

Video 2

Elements of Instruction, Grades 1, 3, and 5

https://resources.corwin.com/ VL-LiteracyK-5

Across Content Areas

When you read the description of Ms. Nguyen's morning in the chapter opening, you may have been surprised to see science content being taught. Because literacy development is essential to learning content, it

Figure 1.4   Sample Weekly Distribution of Time

	Monday	Tuesday	Wednesday	Thursday	Friday
Focused Instruction 20 minutes	Reading (comprehension strategies instruction)	Writing (craft, purpose, organization)	Reading (comprehension strategies instruction)	Writing (conventions and revision)	Reading (comprehension strategies extension)
Guided Instruction 1 20 minutes OR *Collaborative Learning 1* 20 minutes	Guided or Scaffolded Reading (Group 1) Collaborative Reading: Book discussion or reciprocal teaching for deep consolidation (Group 2) Stations for rehearsal (Groups 3 and 4)	Guided Writing (Group 3) Collaborative Writing: Oral planning and composition of text (Groups 1, 2, and 4)	Guided or Scaffolded Reading (Group 3) Collaborative Reading: Book discussion or reciprocal teaching for deep consolidation (Group 4) Stations for rehearsal (Groups 1 and 2)	Guided Writing (Group 1) Collaborative Writing: Peer critiques (Groups 2, 3, and 4)	Close reading, extended discussion, and writing about a complex text
Guided Lesson 2 20 minutes OR *Collaborative Work 2* 20 minutes	Guided or Scaffolded Reading (Group 2) Collaborative Reading: Book discussion or reciprocal teaching for deep consolidation (Groups 3 and 4) Stations for rehearsal (Group 1)	Guided Writing (Group 4) Collaborative Writing: Oral planning and composition of text (Groups 1, 2, and 3)	Guided or Scaffolded Reading (Group 4) Collaborative Reading: Book discussion or reciprocal teaching for deep consolidation (Groups 1 and 2) Stations for rehearsal (Group 3)	Guided Writing (Group 2) Collaborative Writing: Peer critiques (Groups 1, 3, and 4)	
Focused Instruction	Check in with class and reteach as needed	Check in with class and reteach as needed	Check in with class and reteach as needed	Check in with class and reteach as needed	Check in with class and set goals for genius hour exploration
Independent Reading With Conferring 20 minutes	Assess formatively individual students in reading and provide and receive feedback Balance of class is reading teacher-selected texts linked to unit of study	Confer with five students on reading and provide and receive feedback Balance of class is reading teacher-selected texts linked to unit of study	Assess formatively individual students in reading and provide and receive feedback Balance of class is reading teacher-selected texts linked to unit of study	Confer with five students on reading and provide and receive feedback Balance of class is reading teacher-selected texts linked to unit of study	Genius hour: What do these texts inspire you to do?
Independent Writing With Conferring 20 minutes	Assess individual students in writing Balance of class is composing	Confer with five students on writing Balance of class is composing	Assess individual students in writing Balance of class is composing	Confer with five students on writing Balance of class is composing	Oral language development and metacognition
Focused Instruction Closure Goal Setting 10 minutes	Oral language development and metacognition	Oral language development and metacognition	Oral language development and metacognition	Oral language development and metacognition	Oral language development and metacognition

 Available for download at **https://resources.corwin.com/VL-LiteracyK-5**

only makes sense that content areas are incorporated as well as taught at other points in the day. There is simply too much content knowledge to ever be effectively taught in the brief amount of time typically devoted to these subjects.

As well, we are cautious about the uneven use of informational texts in literacy instruction at the elementary levels. Students typically have far more extensive experience with reading stories than with reading non-fiction, and this impacts both their background knowledge and their understanding of how to read these texts. Duke (2000) reported that in some schools, first graders averaged 3.6 minutes per day with informational text. Even with the increased attention in the last decade to the use of informational texts in reading and language arts, some elementary teachers report that relatively little time is devoted to informational text comprehension and composition. Jeong and colleagues' study of second-, third-, and fourth-grade classrooms reported that a decade after Duke's groundbreaking study, instruction in these classrooms had increased by only 1 minute in Grade 2, with a more robust increase of 16 minutes in Grades 3 and 4 (Jeong, Gaffney, & Choi, 2010). However, keep in mind that these findings are for the *entire day*, not just the traditional literacy block. Students simply must have frequent opportunities to read and write informational text within the literacy curriculum if they are to master the many content standards before them. Figure 1.5 on the next page contains a sample schedule of how the this might fit into a balanced curriculum.

SPOTLIGHT ON THREE TEACHERS

To help you further visualize how elementary teachers use the practices highlighted as most effective in *Visible Learning for Literacy*, we will follow the practices of three teachers throughout the remaining chapters:

- Iman Hakim is a first-grade teacher in California. The 29 students in her classroom represent the rich diversity found in her community and include many English learners who speak either Spanish, Arabic, or Tagalog as a first language. Ms. Hakim is a teacher-leader in her school, and she serves as grade-level chair, heads the school's collegial coaching efforts, and has hosted student teachers over the years. An important issue for her is building family and community connections. "These are young children who are profoundly influenced by their families," she noted, "and as a school we are entrusted by families to care for their most valuable assets. I don't think making homes more 'school-like' is the answer. We need to make our schools more 'home-like' so that families feel welcome in meaningful ways."

Figure 1.5   How a Literacy Block Fits Into a Balanced Curriculum

Sample Weekly Schedule for the Entire Day

Time	Monday	Tuesday	Wednesday	Thursday	Friday
8:00–8:15 AM	Morning Meeting	Morning Meeting	Morning Meeting	Morning Meeting	Morning Meeting
8:15–8:30 AM	Independent Reading	Independent Reading	Independent Reading	Independent Reading	Independent Reading
8:30–9:00 AM	Word Study	Word Study	Word Study	Word Study	Word Study
9:00–11:00 AM	Literacy Block *Links to science or social studies*	Literacy Block *Links to science or social studies*	Literacy Block *Links to science or social studies*	Literacy Block *Links to science or social studies*	Literacy Block *Links to science or social studies*
11:00–11:30 AM	Visual and Performing Arts	Music	Physical Education	Library	Physical Education
11:30 AM–12:15 PM	Lunch and Recess	Lunch and Recess	Lunch and Recess	Lunch and Recess	Lunch and Recess
12:15–1:15 PM	Mathematics	Mathematics	Mathematics	Mathematics	Mathematics
1:15–2:15 PM	Science	Social Studies	Science	Social Studies	Science
2:15–2:30 PM	Afternoon Meeting	Afternoon Meeting	Afternoon Meeting	Afternoon Meeting	Afternoon Meeting

Available for download at **https://resources.corwin.com/VL-LiteracyK-5**

- Kiara Mitchell is a third-grade teacher in Virginia. She has 33 students in her classroom, and most qualify for free or reduced-price lunch, a common measure of socioeconomic status. Most of her students speak English as a first language as well as African-American English. Ms. Mitchell is a National Board Certified Teacher (NBCT) in elementary education. When asked about what she sees as being a driving factor in her teaching, she responded, "issues about equitable education and opportunities to learn," and then continued, "I want the students in this school to see possibilities in themselves and in the world."

- Edward Hurley is a Year-5 teacher at a remote primary school in the Northern Territory of Australia. Many of his 26 students identify as Aboriginal and/or Torres Strait Islander, and they speak one or more non-English heritage languages. "Attendance and literacy levels are a major concern for me," says Mr. Hurley, who is a certified Highly Accomplished Teacher (and thus a member of the Australian Highly Accomplished and Lead Teacher HALT association). "I see my role as being one who removes barriers for these children, both through my own practice and in mentoring my colleagues."

These three teachers, although in different regions and contexts, operate under three important assumptions:

- Meaningful change occurs when teachers, families, and communities collaborate to strengthen learning.

- Language and cultural diversity is a strength to be leveraged, not a deficit to be corrected.

- Expert teaching requires monitoring student progress, providing feedback, and adjusting lessons based on the learning of students.

In the chapters that follow, you will encounter these three teachers and view the lesson plans they have developed for themselves (see Figure 1.6 on the next page). The lesson template is not meant to be delivered in a strictly linear fashion, but rather is intended to serve as a way to guide your thinking about the elements of the lesson. In addition, you will more briefly meet a number of teachers from other grade levels whose practices illustrate the approaches under discussion. While no book on literacy instruction could ever entirely capture every context or circumstance you encounter, we hope that the net effect of this book is that we provide you with a process for incorporating visible learning consistently and throughout the day.

CONCLUSION

Literacy instruction that capitalizes on visible learning is established upon principles of learning. A developmental approach to reading and writing is utilized to foster literacy acquisition. This focus on the individual learner makes this approach ideal for students with language or learning needs. In addition, a visible learning for literacy approach leverages high-impact instruction to accelerate student learning through surface, deep, and transfer phases of learning by engaging them in direct, dialogic, and independent learning tasks. Finally, students learn best when there is a solid organizational structure that allows them to learn in a variety of ways and with a variety of materials. In other words,

Figure 1.6   Lesson Plan Template

Assessed Need: I have noticed that my students need:
Standard(s) Addressed:
Text(s) I Will Use:
Learning Intention for This Lesson:
Success Criteria for This Lesson:
Direct Instruction: Model: Strategies/skills/concepts to emphasize Guide and Scaffold: Questions to ask Assess: These are the students who will need further support
Dialogic Instruction: Teacher-Directed Tools (e.g., anticipation guides, 4 Corners activity, K-W-L, to spark discussion) Student-Enacted Tools (e.g., literature circles, reciprocal teaching, debate, Socratic seminar, that are primarily driven by students) Assess: These are the students who will need further support
Feedback Opportunities:
Independent Learning and Closure:

learning becomes visible for students. As we will highlight in each chapter that follows, visible learning students are students who:

- Can be their own teacher

- Can articulate what they are learning and why

- Can talk about how they are learning—the strategies they are using to learn

- Can articulate their next learning steps

- Can use self-regulation strategies

- Are assessment capable—they understand the assessment tools being used and what their results mean, and they can self-assess to answer the key questions: Where am I in my learning? Where am I going? What do I need to do to get there?

- Seek, are resilient to, and aspire to challenge

- Can set mastery goals

- See errors as opportunities and are comfortable saying that they don't know and/or need help

- Positively support the learning of their peers

- Know what to do when they don't know what to do

- Actively seek feedback

- Have metacognitive skills and can talk about these (systematic planning, memory, abstract thinking, critical thinking, problem solving, etc.) (p. 6)

In other words, a visible learner notices when he or she is learning and is proactive in making sure that learning is obvious. As we engage in discussions about literacy learning in this book, we will return to these indicators that students are visible learners to explore how they might look in the classroom.

2

TEACHER CLARITY

© Erin Null

How do you describe a successful lesson? Do you say the lesson was creative? Do you say it used technology in a new way? Do you say that the students really liked it? Or do you say that students learned, and provide evidence to support your claim? We don't have anything against creative and engaging lessons that use technology. In fact, we know that cognitive engagement is an essential component of learning. But visible learning is based on impact. In fact, visible learning assumes that teachers focus their attention on determining the impact that they have had on student learning and that they use that information to determine the success of the lesson.

How do you know whether your students are successful at learning what you wanted them to? How do *they* know whether they're successful? How can students know whether or not they've met the intended learning intentions, or whether they're making progress toward doing so? After completing the monumental feat of studying and consolidating huge amounts of research on quality teaching and learning, John realized that the single most important thing teachers can do is to *know their impact on student learning*.

This impact needs to be assessed daily so that seemingly small yet vital midcourse corrections can be made. In other words, if you're waiting for a project, quiz, or test to find out what your students know, you're waiting too long. These assessments aren't made often enough to provide teachers the information they need to teach their students effectively. The longer the time in between assessments, the less useful the assessments are in helping students achieve. Teachers need tools that allow them to check for understanding frequently. They also need to know when students have met the learning goal so that they can move on. All of this assumes three things:

- The teacher knows what students are supposed to be learning.

- The students know what they are supposed to be learning.

- The teacher and students know what success looks like.

Taken together, these three aspects contribute to *teacher clarity*, which has an effect size of 0.75, and thus remains one of the most robust instructional practices to be described in this book. Fendick (1990) defined teacher clarity as "a measure of the clarity of communication between teachers and students in both directions" (p. 10) and further described it across four dimensions:

1. **Clarity of organization** such that lesson tasks, assignments, and activities include links to the objectives and outcomes of learning

2. **Clarity of explanation** such that information is relevant, accurate, and comprehensible to students

3. **Clarity of examples and guided practice** such that the lesson includes information that is illustrative and illuminating as students gradually move to independence, making progress with less support from the teacher

4. **Clarity of assessment of student learning** such that the teacher is regularly seeking out and acting upon the feedback he or she receives from students, especially through their verbal and written responses

The remainder of this chapter focuses on the first point, what we will call learning intentions and success criteria. *Clarity of explanations* is further described in the chapter on direct instruction and the *clarity of the examples and practice* are explored in the chapter on dialogic approaches. And, as we noted in the introduction, the final chapter focuses on *assessment and feedback*.

Before we explore learning intentions and success criteria further, it is important to note that teacher clarity rests on an understanding of what students need to learn. In other words, teachers have to understand the content and performance standards appropriate for their grade level if they are going to be able to design meaningful learning experiences for students. Lessons should address the gap between what students already know and what they need to know. And this begins with an analysis of the standards.

Visible learning assumes that teachers focus their attention on determining the impact that they have had on student learning and that they use that information to determine the success of the lesson.

EFFECT SIZE FOR TEACHER CLARITY = **0.75**

Video 3
Teacher Clarity
https://resources.corwin.com/VL-LiteracyK-5

It is important to note that teacher clarity rests on an understanding of what students need to learn.

UNDERSTANDING EXPECTATIONS IN STANDARDS

A simple read through the standards documents is not sufficient to teach those standards. Knowing the standards well allows teachers to identify the necessary prior knowledge as well as the expectations for students' success. There are entire books written on unwrapping standards (e.g., Ainsworth, 2014), so we won't repeat that information here. Instead, we want to highlight the need to pay attention to the language in the standards that call for transfer of learning. (See Figure 2.1 for a framework for unpacking each standard.) In nearly all cases, the standards themselves articulate outcomes of learning, and often call upon students to apply what they have learned to an ever-widening set of situations and texts:

- **California State Standards for English Language Arts:** Language 1.4: Determine or clarify the meaning of unknown and multiple-meaning words and phrases based on *Grade 1 reading and content*, choosing flexibly from an array of strategies: c. Identify frequently occurring root words (e.g., *look*) and their inflectional forms (e.g., *looks, looked, looking*).

- **Virginia Standards for Learning:** Reading 3.4.b: The student will expand vocabulary when reading, using knowledge of roots, affixes, synonyms, and antonyms.

- **Australian Curriculum for English Language Arts:** Vocabulary 1512: Understand the use of vocabulary to express greater precision of meaning, and know that words can have different meanings in different contexts.

We selected these to illustrate that knowledge of vocabulary, for example, deepens both within and across school years, and that the standards themselves call for students to transfer present levels of knowledge to grade-level contexts. These outcome standards can't be taught in a day or a week, and therefore are developed over many sustained experiences with spoken and written texts. But these long-range outcomes are difficult for children to understand in the context of daily learning. Therefore, we deconstruct these standards in order to articulate daily learning intentions students can internalize.

> **Teaching Takeaway**
>
> Students should know what they're expected to learn each day and there should be ways to determine if that learning has occurred.

LEARNING INTENTIONS IN THE LANGUAGE ARTS

Standards are statements for teachers that identify what students should know and be able to do at a given point in time. Standards are tough for yet-to-be teachers to understand, and they are often too broad for students to master in a single lesson. Effective teachers start with a

Figure 2.1   Understanding Expectations in Standards

Standard(s)	
Concepts (nouns)	**Skills (verbs)**
Surface Skills and Knowledge Needed	
Deep Skills and Knowledge Needed	
Transfer: Big Idea or Enduring Understanding	

standard, break the learning that standard requires into lesson-sized chunks, and then phrase these chunks so that students will be able to understand them. Each one of these chunked phrases—a daily statement of what a student is expected to learn in a given lesson—is a *learning intention*. Learning intentions can focus on knowledge, skills, or concepts. Effective teachers know where their students are in the learning cycle—at the surface, deep, or transfer level—and design their instruction to foster learning. A teacher who fails to identify where her students are in their literacy learning is likely to undershoot or overshoot expectations for them. The daily learning intentions that are communicated by the teacher are an end product of her careful planning, as she determines the type of expected learning (surface, deep, or transfer) and how to implement instruction for that type of learning. The success criteria provide a means for students and the teacher to gauge progress toward learning, thereby making learning visible.

Learning intentions (which some people call objectives, learning goals, targets, or purpose statements) are where teacher planning begins. Learning intentions are different from standards. Here are some examples of learning intentions that we have seen in language arts classrooms:

- Identify transition words that guide the reader.

- Write a summary of the text using key details.

- Retell events from the beginning of the text.

- Make inferences from the details in a text.

- Find words (verbs) that show action while rereading a story.

- Support your reasons with evidence from the text.

These are common examples of *what* students are expected to learn in elementary language arts classrooms. To our thinking, students should also experience lessons that include *how* they are expected to learn. Some examples of learning intentions that focus on how students might learn include:

- *Listen carefully to the speakers in your group so you can link your ideas with theirs.*

- *You and your partner will arrive at consensus about the author's underlying message of the text.*

- *Draw or write how bees carry pollen from flower to flower.*

The daily learning intentions that are communicated by the teacher are an end product of her careful planning, as she determines the type of expected learning (surface, deep, or transfer) and how to implement instruction for that type of learning.

Video 4

Learning Intentions and Success Criteria

https://resources.corwin.com/ VL-LiteracyK-5

Some teachers might be concerned that statements such as these can rob students of a period of investigation and inquiry. Learning intentions don't have to be used exclusively at the outset of the lesson, and should be revisited over the course of the lesson. Teachers can withhold their learning intentions until after an exploration has occurred. And teachers can invite students to explain what they learned from the lesson and compare that with the initial stated learning intention for the lesson. Interesting class discussions about the alignment (or lack of alignment) can provide a great deal of insight on student understanding.

The *VISIBLE LEARNER*

A visitor walks into a second-grade classroom and observes students. Marco, one of the students in the class, approaches the visitor and says, "Today, I get to learn about bats. So far, I have read three books about bats. I learned about echolocation. And bats are mammals so they have live babies, not eggs like birds. I picked bats for my expert project because we saw some when we went to Texas. We are all writing about our projects but they are all different. I am the only one who picked bats. Like Emily is learning about walruses. Our projects will be on the class [web] page so we can learn from other people."

Visible learners can articulate what they are learning and why.

Learning intentions are themselves evidence of a scaffolded process that unfolds over many lessons. A key to planning a lesson is knowing where your students currently are in their learning. It would be tough to teach students to write summaries using key details if they did not understand how to identify details. Learning intentions can (and should often) have an inherent recursive element in that they build connections between previously learned content and new knowledge. Savvy teachers embed previous content in the new content. The teacher is not only creating a need and a purpose for students to hone learned skills, but also providing opportunities for students to experience those "aha" moments that relate concepts to a previous lesson's content, a sure sign that students are moving from surface to deep learning. There are few other hallmarks of good learning intentions that Clarke, Timperley, and Hattie (2003) have identified:

Video 5

Visible Learners:
"What I learned today"

*https://resources.corwin.com/
VL-LiteracyK-5*

- Explicitly share learning intentions with students, so that students understand them and what success looks like. Recognize that not all students in the class will be working at the same rate or starting from the same place, so it's important to adapt the plan relating to the intentions to make it clear to all students.

- Realize that learning does not happen in a neat, linear sequence; therefore the cascade from the curriculum aim (the standard), through the achievement objective (unit goals), to the learning intention (for a specific lesson) is sometimes complex.

- Learning intentions and activities can be grouped if one activity can contribute to more than one learning intention, or one learning intention may need several activities for students to understand it fully.

- Learning intentions are what we intend students to learn, but it is important to realize students may learn other things not planned for, so teachers need to be aware of unintended consequences.

Student Ownership of Learning Intentions

When Doug speaks to teachers and administrators, he tells them to overtly communicate their learning intentions, because this practice has been shown by extensive research to boost student learning and achievement (Hattie, 2012). But he has found that people actually take this advice more seriously when he frames learning intentions as a students' rights issue. Students have a right to know what they're supposed to learn, and why they're supposed to learn it. After all, teachers are going to evaluate student performance and mark report cards that last a lifetime. These records can open doors to colleges and careers, or close them. It's only fair that students understand what they're expected to learn if teachers are going to evaluate that learning.

John notes that the New Zealand Privacy Commission ruled that "students owned their data," and this led to major improvements in creating systems for maintaining data where data followed students through school. It is an interesting thought to consider that your students "own" their data (information about what they have and have not yet learned), and one of our roles is to teach them how to interpret what they own. This approach has led to the development of the notion of "student assessment capabilities," which involve teaching students when to best assess their knowledge, how to interpret their assessments, and where to go next in their learning process. It also emphasizes the importance of the teacher sharing with students the learning journey and especially the destination—the learning intentions and the success criteria. In other words, these two practices can provide a means for promoting student ownership of their learning, rather than continuing to perpetuate an ineffective system that attends to the act of teaching, rather than the facilitation of learning. In the next section, we will zoom

Teaching Takeaway

Students have a right to know what they're supposed to learn, and why they're supposed to learn it.

in further on learning intentions before turning our attention to success criteria.

Connecting Learning Intentions to Prior Knowledge

The learning intention itself is important—it needs to be based on an agreed-upon standard, phrased in a way that's easy for students to understand, and appropriately constructed around where students are in their learning. But the learning intention should also link to students' prior knowledge. Activating prior knowledge going into a lesson is an important consideration as teachers explain the learning intentions (Bransford et al., 2000). Many teachers begin their classes with a warm-up exercise. Unfortunately, some teachers do this solely for management purposes—taking attendance, making sure everyone has a pencil—thereby squandering an important learning opportunity. Bell work should be an opportunity to cultivate and activate prior knowledge through written work or classroom discourse. An effective teacher uses opportunities like this to assist students in preparing for new knowledge acquisition. You want to be actively engaged with your class so that you can gain a solid sense of what they know, so that you can capitalize on this. Second-grade teacher Darnell James keeps a chart near his classroom door so that each morning his students can respond using their prior knowledge. The poster is set up in a grid, with each 2″ × 2″ square labeled with a student name. Mr. James changes the prompt each morning, but it is always linked to one of his lessons:

> Teaching Takeaway
>
> Tie prior learning to new learning intentions by embedding previous content within new content.

- *We're going to learn about volcanoes today! Can volcanoes be under the ocean? How do you know?*

- *We'll be reading another poem by Shel Silverstein today. List three things you already know about this poet.*

- *Our city's name comes from a local Native American tribe. What do you already know about the Choctaw Indians?*

As students arrive each morning, they write their short responses on a sticky note and post it in the square that corresponds with their names. "I can take attendance at a glance because I can see immediately who's not here," said Mr. James. "The real benefit, though, is that I collect the stickies and use them on the doc cam [document camera] to discuss what individual students are already thinking about," the teacher continued. "I can ask them more questions and get them to elaborate. It's a great launch for my lesson."

Students can write or talk about what they already know about the concept or skill they'll be learning, pose questions about it, or write about concepts they need to understand before they can tackle the day's learning. Bell work can be a good opportunity to cultivate and activate prior knowledge. The point is to get learners ready to learn the new content, by giving their brains something onto which to connect their new skill or understanding.

Make Learning Intentions Inviting and Engaging

The ways in which teachers talk about learning intentions makes a difference. William Purkey (1992) described four patterns with which students perceived lessons: intentionally disinviting, unintentionally disinviting, unintentionally inviting, and intentionally inviting.

Teachers who were intentionally disinviting were easily recognizable because of their dismissive and harsh tone. Most of us would, thankfully, not be in that category. However, teachers who were unintentionally disinviting were negative and pessimistic about their students' capabilities, and their low expectations were apparent to the learners (and they were often successful in having a low impact on student learning!).

Take, for example, this introduction to a lesson on multisyllabic words. The teacher starts by saying, "Today we are going to work on reading long and hard words. This is a really difficult and I know that most of you are going to struggle with being able to do this, so you are going to have to pay close attention." Little does the teacher realize that she has just told the students that they will likely be unsuccessful in this lesson. In addition to being disinviting, using this type of introduction elicits a negative response in students who are thinking, "This is going to be hard and I probably won't be able to do it."

On the other hand, there are a group of teachers Purkey categorizes as unintentionally inviting. They are energetic and enthusiastic, but they lack a plan for their journey. Students like being with them, but don't benefit as fully as they could from instruction because it is inconsistent and naïve. An unintentionally inviting teacher might begin the same lesson by saying, "Good morning scholars, today we are going to learn more about multisyllabic words! It's exciting to know more words and I think you'll find this interesting work and I cannot wait to get started!" This is unintentionally inviting because the teacher is all about getting students excited and interested in the lesson, but notice how the statement doesn't talk about exactly what students are going to learn or why it is important. It may not take long before the students realize that despite their enthusiasm, they have no idea of what is going on.

The final category, those who are intentionally inviting, are consistently positive and are sensitive to the needs of students. They take action,

Bell work can be a good opportunity to cultivate and activate prior knowledge. The point is to get learners ready to learn the new content by giving their brains something onto which to connect their new skill or understanding.

and promote a growth mindset. Most of all, they are purposeful and effectively transmit a sense of instructional urgency. As teachers set the learning intentions, they also set the tone for their classroom.

First-grade teacher Iman Hakim's students have been learning about writing to inform others, and their science content has focused on learning about California plants and animals. However, she has determined that when they are writing, the information they share is often disjointed and doesn't build in a logical way. Therefore, she has decided that she will have them compose a class book on trees in southern California. "They already know a lot about this topic, so it's going to allow me to focus on how we organize the information, rather than on having to gather all the topic information," she says. However, she also knows that telling them they are not good at something isn't exactly inspiring. Instead, she intentionally invites them into the project by telling them, "You've learned so much about our environment in this first quarter, and your families are going to be so proud of you! Since we have our first Open House in two weeks, I thought it would be great to be able to show them how much our class has learned about this topic." After explaining what a class book is (individual pages composed as partners and assembled as a coherent book) and discussing the qualities the children would like to see in their final product, she turns to the learning intention for the lesson.

> You've said that it's going to be important that your families are able to learn a lot about trees from your book, which means that we will need to organize our writing. That means we need to make a plan. Let's use one of the books we read together, called Seed to Plant. Remember this one? One of the reasons it is such a good book is because the author does a really good job of giving us the information in an organized way. I'm thinking we can use her table of contents to help us organize our book. We'll make our own table of contents for our book, so we can know what information is needed, and in an order that makes sense for our readers, your families.

Ms. Hakim ably communicated the learning intention, to be sure, but she took the extra step of making sure it was inviting by including mention of their families as their readers. "The children are so proud to show what they know, and linking this work to an authentic audience is even more motivating," she says. See Ms. Hakim's complete lesson plan in Figure 2.2.

Social Learning Intentions

Since high-quality lessons involve a good deal of collaboration, it makes sense for teachers to set social learning intentions as well. Social learning

Figure 2.2   Lesson Plan for First-Grade Organization in Writing

Assessed Need: I have noticed that my students need: To organize the presentation of facts in their informational writing.
Standard(s) Addressed: W.1.2: Write informative/explanatory texts in which they name a topic, supply some facts about the topic, and provide some sense of closure.
Text(s) I Will Use: Seed to Plant (Rattini, 2014)
Learning Intention for This Lesson: We will examine the table of contents for this book to brainstorm the information we will need to plan our class book on trees.
Success Criteria for This Lesson: We will make our own table of contents for our class book.
Direct Instruction: Model: Strategies/skills/concepts to emphasize Model and think aloud about what I expect to learn from this book, based on the table of contents. They have read this book before and are familiar with the content. I will confirm the alignment between the TOC and the topics addressed in the book. Guide and Scaffold: Questions to ask 1. What would our readers expect to learn from a book titled Trees of Southern California? 2. How could I be sure that we are organizing our writing efforts so we don't skip information or keep repeating ourselves? Assess: These are the students who will need further support Pair Ahmed with Sabah, as she speaks the same dialect as he does and can broker language. I will partner with Jeremy, so that I can support his occupational therapy goals as they relate to handwriting.
Dialogic Instruction: Teacher-Directed Tools Assigned partners share ideas and write them on their whiteboards. Student-Enacted Tools Partners will verbally compose, and then write on their assigned topic, in the next segment of this lesson. I will need to review the rubric for informational writing with them. Assess: These are the students who will need further support Meet with Arturo, Angel, and Marissa before lesson to discuss ideas they will be sharing with partners.
Feedback Opportunities: We will analyze our table of contents to see if we have met the learning intention of planning our class book. I will also meet with Precious, Suha, Adriana, and Francisco to look at the items they generated for this lesson.
Independent Learning and Closure: Students will meet with their writing partners to begin composing their sections for the class book. They will also review their success and compare it with the learning intentions.

Available for download at **https://resources.corwin.com/VL-LiteracyK-5**

intentions are those that focus on the social skills that foster effective collaboration and communication. Nancy saw one frustrated teacher post the social goal, "Raise your hand before talking!" This is *not* the type of social goal that we mean here. However, a social goal of "taking turns while speaking and tracking the speaker" is a valued skill in small and large group work. It makes sense to attend to the social skills of students as they learn. After all, Vygotsky (1962) and others have certainly shown us that all learning is a social endeavor. The ways in which peers interact and work with one another, and with their teacher, are an engine in the classroom.

Social learning intentions can include things like

- *Ask your teammates for help.*

- *Listen to really understand what your group members are saying.*

- *Explain your reasoning.*

- *Give helpful feedback to others.*

These and other communication skills contribute to a sense of classroom cohesion, which Hattie (2009) describes as "the sense that all (teachers and students) are working toward positive learning gains" (p. 103). As with other learning expectations, social learning intentions should be based on what teachers learn from their students as they watch them work and review individual and group products. Listening to and observing the interactions of students in small and large group settings is essential for making such decisions.

Shortly into the school year, Year 5 teacher Edward Hurley asks his students to create a list of class norms they will agree to as they work together throughout the school year. Using the communities of practice work outlined by Wenger (1998), he had introduced these concepts in previous lessons:

- **Learning as Belonging** through trusting and respectful relationships

- **Learning as Experiences** using collaborative, participatory conversations

- **Learning as Doing** by fully engaging in the work and honoring commitments to self and others

- **Learning as Becoming** by telling one's own story, challenging views held by self and others, and becoming a steward of one's world

> Social learning intentions are those that focus on the social skills that foster effective collaboration and communication.

> EFFECT SIZE FOR CLASSROOM COHESION = **0.53**

> **Teaching Takeaway**
>
> Social goals can include things like "Ask your teammates for help," "Listen to really understand what your group members are saying," "Explain your reasoning," or "Give helpful feedback to others."

Mr. Hurley began by stating that the learning intention focused on developing some norms that aligned with the communities of practice work they had done in previous lessons, and he reviewed the language charts they had developed. He posed several questions about the need for norms in families and groups as well as what happens when norms are violated. He then handed out colored adhesive dots to students and asked them to "place your dots on the charts next to the norms you believe are most important for us. You've each got 10 dots, and you can 'spend' them anyway you like." The students completed a gallery walk in which they discussed items hanging on the wall with a group of peers moving from item to item. Gallery walks are a student-enacted form of dialogic instruction, because conversations are student-led. Following the gallery walk, Mr. Hurley invited his students into the learning circle, their chairs positioned so that they could clearly see one another. He guided students through a tallying of the results, which clustered in three domains: Learning by Belonging, Learning by Experiences, and Learning by Doing. From there, Mr. Hurley relied on several teacher-directed dialogic methods to structure their discussion, including using the class talking piece (a miniature souvenir ball from the local football club) so he could hear from some silent students. Here is a list they developed.

We will listen when others are speaking. That means

- ☐ Looking at the speaker
- ☐ Waiting to talk and avoiding talk with others

We will work to support each other in our collaborative groups. That means

- ☐ Answering questions from others
- ☐ Sharing our thinking without telling others how to do it
- ☐ Asking good questions of one another

We will come to class prepared to work hard to learn. That means

- ☐ Being ready to start when the bell rings
- ☐ Having the correct supplies (paper, pencil, notebook, textbook) ready

As the year progressed, students added other norms to this list. Mr. Hurley did not have to spend time nagging students about their behavior or being prepared for class. When needed, he could instead refer back to their agreements about the norms that had been chosen by the entire class, allowing the students to take a greater degree of responsibility for their behavior and work. Mr. Hurley's lesson plan can be viewed in Figure 2.3 on the next page.

EFFECT SIZE FOR CLASSROOM MANAGEMENT = 0.52

SUCCESS CRITERIA IN LANGUAGE ARTS

Effective teachers establish not only the learning intentions but also the success criteria. Note that a key notion here is that learning intentions alone are not satisfactory; it is the quality of learning intentions *and* success criteria that make the difference. We need both! In addition to knowing what they're supposed to learn, students should know how they will know they've learned it, and how they can assess themselves along the way.

Success Criteria Are Crucial for Motivation

The good news about learning intentions and success criteria is that they have been shown to increase students' internal motivation. And a very convincing case could be made that internal motivation to succeed is one of the most important things your students can learn.

Success criteria work because they tap into principles of human motivation (Bandura, 1997; Elliot & Harackiewicz, 1994). People tend to compare their current performance or ability to a goal that they have set or that a caring teacher has set with them. When there is a gap between where they are and where they want to be, it creates cognitive dissonance. Students are motivated to close the gap and get rid of the dissonance by working and learning. The more explicitly and precisely they can see the goal, the more motivated they will be.

Video 6

What Changes When You Use Learning Intentions and Success Criteria?

https://resources.corwin.com/ VL-LiteracyK-5

It may seem obvious that teachers should know whether or not their students are learning what they're supposed to. But students need to know whether they're on the right track, too. Self-reported grades reflect the extent to which students have accurate understandings of their levels of achievement. It matters that students can describe their current performance accurately, whether that performance is high or low (Hattie, 2012). When we think about it, though, it's hard for learners to know whether they are learning something without having some criteria against which they can measure themselves. Teachers should have success criteria in mind for the lesson. Put simply, success criteria describe what success looks like when the learning goal is reached. It is specific, concrete, and measureable.

EFFECT SIZE FOR SELF-REPORTED GRADES = 1.44

Figure 2.3   Lesson Plan in Year 5 Social Language

Assessed Need: I have noticed that my students need: *To arrive at agreed norms for how we work together.*
Standard(s) Addressed: *Language for social interactions: Understand that patterns of language interaction vary across social contexts and types of texts and that they help to signal social roles and relationships (ACELA1501)*
Text(s) I Will Use: *Language charts developed during previous lessons on communities of practice*
Learning Intention for This Lesson: *To develop a list of class norms that name how we learn by belonging, experiencing, doing, and becoming.*
Success Criteria for This Lesson: *We will come to consensus about our norms.*
Direct Instruction: Model: Strategies/skills/concepts to emphasize *Review communities of practices language charts.* Guide and Scaffold: Questions to ask 1. *What are the norms your family relies on? What happens when the norms are violated?* 2. *What can happen in a community where there are no norms for how people interact?* 3. *What do you consider to be the most essential elements of each, and why?* Assess: These are the students who will need further support *Melissa may need redirection to gain her attention.*
Dialogic Instruction: Teacher-Directed Tools *After the gallery walk (below) we will sit in a learning circle to view the norms we listed during the classroom discussion. I will ask for proposed norms for the class, and ask for fist-to-five hand signals to work toward consensus. I will use the talking piece as needed to ensure that every voice is heard.* Student-Enacted Tools *Use a gallery walk process so that students can meet in small groups in front of each poster. Students will be given colored dots to affix to the poster statements they consider to be essential.* Assess: These are the students who will need further support *Check in with Getano frequently to make sure he is following the discussion.*
Feedback Opportunities: *Students will write a short exit slip about the process we used, so I can address any individual concerns.*
Independent Learning and Closure: *Students will apply norms with my assistance for the next week, and we will revisit these after this time period to revise as needed. For closure, students will be asked to review major aspects of the lessons and identify what they learned from each.*

Suppose that a teacher establishes a learning intention that students should compose a response to a writing prompt. How would a student know whether she can do this? Would writing three sentences be enough? Should students compose the response independently, or as part of a team? What if her spelling and conventions are correct, and she used evidence from texts to support her opinion? Each of these questions can guide teachers in determining what success looks like for their students. In writing, for instance, success is demonstrated by more than simply writing a certain number of words or sentences. Teachers who focus only on the correctness of a student's use of conventions do so at the peril of misunderstanding the students' conceptual understanding of the topic and the purposes of writing.

> Success criteria describe what success looks like when the learning goal is reached. It is specific, concrete, and measureable.

Without clearly defined criteria, teachers and students are not sure what type of learning has occurred, if any. As we noted earlier, some learning intentions focus on surface learning, and thus the success criteria should be aligned with that level of learning. Other times, the learning intention focuses on deep or transfer levels of learning, and the success criteria need to align with those levels.

The *VISIBLE LEARNER*

Fifth grader Ashley was reviewing her writing fluency log and wrote in her writer's notebook, "I will increase my writing fluency to 40 words in a minute and only have 8 errors." When asked about this, Ashley noted that she already writes 34 words on average per minute during timed writing and that having a goal keeps her focused. "I think about my goals before we write so that I can stay focused on writing better. I like to write a lot so that I have a lot of ideas to edit later." Ashley understands that writing is more than fluency and has identified other areas for mastery, including "changing the sentence lengths inside of paragraphs to keep the reader interested" and "writing better hooks to make sure that readers want to read what I write."

Visible learners can set mastery goals.

Students are much more motivated to work toward success criteria if those criteria are specific (Locke & Latham, 1990). Criteria such as "do your best" and "try hard" are not very clear or actionable. It may well be worthwhile to ban these phrases from your vocabulary, as they set very low targets. (Whatever the student does is often claimed as his best, when this best may not be good enough.) Instead, criteria such as these are more likely to produce results:

"I will be able to clearly support my opinion using evidence from the text."

"I can use correct spelling and punctuation so my reader can understand my writing."

The more specific the learning intentions and the criteria for reaching those intentions, the more likely it is that your students will achieve them. Learning intentions should be proximal (Bandura, 1997). In other words, they shouldn't be too distant in the future. This is important to keep in mind when assigning long projects—it really is worth establishing daily success criteria that your students can keep in mind as they work on long-term projects, especially for younger students.

Success criteria for longer projects often come in the form of rubrics and checklists, but more common ones are specific to the individual lesson and are used many times:

- Show how you checked your work before turning it in.

- I can ask questions about words I don't know in a text.

- Be sure your story includes an opening that grabs the reader's attention, and end with a cliffhanger.

- I can describe the main character and the problem she is facing at this point in the book.

- I use spaces between words.

Success criteria can be developed with students, and this is especially effective because it ensures that you are truly using child-friendly language, which is especially important in the earlier grades.

Kiara Mitchell created a checklist of success criteria for identifying main ideas and supporting details with her third-grade students. "They've already had some experience at doing this," she explained, "and now I want to deepen their knowledge a bit more by showing them how to be more mindful of how they go about doing it."

While she conceded that she could furnish them with a checklist, she said she was interested in increasing their opportunities to think metacognitively. "I know they could probably do this with a checklist I give them, but I want them to notice my thinking and theirs as we create and then test our own Room 7 checklist."

Using a previously read and discussed passage from their basal reading series, Ms. Mitchell explained that the learning intention was to "identify the ways we determine the main idea and supporting details in informational text," and that today's success criterion was to "develop a checklist we can use to help us locate these in other informational texts." She began by modeling and thinking aloud while the passage was displayed on the document camera, inviting students to record the questions she asked herself. She then wrote down their answers, using the language the children used to describe her sentences. "I was glad to hear how much academic language they were using," she remarked later.

Using questions to further scaffold their thinking, she queried them about the need to use main ideas and supporting details, both as a writer and a reader. Titus said, "Without a main idea, the author's ideas can get all messed up," and Janelle added, "Sometimes when I read I get kinda lost, and then if I remember to look for the main idea it can help."

Together, the students and Ms. Mitchell created the following checklist:

To find the main idea, make sure you:

- ❏ Can name the topic the author is writing about
- ❏ Can figure out why the author thinks it is important (author's purpose)
- ❏ Check to see if there are text features that can give you a clue
- ❏ Find a sentence that has the most important idea in it
- ❏ See if there are other facts that are related (supporting details)
- ❏ If you still can't find the main idea,
- ❏ Read the passage again, and then ask yourself these same questions.

Using the checklist they developed, students then did a "test drive" using another reading passage to see if their suggestions worked. In the meantime, Ms. Mitchell added the terms *author's purpose* and *supporting details* to the checklist to further expand their academic language.

"We'll use these questions a few more times and then convert our list into a checklist. We're developing a wall of success criteria for readers and writers that we can refer to many more times throughout the year," Ms. Mitchell told her class. Her lesson can be seen in Figure 2.4.

Figure 2.4   Lesson Plan in Third-Grade Reading Comprehension

Assessed Need: I have noticed that my students need: Experience locating main ideas and supporting details, especially in texts where portions of the main idea appear in more than one sentence.
Standard(s) Addressed: The student will continue to read and demonstrate comprehension of nonfiction texts. (g) Identify the main idea. (h) Identify supporting details.
Text(s) I Will Use: Passage we read yesterday from our basal reader
Learning Intention for This Lesson: We will identify the ways we figure out the main idea and supporting details in informational text we read.
Success Criteria for This Lesson: We will develop a checklist we can use when we need to figure out the main idea and supporting details in informational texts we read.
Direct Instruction: Model: Strategies/skills/concepts to emphasize I will think aloud about how I locate the main idea and supporting details of the passage. I ask myself questions about the topic. Do I know what the topic is? I look at the text features to give me clues about the main idea. What text features does the author use? I look for evidence of the author's purpose. What does he or she want me to know about this topic? I look for a sentence that summarizes the most important idea in the passage. Does this make sense? I look for supporting details that link to the main idea. Do they give more information about the main idea? If I am not sure, I begin again. Guide and Scaffold: Questions to ask Why do writers need a main idea? Why do readers need to understand the main idea and supporting details? Assess: These are the students who will need further support Andre and Janette were absent yesterday and have not read the passage. I will need to read it with them before the lesson.
Dialogic Instruction: Teacher-Directed Tools Students will work in groups of four with another passage and the checklist to see if they can locate the main idea and supporting details. Student-Enacted Tools N/A Assess: These are the students who will need further support Check for understanding with Andre and Janette to see if have further questions.
Feedback Opportunities: I will meet with Kenneth, Rico, Jamal, and Ashleigh for guided instruction so they can get feedback about how successfully they are using the checklist.
Independent Learning and Closure: Students will use the checklist we develop in their independent reading, and then we will discuss what worked and what didn't work for them. We will also revisit the learning intentions and success criteria, providing students time to consider their own learning.

CONCLUSION

Learning intentions and success criteria contribute greatly to teacher clarity, but only if they are adequately and consistently communicated to students. There is another benefit from spending time figuring out what you want out of a lesson, and that is in its contribution to your planning processes. As we have stated before, this book is not about writing extensive lesson plans that consume huge amounts of precious time. However, if we cannot articulate what we are pursuing in our lessons, how will our students ever know? And without coherent learning intentions and success criteria, how would we ever know our impact on learning?

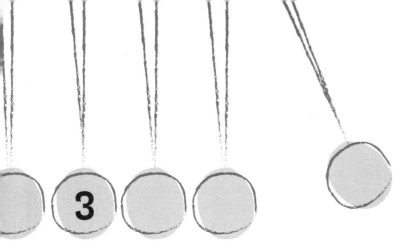

3

DIRECT INSTRUCTION

© Spencer Grant/PhotoEdit

"So why eat insects?" Year 5 teacher Edward Hurley asks his students. The students in his Northern Territory classroom have been studying the history of their aboriginal ancestors. Mr. Hurley has selected an informational article that draws on a more contemporary argument: that insects are an excellent source of protein, and the consumption of termites, crickets, and ants is growing in Western societies, even as it has been practiced for thousands of years by nearly 80% of the planet.

Mr. Hurley recognizes that simply handing students an article and wishing for the best isn't likely to have the impact he wants. The article he selected is a challenge for these 10-year-olds, and the author has a decidedly strong point of view, one that might cause students to simply go with the author's opinion, rather than question it. The teacher has determined that direct instruction is an essential aspect of his teaching. "I've tracked my impact for years now, and it's helped me to figure out how I can maximize my effectiveness." (Mr. Hurley's full lesson plan can be found in Figure 3.1 on pages 52–53.)

To be sure, direct instruction has gotten a bad rap in some quarters. In fact, it might be one of the most misunderstood instructional approaches out there. Impressions about direct instruction usually cluster into four categories:

1. It is scripted and didactic.

2. It is inflexible.

3. It devalues teacher judgment.

4. It relates only to surface or content knowledge.

Yet walk into virtually any effective elementary classroom and you will see direct instruction in action. Don't believe us? Interview colleagues you have identified as being highly successful with their students, and ask them to reflect on the methods they frequently employ. You might ask

- When planning, do you have a clear idea about your learning intentions?

- Do you consider it important for students to know what the criteria for learning success are, and to be held accountable for their learning?

- Is it important to draw students into the lesson by appealing to their interests, curiosities, and wonderings?

- Are modeling and demonstrating skills and concepts part of your repertoire?

- Does checking for understanding have a place in your lessons?

- Should a lesson include guided instruction such that learners can practice new skills and concepts, with feedback from the teacher?

- How important is it to close a lesson with a summary to organize student thinking and consolidate learning?

- Should students have time to try on new learning independently in novel situations?

These are the essence of direct instruction. It is deliberate planning, sharing the notions of success with the students, and continually monitoring your impact.

To limit one's understanding of direct instruction to highly scripted programs is to overlook the practices that make it highly effective for developing surface level knowledge.

Video 7

Creating Visible Learners: The Visible Learner Seeks, Is Resilient, and Aspires to Challenge

https://resources.corwin.com/ VL-LiteracyK-5

The *VISIBLE LEARNER*

When asked about reading hard texts, fifth grader Tristen said, "Yeah, they're hard. I mean really hard. But it's like being a detective. You can figure it out, with some help. If it's not a challenge, it can get boring. It's better to better to not totally get it at first because you stay interested and times goes really fast."

Similarly, second grader Justine said, "My teacher says that that I'm really good at trying. I don't give up and that is good because you get to learn things that are interesting."

The visible learner seeks, is resilient to, and aspires to challenge.

Chances are good that the talented teachers you identified affirmed that each of these actions is vital for students' learning. Adams and Engelmann (1996), in their meta-analysis of direct instruction, named each of these as necessary components of direct instruction. To limit one's

Figure 3.1   Lesson Plan for Year 5 Using Texts in Context

Assessed Need: I have noticed that my students need: *To evaluate texts by looking for loaded language to determine an author's opinion.*
Standard(s) Addressed: *Use metalanguage to describe the effects of ideas, text structures, and language features on particular audiences (ACELT 1795)*
Text(s) I Will Use: *"Why Eat Insects?"*
Learning Intention for This Lesson: *We will consider the author's message and point of view so that we can evaluate the information presented.*
Success Criteria for This Lesson: *I will write a response to this information that includes my opinion and supporting evidence, and compare or contrast it with the author's point of view (use argumentation rubric).*

Direct Instruction:

Model: Strategies/skills/concepts to emphasize

Use of loaded vocabulary to convey opinion

Name the strategy, state its purpose, explain its use: Use title to set the author's purpose (poses a question). I am modeling how I look for loaded vocabulary that suggests the author's point of view. When I am reading an opinion piece, I look carefully for terms that show the author's opinion.

Analogy: Loaded words are like weights on a balance scale. They tip the scale in one direction, which is what authors will do when stating their opinion.

Demonstration: Underline words in first paragraph: rightly considered, excellent, plentiful, resource-plentiful, normal, good reason, and incredibly rich source of protein

Errors to avoid: I have to be careful that I don't form my own opinion too soon and stop reading altogether just because I might disagree. I need to keep reading and give the author time to make his case, before I settle on my opinion.

Assess the skill: Write at least one question in the margin that challenges the author's message.

Guide and Scaffold: Questions to ask

1. How does the author use different techniques for conveying his message?

2. The author claims that agriculture consumes 92% of freshwater. What are some of the sustainability implications for NT?

3. What do you want to independently verify in this paragraph? What statements might you challenge?

Assess: These are the students who will need further support

Alkina, Waarrar, and Koorine will need me to support them through the second paragraph, while the rest of the class is reading independently.

Dialogic Instruction:

Teacher-Directed Tools

N/A

Student-Enacted Tools

After reading, I will direct all the students who strongly agree with the author to meet in one corner of the classroom, and I will indicate that others who simply agree, who disagree, and who strongly disagree should meet in the other three corners, respectively. The students in each corner will work together to list arguments in favor of or opposed to eating insects as a protein source.

Assess: These are the students who will need further support

Check in with Peter about his opinion, as he will usually just follow his friends rather than consider his own thoughts.

Feedback Opportunities: *I will meet with the smallest group first so that they receive feedback about their list. Given a smaller number, they may need further support.*

Independent Learning and Closure: *Students will write an opinion with evidence exit ticket, using the argumentation rubric as a way to self-assess before submitting. As part of the closure, I will summarize the main points of the lesson and foreshadow the next lesson.*

Available for download at **https://resources.corwin.com/VL-LiteracyK-5**

understanding of direct instruction to highly scripted programs is to overlook the practices that make it highly effective for developing surface level knowledge. With an effect size of 0.59, direct instruction offers a pedagogical pathway that provides students with the modeling, scaffolding, and practice they require when learning new skills and concepts. John notes that

EFFECT SIZE FOR DIRECT INSTRUCTION = 0.59

> when we learn something new . . . we need more skill development and content; as we progress, we need more connections, relationships, and schemas to organize these skills and content; we then need more regulation or self-control over how we continue to learn the content and ideas. (Hattie, 2009, p. 84)

In other words, whether we are 5 or 45, we follow a trajectory that moves from surface learning to deeper learning, and we transfer some of that learning such that we can utilize it in lots of new and seemingly dissimilar situations. It is quite possible that you have applied a teaching technique or two over the years to your own unsuspecting family members, even though no one told you to do so.

Perhaps you are still reluctant to entertain the possibility that direct instruction might be effective. We invite you to try it and evaluate it yourself using your students' learning as a measure. We would be remiss, and would fail to convey the full message of visible learning, if we did not restate that knowing your impact on your students is the truest yardstick you'll ever possess (Hattie, 2009). We don't mean your gut instincts, or your impressions, or your anecdotes, but the fact that you determine the impact of your teaching on your students and adjust accordingly. Finding out what they know and don't know at the beginning of a unit of study, teaching, and then assessing again at the end of the unit furnishes feedback to you about the impact of your teaching.

Imagine meeting a kindergarten student who did not know all of the sound-symbol relationships. It hardly seems fair to ask the student to guess the sounds for each of the letters. Of course telling students the sounds that correspond to given letters does not mean that they will master the language. They also need to practice and receive feedback. Telling students the sound-symbol correlations speeds up the process of students learning to break the code. For example, let's say that there is a small group of five-year-olds in class who do not yet match sounds and letters. The teacher might say, "Today we are going to learn a new letter sound. We use this letter's sound to read words." Pointing to the letter *s*, the teacher could model, saying, "The sound for this letter is */sss/*. Listen as I say this sound */sss/*." The teacher might then provide students with opportunities to see a number of different fonts, each time asking the students to practice the letter sound, saying, "The sound for this letter is */s/*." "What is the sound for this letter? " */sss/* "Yes, the sound for this letter is */sss/*." Over time, and with practice, the student will recognize the letter and its corresponding sound.

But that's not really reading. To read, students have to use their knowledge of sight words and decodable words (words for which the phonics rules work) to make meaning. Following the recognition of individual letters, teachers work on blending. For example, teachers might focus on consonant-vowel-consonant words, such as *sat, cat, rat, bat,* and *mat.* Through direct instruction, the teacher may model sounding out each of the letters in the first word, noting the sound for each of the letters: *s, a, t.* The teacher could say: */s/, /sa/, /sat/.* After the student practices a bit, the teacher might change the onset letter, maintaining the rhyme (at) having the students practice a number of CVC words that end with *–at.* The role of direct instruction cannot be minimized.

This chapter is not about phonics instruction per se. Rather, we will profile the ways teachers provide direct instruction for students who are learning a wide range of skills, strategies, or concepts. Because the first two steps in the list—learning intentions and success criteria—have already been examined in the previous chapter, we will confine our discussion in this chapter to

- Relevance

- Modeling

- Checking for understanding

- Guided instruction

- Closure

- Independent learning

RELEVANCE

All learners, whether they are 6 years of age or 36-year-old educators, crave relevance. By that, we mean that an important driver of learning is in understanding why the acquisition of a new skill or concept is important in one's life. Think about all of those ubiquitous how-to videos on YouTube. Quite frankly, many of them are boring, unless you actually have a need and desire to learn something. Figuring out how to tie a necktie, or making the new tortilla iron work (something Doug had to figure out one evening), makes those videos infinitely more interesting, because there's a reason to learn something. Moreover, by looking at the video, Doug realized what success looked like and how best to work to this success.

Video 8
Relevance

*https://resources.corwin.com/
VL-LiteracyK-5*

Importantly, relevance facilitates intrinsic motivation, and those who are intrinsically motivated to learn tend to persist in their learning when they confront challenges (Meece, Anderman, & Anderman, 2006). Relevancy doesn't mean that all your lessons need to ensure success in a career, but rather that learners can see how the learning intentions apply in their lives. Why are syllables important? They help us spell more accurately. Why are adjectives important? We can use them to write more descriptively so that our readers understand our ideas.

Kindergarten teacher Saul Romero knows that relevancy is key for his young students. As part of the opening of his lessons, he posts and discusses the importance of the lesson using a sentence frame: "This helps me _____." For instance, at the beginning of a lesson on writing lowercase letters that descend below the line (*g, j, p, q,* and *y*), Mr. Romero set the learning intention and success criteria, and then he said, "It's always important that we think about why we are learning something. If you're not sure, you should always ask, 'Mr. Romero, why are we learning this?' I want to make sure we can always explain why we are learning something. I'll read this sentence to you, and then we will read it together: "I practice

> Relevance facilitates intrinsic motivation, and those who are intrinsically motivated to learn tend to persist in their learning when they confront challenges.

printing letters that go below the line because it helps me read my own writing." After Mr. Romero repeats it, the students read it chorally, and he moves forward with the lesson.

The *VISIBLE LEARNER*

Keoni, a student in Mr. Romero's kindergarten class, asks his teacher during a small group conference, "After we learn letters below the line, can we learn letters that go above the line?" Mr. Romero responds, "That would be a very interesting lesson. I think we should talk about it as we learn more about letters. Thank you, Keoni. And for this lesson, which letters are you comfortable writing and which ones do you still want to learn?"

Keoni responded, "I am not good with any of them. But I will be. I want to start with the letter *p*. Can we practice that one?"

Visible learners can articulate their next learning steps.

Video 9
Modeling Academic Language
https://resources.corwin.com/VL-LiteracyK-5

Teaching Takeaway

Model for students such that they can approximate the thinking of an expert.

TEACHER MODELING

There was a fascinating series of studies that began with neuroscientists in the 1990s who noticed something surprising. When they measured brain cell activity of monkeys that were watching the movements of other monkeys, such as picking up a banana, they found that specialized brain cells called motor neurons in the observing monkeys were active, even though these observing monkeys were sitting still. Interestingly, these were some of the same neurons that became active when the observing monkey was the one doing the motion. So, the monkey *watching* and the monkey *doing* used a lot of the same brain cells, and the cells were similarly active (Rizzolatti & Craighero, 2004). Later, researchers showed that these mirror neuron systems in the human brain function similarly to understand the intentions of others (Iacoboni et al., 2005). When you observe someone else do something you use many of the same neural pathways as when you perform the same action yourself. These mirror neuron systems may help explain the power of teacher modeling, not to mention how babies learn and why fads and trends spread so quickly.

Teacher modeling processes can trigger similar responses in observing students. Through modeling, students can be taught to think aloud about their own cognitive decision making and problem solving, providing teachers with further insight into students' grasp of skills and concepts. Providing examples of thinking is useful, but effective modeling includes an explanation of why teachers are doing what they are doing, so that students understand *how* the teacher was thinking, not just *what* the teacher was thinking.

Pair With Think-Alouds

When teachers explain their expert thinking in a way that students can understand, students are better able to imitate the thinking of their teachers. We're not looking for students to simply replicate the work of the teacher but rather to explore the ways that other people think. Thinking is invisible, so teachers have to talk about their thinking. By listening to a teacher think, students are guided through the same cognitive processes that the expert uses, as if they were apprentices. Teachers who open up their minds to describe their cognitive and metacognitive processes for their students call these narrations *think-alouds* (Davey, 1983). As noted in Figure 3.2, there are common steps in teacher think-alouds (Fisher, Frey, & Lapp, 2009). Of course, teachers don't use all of these each time they think aloud. They pick and choose the aspects of the think-aloud necessary to build students' strategic thinking.

> By listening to a teacher think, students are guided through the same cognitive processes that the expert uses, as if they were apprentices.

The "I" and "Why" of Think-Alouds

Think-alouds use "I" statements. A lot of teachers say "we" or "you" in their explanations, but "I" statements—using a first-person pronoun—do something different and more powerful for the brains of students. They activate

Figure 3.2   Design a Think-Aloud

Possible Features to Model	Features You Plan to Model
1. Name the strategy, skill, or task.	
2. State the purpose of the strategy, skill, or task.	
3. Explain when the strategy or skill is used.	
4. Use analogies to link prior knowledge to new learning.	
5. Demonstrate how the skill, strategy, or task is completed.	
6. Alert learners to errors to avoid.	
7. Assess the use of the skill.	

Source: Adapted from Fisher, D., Frey, N., & Lapp, D. (2009). *In a reading state of mind: Brain research, teacher modeling, and comprehension instruction.* Newark, DE: International Reading Association.

 Available for download at **https://resources.corwin.com/VL-LiteracyK-5**

"I" statements do something different and more powerful for the brains of students. They activate the ability—some call it an instinct—of humans to learn by imitation.

the ability—some call it an instinct—of humans to learn by imitation. We have worked with teachers who actually think that they are using "I" statements, when they are saying the word "you" (a second-person pronoun) in their explanations. Or, they will start their think-alouds with "I" and then switch to "you" at some point in their explanations. The second-person pronoun is directive; the first-person pronoun signals the sharing of intentions.

These people are not delusional. Rather, teaching is such a complex skill that it can be difficult for teachers to use the exact words that they'd planned on using, or to remember exactly what they said at a time when they were also thinking about 32 (or more) young people, considering formative evaluation results, wondering whether they'd been talking for too long, and thinking as an expert, all simultaneously. Allowing teachers to video- or audio-record their think-alouds, and then giving them the opportunity to watch or listen to the recording, has been very useful in helping teachers over this hump. Knight (2014) and his colleagues at the University of Kansas have analyzed the work of teachers and instructional coaches as they interacted with video and audio recordings of lessons, and found that these tools propelled improvements in instructional quality more effectively than lesson debriefing alone. Similar effects were seen with individual teachers who coached themselves by watching videos of their own teaching. Advancements in digital technology have made it possible for teachers to wear a small device that remotely signals the video camera to turn and follow them as they teach, eliminating the need for another person to operate the camera.

Another strategy is for teachers to use written notes that include the word *because*. It's important to explain *why* you're thinking what you're thinking. If not, students experience an example but do not know how to do this on their own. Using *because* reduces the chance that students will be left wondering how you knew to do something or why you think a certain way. For example, while modeling the comprehension strategy of predicting, you might say, "I can make the following prediction [insert the prediction] because the author told me. . . ." A teacher modeling word solving might say, "I am going to try to figure out this word by looking inside the word for prefixes, suffixes, and bases, because many English words have clues inside them that help readers figure out their meaning." Including the *why* and *because* while modeling increases the chance that students will be able to imitate the expert thinking they have witnessed, because they are provided with examples and the reasons for those examples. Thinking about your thinking is a metacognitive act, and students will start to think more metacognitively when they hear others, including their peers, do so.

EFFECT SIZE FOR METACOGNITIVE STRATEGIES = 0.69

First-grade teacher Iman Hakim's students have been working on developing their ability to infer the emotions and motivations of characters using multiple clues, including words, characters' actions, and the visual clues to be found in the illustrations. This is a complex skill that is developed over many lessons, so Ms. Hakim routinely models how she applies this comprehension skill using the many texts they read. The previous day, she read *Music Over Manhattan* (Karlins, 1998), a picture book about a boy who gains confidence by learning how to play the trumpet. The story features two young cousins who are at times jealous and resentful of each other's accomplishments. Now that her students have a foundational knowledge of the arc of the story, Ms. Hakim returns to the first page to model and think aloud about how she understands the clues. (Her full lesson plan can be found in Figure 3.3 on the next page.) After establishing the learning intention and success criteria, she begins,

> *Today I'm going to model and think aloud about how I use the words the author uses, the actions of the character, and the picture clues to help me figure out how a character feels.* [names strategy]
>
> *We've done this many times before, and today I'm going to use it with* Music Over Manhattan, *the story we read yesterday.* [purpose]
>
> *Authors can't give us every detail, because if they did every story would be really long and kind of boring. The author and the illustrator give us clues to find, just like a detective who's trying to solve a mystery.* [analogy]
>
> *My clues are words, actions, and picture details.* [explains use]

Ms. Hakim reads the first page aloud—it is a passage consisting of seven sentences—and then she demonstrates where she locates clues.

> *When I read I keep my eye out for clues, like a detective. I see a word clue! The author says Bernie is grumpy. I know grumpy means he's not happy, but I wonder why? I expect that his actions will show me how he feels, because authors will let us see how a character feels through actions. It says Bernie mashed the potatoes harder* [makes a gesture of pushing her fist into the palm of her other hand to simulate mashing potatoes]. *Sometimes when I am not happy I push things harder than I really have to. But I still don't know why he feels grumpy. I'll look for another clue.*

Rereading, she pauses on the phrase "but any minute perfect Cousin Herbert would arrive."

> *THAT'S an important clue! People don't say their cousin is "perfect" unless they mean it in a sarcastic way. Like when my sister and I would argue when we were little, and she would say, "You think you're so perfect!" and I would know she meant the opposite. She would be angry with me. I am going to say that sentence again and use my voice like my sister did* [repeats the sentence using a sarcastic tone].

Figure 3.3   Lesson Plan for First Grade Inferring the Emotions and Motivations of Characters Using Multiple Clues

Assessed Need: I have noticed that my students need: To infer characters' feelings using words, actions, and pictures.
Standard(s) Addressed: RL.1.4: Identify words and phrases in stories or poems that suggest feelings or appeal to the senses.
Text(s) I Will Use: Music Over Manhattan (Karlins, 1998)
Learning Intention for This Lesson: We will look for word clues and picture clues in this book to figure out how Bernie and Herbert are feeling.
Success Criteria for This Lesson: I can find and explain evidence of these characters' feelings on my graphic organizer.

Direct Instruction:

Model: Strategies/skills/concepts to emphasize

Use the first page of the book to model my thinking about the word and visual clues I find about Bernie's feelings. Since we read the entire book yesterday, this will be a closer inspection of the text.

Name the strategy, state its purpose, explain its use: Authors don't explain every detail of a story. If they had to tell us everything, the story would be really long! They expect the reader to infer the character's feelings by using the character's words, actions, and pictures. I am going to look closely at the first page of the story to find these clues.

Analogy: When I read, I am always looking for clues like this, just like a detective does when she's solving a mystery. I gather up the clues to figure out what might be happening.

Demonstration:

Words to model: grumpy, perfect Cousin Herbert (sarcasm)

Actions: "Bernie mashed [the potatoes] harder."

Visual: Bernie's frown, creased forehead, and sideways glance

Errors to avoid: If I don't match my tone of voice with the character's feelings, I might miss the inference the author wants me to make.

Assess the skill: Read the passage again using the correct vocal tone.

Guide and Scaffold: Questions to ask

(pp. 3-4): What are the words, actions, and picture clues that tell us how Bernie is feeling?

(pp. 11-12) What clues can we find that show us how Herbert's feelings have changed? Why do we think they have changed?

(pp. 14-17) Herbert's behavior is awful now. But why? What words, actions, and pictures help us understand this?

Assess: These are the students who will need further support

I will reread the text with Aubrey, Ignacio, David, and Alexis because they struggled with the fantasy element of the story yesterday when we read it for the first time.

Dialogic Instruction:

Teacher-Directed Tools

Students will complete a simple graphic organizer about Bernie and Herbert, listing three other confirming pieces of evidence (words, actions, or visual clues) that explain their feelings.

Student-Enacted Tools N/A

Assess: These are the students who will need further support N/A

Feedback Opportunities: I check for understanding with students at tables 2, 4, and 5 to listen to their evidence. These same students will then partner with classmates at Tables 1, 3, and 6 to share their evidence.

Independent Learning and Closure: Students are finding evidence on their own, and after meeting with partners, will add any new examples. They will be provided opportunities to reflect on this experience and ask questions about areas of confusion and what they still would like to learn.

Available for download at **https://resources.corwin.com/VL-LiteracyK-5**

Ms. Hakim continues, now demonstrating how she uses picture clues. She and the children study the face of Bernie, noticing his scrunched up forehead and frowning expression.

> *Look at how his eyes are going sideways in little slits!* exclaims Ms. Hakim. *That's another great clue for me that Bernie is not happy that cousin Herbert is coming over to his house for dinner, and that he is feeling like he is not as good as his cousin.*

She then explains that she needs to put these clues together to avoid an error:

> *When I read, I hear a voice in my head, like I am reading to myself. But if I don't let the voice change using the clues I find, I might miss the meaning. So I am going to read it one more time, and I want to use a grumpy voice as I read to myself.* [rereads] *Yes, that worked. My voice matched how the character seems to be feeling, and I figured out how Bernie felt by paying close attention to clues such as the words, actions, and pictures of the character.* [assess the skill]

In the next part of her lesson, Ms. Hakim will use questions to scaffold their learning, in order to check for their understanding of the comprehension strategy she modeled for them.

STUDENTS SHOULD THINK ALOUD, TOO

Have you ever had a student come to the front of the room to show how she figured out a solution, only to watch her explain it in a way that guarantees nobody else will learn from it? Students leading the class through their solution paths can be very powerful, and the way this is done shouldn't be left to the pedagogical skills of an untrained child. Rather, if you want students to explain their thinking or their solution, you will need to teach them how to do this explicitly. One way to do this is to debrief after your think-alouds, explaining what you did. Figure 3.4 includes a checklist useful in self-assessing aspects of a think-aloud. If you use this checklist to debrief your think-alouds, your students can use it as a guide when they are leading. Other students can hold the demonstrator accountable for following the guidelines, and, ideally, they will hold you accountable when you do yours as well.

> EFFECT SIZE
> FOR SELF-
> VERBALIZATION AND
> SELF-QUESTIONING
> = 0.64

The third-grade students in Kiara Mitchell's class have been studying the works of artists featured in the book *Honoring Our Ancestors* (Rohmer, 1999). In this book, 14 contemporary artists explain a painting of theirs that features a family member, and they discuss their inspiration. For example, artist Mark Dukes paints himself in a portrait of Ethiopian

Figure 3.4   Student Think-Aloud Checklist

☐ Let your listener(s) read through the entire question or text before you begin your think-aloud.
☐ Use "I" statements.
☐ Explain why you think you are correct, or how you know you are.
☐ Speak loudly enough for your partner(s) to hear.
☐ Don't go too fast or too slow.
☐ Make sure your think-aloud doesn't go on for more than 5 minutes.

Available for download at **https://resources.corwin.com/VL-LiteracyK-5**

saints, armed with a paintbrush because "that enables me to travel back in time" (p. 10). Ms. Mitchell and her class have read all of the selections previously, and she wants her students to use the think-aloud checklist to explain how their thinking uses visuals from the book.

To refresh their memories, she reviews the checklist using one of the readings from the book. "I chose Devon to be my partner because I've noticed she can get distracted easily. This gives her a really important job as we fishbowl for the class," said the teacher.

After completing the teacher think-aloud, Ms. Mitchell hosts a short discussion, using questions to guide students' thinking in order to circumvent possible difficulties. She asks students, "What did you notice that I did when we got stuck?" and "Which words did we use to provide you with information about our thinking?" After the class discussion, she has each student partner with another student to think aloud about a painting and accompanying text of their choice from the target book. Ms. Mitchell's lesson is in Figure 3.5 on the next page.

> If you want students to explain their thinking or their solution, you will need to teach them how to do this explicitly.

The *VISIBLE LEARNER*

Jacy and Leslee, students in Kiara Mitchell's third-grade class, do not tell each other answers. Rather they support each other through questions and prompts. They provide hints to one another, much like their teacher has modeled. For example, when Jacy gets frustrated with a section of the text, Leslee says, "We got this. Just take it slow and go back to read it over. This is interestin' so it's worth it to get it right."

Later, when Leslee writes some vocabulary words in her personal journal and spells them incorrectly, Jacy says, "I think you want to check those again. I'm not sayin' which is right or wrong, but I think it would be good to check again."

Visible learners positively supports their peers' learning.

Jacy and Leslee choose artist Caryl Henry's portrait of herself with her grandmother, a cosmetologist, and Madame C. J. Walker, the first Black female millionaire in the United States. (The artist's grandmother studied at Madame Walker's School of Beauty Culture in 1916.) After the girls reread the checklist, Jacy begins:

> *The grandma is in the middle of the three ladies, and I know I'm right because she looks like the photograph on the other page* [points]. *And the lady on the right is the person who made the painting. She doesn't look so much like her picture, but it says right here* [points at text]

Figure 3.5   Lesson Plan for Third-Grade Lesson

Assessed Need: I have noticed that my students need: To use academic language to express ideas.
Standard(s) Addressed: Oral Language 3.1: The student will use effective communication skills in group activities. Oral Language 3.2: The student will present brief oral reports using visual media
Text(s) I Will Use: <u>Honoring Our Ancestors</u> (Rohmer, 1999)
Learning Intention for This Lesson: We will use spoken language and visuals to share ideas with others.
Success Criteria for This Lesson: Think-aloud checklist

Direct Instruction:

Model: Strategies/skills/concepts to emphasize

Review the student think-aloud checklist to reinforce knowledge of elements.

Name the strategy, state its purpose, explain its use: I am going to model how I use the think-aloud checklist to help me remember all the things I should do when I think aloud for a partner. When I remember to do these, I help my partner understand

Analogy: When I go to the grocery store, I have a list so I don't forget to buy something I need. The think-aloud checklist helps me remember everything.

Demonstration: [think-aloud using the painting by Nancy Hom (p. 17)] I am going to think aloud today with Devon. First, I'll read the checklist to myself to remember all the elements. The first reminder is to let the listener read first before I start talking. I know we read about this artist yesterday, so I can start. Next, use "I" statements. When I look at the painting, I see how large her father's arms are. I remember in the text she talked about her dad being so strong "from lifting huge plates of food." Explain why you know you are correct. I know I am correct because I can find the sentence with that information.

Errors to avoid: One mistake would be to talk too softly. It would be hard for my partner to hear if I am too quiet.

Assess the skill: I will check with my partner to ask how I have done. Devon, can you give me feedback using the checklist?

Guide and Scaffold: Questions to ask

What can be hard about thinking aloud?

How will you know you have been successful?

If you are having a difficult time, how could you get help?

Assess: These are the students who will need further support

I am thinking aloud with Devon as my partner so she can be more actively engaged in this lesson.

Dialogic Instruction

Teacher-Directed Tools

All students will complete the checklist with their partners to rate how they did

Student-Enacted Tools

N/A

Assess: These are the students who will need further support

Listen to Devon and Katie as they discuss their checklists to make sure Devon is applying new concepts.

that she is pictured on the right. So the directions and the photographs helped me. Now it's your turn.

Now Leslee continues:

When we read the story, Ms. Mitchell told us that the artist didn't like hot combs when she was little. She wears her hair in dreads [dread-locks] *now so she don't need a hot comb. That's in this sentence* [points]: *"I threw away my combs and went natural with dreadlocks"* (p. 14). *Look at the painting! She got those combs on fire!*

The girls then evaluate each other's performance, agreeing that they both used "I" statements, spoke loud enough to be heard, and used the text to show they were right.

And we didn't talk too long and get all boring! said Jacy.

CHECKING FOR UNDERSTANDING

Effective teachers check for understanding throughout their lessons, using a variety of approaches, especially by examining the oral and written language of their students. Durkin (1978/79) studied reading comprehension instruction of elementary teachers and found that by far the most common method for doing so was questioning. She observed teachers identified by district administrators as being "exemplary" in 39 classrooms, and she found that these teachers were in fact "primarily mentioners, assignment-givers, and interrogators" (1981, p. 454). Durkin argued that the effective teaching of comprehension required modeling and thinking aloud, feedback, and especially questions that scaffold and probe, rather than interrogate.

Video 10
Checking for Understanding

https://resources.corwin.com/ VL-LiteracyK-5

Use Questions to Probe Student Thinking

Questions that check for understanding are a crucial aspect of direct instruction. But the best teachers probe deeper, for more specific information. They don't just want to know whether or not a student understands something. If the student does understand, they want to see if he can explain his thinking and apply what is understood. If the student doesn't understand, these teachers probe deeper to find the point at which a misconception, overgeneralization, or partial understanding led her astray. Lurking in the back of the teacher's mind is the question, "What does this child's answer tell me about what he or she knows and doesn't know?"

The purpose of the question matters. Closed questions that constrict student speculation limit student thinking to trying to determine what the "right" answer might be (Doug calls it, "Guess what's in the teacher's brain.") A series of closed questions strung together is called a *funneling pattern,* because the purpose is to lead the student through a procedure without adequate attention to connections (Herbel-Eisenmann & Breyfogle, 2005). In contrast, open questions require students to notice their own thinking, and a string of these is called *focusing questions*. The difference at times may seem subtle, but it is the outcome that is more telling. A series of funneling questions results in channeling the student toward the predetermined correct answers, with little room left for students to consider possibilities and notice their thinking. On the other hand, a series of focusing questions can open up student thinking, and provide you with more insight into their thought processes. Fourth-grade teacher Gloria Hansen worked with her grade-level colleague Diane Lincoln, a first-year teacher, to develop focusing questions that would open up student thinking. After examining questions Ms. Lincoln had developed to use with the following day's reading, they discussed the concept of funneling and focusing questions, and then changed Ms. Lincoln's questions just enough so that the revised ones might prompt richer responses (see Figure 3.6). After school the next day, Ms. Lincoln came back to Ms. Hansen's room and said, "I was surprised at how much longer their answers were when I asked those focusing questions. I learned a lot more about what they were thinking."

GUIDED INSTRUCTION

Using focusing questions is an excellent way to begin guided instruction, because it has the potential of expanding, rather than constricting, student thinking. Direct instruction requires that the teacher scaffold—only as much as needed—through strategic questions, prompts, and cues, with the goal of elevating students' learning. It does *not* involve giving students the answers, or telling them how to solve a problem. Many teachers default to

> Effective teachers don't just want to know whether a student understands something, they want to see if the child can explain his thinking and apply what is understood.

Teaching Takeaway

Use questions to better understand student misconceptions or partial understanding.

EFFECT SIZE FOR QUESTIONING = 0.48

Figure 3.6   Funneling and Focusing Questions

Funneling Questions	Focusing Questions
What did the character mean when she said, "I need a change of scenery"?	The character said he needed a "change of scenery." What might have caused him to say that?
What two problems is the character facing at this point in the story?	Are there any connections you could make between that remark and any problems the character might be having?
Which problem would be solved if the character left town? Which problem would be made worse?	Would a change of scenery solve the character's problems or make them worse? Why do you say so?
Can you predict what the character will do next?	Based on what you know about the character so far, what might he do next? Do you believe that is a wise thing for him to do? How would you advise him?

Available for download at **https://resources.corwin.com/VL-LiteracyK-5**

a pattern of questioning that has been labeled initiate-respond-evaluate, or IRE for short. In an IRE pattern, a teacher asks a question, a student provides an answer, and the teacher decides whether the answer is right or wrong. This is Durkin's (1978/79) major criticism of teachers' questioning—that it too often consists of interrogation, rather than activation of thinking.

One of the problems with IRE is that students tend to stop thinking the minute you tell them they're right (Cazden, 1988). More damaging, however, is that giving students feedback that is limited to the correctness of their answers or methods hurts their long-term understanding and prevents them from transferring their knowledge to new situations (Schroth, 1992). They also learn that learning is about knowing the answers to questions—knowing lots. In contrast, what they need to learn is as much about knowing how, addressing Why as well as What questions, and welcoming what they do not know as an opportunity for future learning. Most harmful of all, however, is feedback that is limited, infrequent, and focused on the personal attributes of the student, rather than on the task, process used, and ability to influence their own learning. It takes away their ability to self-regulate (Hattie & Timperley, 2007). When you're guiding students' learning using questions, prompts, and cues, let students do as much cognitive work as possible to evaluate their own learning—especially if they're correct. When they ask you, "Is this right?" reply, "Tell me why you think it's right and I'll listen."

> Giving students immediate feedback on the correctness of their answers or methods hurts their long-term understanding and prevents them from transferring their knowledge to new situations.

When we ask teachers to explain what they mean by feedback, they most often answer by saying feedback relates to the questions *Where are we going?* and *How are we going?* Indeed, these are critical and powerful questions. Students, however, see feedback as answering the question *Where to next?* They want to know where they go next—the action, the consequence—and of course this is more valuable when the *Where to next* question is based on the *How am I going* and *Where am I going* questions. These could be the three most important questions to keep in mind when questioning in the class.

And most critical of all is to increase the focus on "where to next" feedback. Many students will claim they did not receive feedback if this aspect is not included, so you could spend hours giving "where am I going" and "how am I going" feedback, only to be thwarted because the students are then seeking "where to next" feedback. (Of course, "where to next" should be based on the other two feedback questions.)

One way to develop skills in this area is to video-record your own teaching and then watch the video later, ideally with another person, so that you can analyze your moves and determine if you are guiding students, using direct explanations, or telling them what to think.

Structure the feedback so they have the space to hypothesize, reflect on their own learning, and evaluate their own approaches as well as those of their peers.

At times, of course, students' responses are incorrect or show only a partial understanding of the concept or skill in question. This is point of departure that separates expert teachers from novices. Nonexpert teachers respond more often with corrections, rather than asking another question or two to uncover students' thinking. The knee-jerk reaction is to give students the right answer—"No, that word is *implements*"—rather than being confident enough to explore why the student might have misread it. When the teacher says, "Read that sentence again and think about the meaning. Does *interest* work in the sentence?" You're posing a question, one that should cause the student to think. At the same time, you're providing a prompt (a reminder) for the student to monitor sense-making while reading.

If that isn't sufficient, and the student is still stumbling, then provide him with a cue, which is a more overt signal designed to shift his attention to a physical space or cognitive task (e.g., pointing to the word wall). A possible cue might be to cue the student to look in the glossary to check the word. Now you have a lot more information to work with: Is the difficulty because he isn't monitoring his understanding, or he doesn't have a good schema of the topic, or possibly that he doesn't know how to repair his errors when the meaning is lost? These are the "pivotal events" that Ross and Gibson (2010, p. 197) attribute to expert teaching—the ability to rapidly hypothesize what instructional move should come next to move student learning forward. Simply correcting errors over and over isn't going to result in learning that lasts. However, getting students to think metacognitively, although it takes a bit longer, will.

Formative Evaluation During Guided Instruction

The benefit of noticing errors and misconceptions is that it allows for additional instruction. By observing and taking notes, you'll know which groups or individual students are stuck or need help, which ones are flying and need enrichment, and who misunderstands the concepts or lacks foundational knowledge that you will need to scaffold for them. When you do move in to guide the learning, you will be able to do so in a strategic way that provides the right amount of feedback, differentiation, and support that your students need—and not the excessive scaffolding that takes the rigor and engagement out of your math tasks.

As the first-grade reading comprehension lesson evolved, Ms. Hakim transitioned from modeling and thinking aloud to guided instruction, using a series of questions to probe her students' thinking and monitor their understanding. She had prepared a few of these scaffolding questions in advance, primarily focusing ones that drew their attention to incidents in the book when Herbert reacts badly to Bernie's growing confidence:

1. (pp. 3–4): What are the words, actions, and picture clues that tell us how Bernie is feeling?

2. (pp. 11–12) What clues can we find that show us how Herbert's feelings have changed? Why do we think they have changed?

3. (pp. 14–17) Herbert's behavior is awful now. But why? What words, actions, and pictures help us understand this?

She uses these questions to check in with children sitting at tables 2, 4, and 5. They'll later "pollinate ideas" as the teacher calls it, by partnering with students at Tables 1, 3, and 6.

INDEPENDENT LEARNING

The learning continues, and in fact deepens, when students are able to employ what they have been learning. This can occur in four possible ways (Fisher & Frey, 2008):

- Fluency building

- Application

- Spiral review

- Extension

Fluency Building

Fluency building is especially effective when students are in the surface learning phase and need spaced practice opportunities to strengthen automaticity. For instance, young children who play games using flashcards of sight words, or who read books independently, are engaged in fluency-building independent learning.

Application

Application is arguably the most common approach to independent learning. Students engaged in application of learning are consolidating their knowledge through the transfer of skills to contexts similar to the situation in which they initially learned. As an example, Mr. Hurley's Year 5 students wrote an exit slip using evidence to support their opinion about the author's advice to eat insects. Like the author, they are applying loaded language to support their claims.

Spiral Review

Spiral review, a third approach to independent learning, is one in which students revisit previously mastered content in order to prevent learning recidivism due to infrequent use. For instance, fourth-grade teachers Gloria Hansen and Diane Lincoln keep the learning alive by requiring that their students compare previously read class texts to current ones.

Ms. Lincoln said, "This is something Gloria has been using for several years, and I really see the benefit. When I'm teaching a literary device like foreshadowing, say, I not only ask them about how it's being used by the author in the text we're reading right now, but also to give me another example."

Ms. Lincoln's students, she noted, end up consulting texts read earlier in the year to locate examples. "What I really like about this is that it casts a new light on something they've already read. They realize that the author was using foreshadowing all along, but now they're noticing it."

Her colleague, Ms. Hansen, added, "There's so much I could potentially teach with each text, and it used to be hard for me to narrow it down. You know, to decide what to leave out. But with spiral reviews, I get to teach those concepts again and again, instead of just using one text as an example. They can't transfer their knowledge if they don't get lots of chances to see patterns in how text is universally constructed."

Extension

Extension is a fourth kind of independent learning in which students are asked to use what they have learned in a new way. This often requires that they research on their own and find additional information. The text-dependent question, "What does this text inspire you to do?" (Fisher & Frey, 2014b) is an organizing tool that can be used to design extension learning. Independent learning through extension includes

- Writing

- Presenting information to peers

- Participating in debates and Socratic seminars

- Engaging in investigations

> **Teaching Takeaway**
>
> Use spiral review to foster transfer.

This is especially effective when the text has been utilized over multiple lessons, including those that require close and critical reading. Third-grade teacher Kiara Mitchell did just that as an extension of the study her students did with *Honoring Our Ancestors*. Her students were still learning how to do investigations, so Ms. Mitchell curated websites using Sweet Search4Me, a search engine designed for students. The sites included are vetted by teachers, and Ms. Mitchell was able to add specific sites for her students to use.

"I had them research the artists in the book, but I wanted to limit their searches so they returned a manageable amount of results and had content appropriate for 8-year-olds," she said. One team investigated JoeSam's current work, locating commissioned outdoor public art at public libraries, a children's center, and several train stations around the country.

One team member, Marcus, said, "When we read about him he said he liked bright colors 'cause his aunts from Trinidad did. And boy, did we see bright colors!"

His friend Roberto added, "They're sculptures, but they're like his paintings, but bigger!"

CLOSURE

A robust lesson will fall short of its full potential if the lesson doesn't include a solid closure. This is the time to return to the learning intention and success criteria in order to reestablish purpose and consolidate new knowledge. Importantly, it doesn't necessarily mean the temporal end of the lesson. Rather, consider it to be a time when you are checking for understanding more globally and inviting students to consider their own learning so far. Lesson closure can include a combination of the following:

- Revisiting the learning intention and success criteria

- Reviewing the key points of a lesson

- Posing a question that asks students to summarize (e.g., "Tell me the three most important ideas you learned this morning.")

- Inviting students to draw conclusions or to notice similarities and differences based on the learning

- Asking students to rate their level of understanding (e.g., a fist-to-five method displaying the number of fingers that correspond to the level of understanding)

- Inviting further clarifying questions from students

- Previewing future learning opportunities and lessons

- Exhibiting evidence of student learning

- Creating a smooth transition to the next lesson

Using a direct instruction approach, Edward Hurley has led his Year 5 students through modeling with think-alouds, guided instruction, and peer collaboration as they read and discussed the informational article on eating insects. Satisfied with their progress through frequent checks for understanding, he will soon be releasing them to further independent learning as they compose an exit ticket summarizing the author's use of loaded language in the informational article, using evidence from the text. However, before he does so, he spends a few minutes on closure to further consolidate their learning and invite self-assessment of progress toward goals. He begins with questions about the content, asking them for the most surprising facts they learned, before turning his attention to the learning intention, which concerned looking for loaded language to determine the author's point of view.

"I'd like to hear a summary of that," says the teacher.

Kyana responds, "Authors want you to know what they think, and they can use words that tell you their opinion. Like *rich source* and *good reason* show this author thinks it's a good idea."

After fielding a few more responses, he tells his students, "Check the writing goals you made for yourself on Monday. We're going to be writing in a few minutes, so now is the time to check them for yourself."

The *VISIBLE LEARNER*

It is important for students to know what they are learning and why, but equally important is for students to know *how* they are learning. If students are able to articulate the strategies that they are using to learn, they are more likely to try those approaches again when the learning gets hard.

Kaila, a fourth grader, is learning when to summarize. She knows how to summarize but does so only when her teacher asks her to. As she says,

> I have to think about the text and then see if I need to keep a summary. This makes me think about the purpose for the reading and what I will do with the reading. Like, I was reading *Fish in a Tree* because my friends read it. I didn't really need to summarize but I wanted to remember a few places to talk about. But when I was reading about climbing Mount Everest, I had to keep a better summary because I needed information for our group presentation. But then, later, when we were in reciprocal teaching, I had to be really careful because my job was to summarize and I had to think about the most important information so that I didn't waste time for my group.

Visible learners can talk about how they are learning—the strategies they used to learn.

CONCLUSION

Direct instruction has a solid track record for promoting acquisition, consolidation, and transfer of learning through intentional lesson design that uses an explicit approach. Although sometimes narrowly defined as a heavily scripted program, direct instruction has elements that trace their roots to Madeline Hunter's (1982) model of mastery learning. These elements of instruction include clear statements about the learning intention and success criteria, teacher modeling and think-alouds, guided instruction through scaffolding, checks for understanding, closure, and independent learning. These practices form a solid set of practices for making skills and concepts clear to learners. However, we do not suggest that these are the only valuable teaching practices. In the next chapter, we will turn our attention to the value of dialogic teaching, instruction that requires the effective use of talk to accomplish the learning. You might be wondering about the difference between direct and dialogic approaches, given that there has been a lot of talking described in this chapter. In the next chapter, we hope you'll see a different type of talk, one in which the discussions rely on argumentation and inquiry.

4

TEACHER-LED DIALOGIC INSTRUCTION

© Jeff Greenberg/PhotoEdit

Second graders Jesse and Ray settled into two small chairs below a sign that said, "Writers at Work." They were joined by their teacher, Francisco Reynoso, who was facilitating peer critique sessions with his students. On the table was a tented reminder, with notes about how fellow writers talk and listen to one another. Mr. Reynoso reviewed the norms with the two boys, and then asked them to begin.

"I'll be here to help if you get stuck," he said, *"but otherwise this is your conference."*

"I'll start," said Ray, turning to Jesse, who had written a report about spiders. *"I liked reading about spiders 'cause I like spiders, too,"* began Ray. *"It was interesting. I liked the part about wolf spiders best."*

"Why is that, Ray? Can you tell Jesse why you liked it?" asked the teacher.

"Sure," said Ray. *"I was surprised they can kill a toad!"*

"I liked that part, too!" said Jesse, warming to the topic.

The teacher added, *"Go ahead, Ray. Can you retell Jesse's story to him? And Jesse, as he does, think about whether those are the ideas you had in your report."*

Ray said, *"You said spiders are mostly good and they eat bad insects and they're mostly not poisonous. Then you told about weird spiders, like the wolf spider."*

"Can you say more about that, Ray?" said Mr. Reynoso.

"There's stuff about funnel spiders and Brazilian wandering spiders," offered Ray.

Jesse responded, *"That's right. That's what my report is about. I want to draw pictures of them, too."*

"What do you think about Jesse's idea of adding pictures?" Mr. Reynoso asked Ray.

Many teachers state that student discussion is critical for learning, yet despite all the talk about talk, the discouraging news is that it isn't as prevalent as one would like to believe. Among a sample of more than 1,000 teachers, only about one in three was able to lead a classroom discussion or communicate with students at the level defined as "proficient" by the rubric used in the study (Kane & Staiger, 2012). One review of the research on student discussion reported that its use in middle and high school classrooms varied from 14 seconds to 68 seconds per class period (Wilkinson & Nelson, 2013). Discussion time in elementary classrooms is somewhat longer. However, here the dominant talker remains the teacher, who relies primarily on a repertoire of recitation (question-answer sequences asking students to furnish information that is already known) and exposition (explaining and imparting information) (Alexander, 2008).

> Despite its importance, one review of the research on discussion reported that its use in middle and high school classrooms varied from 14 seconds to 68 seconds per class period.

If you're questioning the results of these published studies and thinking to yourself, "Well, that's not me!" that may be entirely true. However, we challenge you to use a timer for yourself for one week to measure the amount of time you allot to discussion. To do so, use Applebee, Langer, Nystrand, and Gamoran's definition of discussion: "a free exchange of information among students and/or between at least three participants that lasts longer than 30 seconds" (2003, p. 700).

The dearth of meaningful discussion about texts, ideas, and concepts is especially unfortunate for students who are not making expected progress. Ironically, they are the ones who seem to profit most from discussion, as measured by improved reading comprehension (Murphy, Wilkinson, Soter, Hennessey, & Alexander, 2009). As we noted in the previous chapter, direct instruction is an essential instructional practice. However, it should not come at the expense of discussion. In fact, the benefits of classroom discussion, with an effect size of 0.82, are even

> EFFECT SIZE FOR DISCUSSION = 0.82

stronger than the benefits of direct instruction. As is the case for most good things in life, though, there should always be a healthy balance between them.

EFFECTIVE TALK, NOT JUST ANY TALK

Just because children are chattering away doesn't mean they're learning or talking about learning. Most will chatter with little prompting—on the playground, waiting in line, or sharing morning snack. Those interactions are of value, especially as they develop the social and communication skills needed in everyday life. But classroom talk differs from social exchanges, and in fact represents a specific language register— what Joos (1961) describes as the *consultative mode*. This consultative mode is one of five registers he has identified—each of which sits along a broader continuum of formality:

- **Fixed or frozen:** Unchanging speech, such as reciting the Pledge of Allegiance each morning in class.

- **Formal:** As in delivering a presentation to the class, where interruption is not expected or elicited.

- **Consultative:** The academic discourse of the classroom, where information is exchanged, and background information is provided. The consultative register is regularly used in work settings as well.

- **Casual:** The informal exchanges between friends, where prior knowledge is assumed due to shared experiences.

- **Intimate:** Private exchanges between family members and the closest of friends.

Students arrive to school already immersed in the intimate and casual registers, but the others are first learned in school. Of the three others (fixed, formal, and consultative), it is this last one that should occupy the greatest amount of time. However, in truth students seem to spend more time on the receiving end of the formal register, listening to the uninterrupted speech of the teacher. Yet what lies within the consultative register are some of the most significant functions in which school-aged children engage. Specifically, they use oral language to do the following:

- Share facts and information (e.g., "The microraptor was a tiny dinosaur that had four wings.")

- Speculate or find out about something (e.g., "How tiny was the microraptor? Was it bigger than an iPad?")

- Think imaginatively (e.g., "Once there was a tiny microraptor named Fiona, but her mom called her Doodlebug.")

Talk, in this case, serves as a platform for written expression. After all, if students don't get to explain, pose questions, and narrate routinely, it's going to be much more difficult for them to do so in writing. Having said that, children must be taught how to engage in productive discussions that build and extend their knowledge.

Teachers who create space for students to pose questions, wrestle with complex issues, clarify thinking, speculate, probe, disagree, resolve problems, and reach consensus are employing a dialogic approach to instruction. Unlike the initiate-respond-evaluate cycle of teacher questioning and student recitation (Cazden, 1988), this form of instruction assumes a higher level of authority on the part of the learners, who coconstruct knowledge under the guidance of a teacher who facilitates the discussion rather than presents information. Dialogic instruction assumes many forms, including those that are facilitated primarily by students, such as reciprocal teaching and talking circles (the subject of the next chapter). However, many other forms of dialogic instruction are led by the teacher, who remains the chief mediator of the discussion. Using the collective knowledge of the learning community, students consolidate, deepen, and extend their learning.

> Teachers who create space for students to pose questions, wrestle with complex issues, clarify thinking, speculate, probe, disagree, resolve problems, and reach consensus are employing a dialogic approach to instruction.

FOSTER DEEP LEARNING AND TRANSFER

Discussions can have a profound effect on shaping and transforming the understanding of a student. You'll recall that in Chapter 1 we discussed that the process of moving from surface to deep and from deep to transfer learning involves students moving initially from one idea to many ideas. The deepening really accelerates when students begin to transform concepts such that they see how ideas are related. In the transfer phase of learning, students are extending ideas to new and novel situations.

How does this deepening actually occur? It is accomplished in a multitude of ways:

- At the surface phase of learning, students figure out what they already know about a topic, and determine where their gaps may lie.

- They share their opinions with one another and listen to those who agree and disagree with them.

- This acquisition and consolidation of knowledge continues as learners deepen their understanding, especially as they find connections and further organize their thinking.

- They read with texts and then against them, thinking critically about what is told and what is not. They consider bias and question the commonplace.

- They further deepen their knowledge as they read *across* texts, especially those that offer contradictory perspectives.

Discussion, in small groups and with the whole class, is fodder for thinking. But meaningful discussion doesn't just spontaneously happen, or at least not without a teacher's intention to cultivate a climate where exchange is expected.

If we could sum up our advice to teachers who want to encourage classroom discussion, we would say, "Teachers, stop talking so much." This signals to students that they have a hand in controlling the conversation. As John has noted many times, we would never tolerate a personal conversation that adhered to the same rules as much of the classroom talk encountered worldwide. Would you ever want to spend time talking to someone who decided what could be discussed and when it would end, asked questions but never gave you space to do the same, and spent most of the time interrogating you to find out if you were paying attention? Yet that's the dynamic in too many classrooms, for too many instructional minutes. No wonder so many students become progressively more disengaged the longer they attend school. They figure out that we're not listening.

LISTEN CAREFULLY

When was the last time you read research on teacher listening? If your response is "never," it's possibly because there is very little on the topic, despite its importance in classroom discussion. Much of the research on adult listening in schools skews toward empathetic listening as a counseling tool to employ when a student is troubled or upset. Empathetic listening—maintaining eye contact, using body language that signals acceptance, revoicing student statements—is of great value in these situations.

Yet these tools can be applied in discussions of academic content, too. A teacher's nonverbal signals and compassionate listening can encour-

---

Teaching Takeaway

Stop talking. Allow for silences that give students time to think and then chime in. When they do, listen, then let another student speak. Fight the urge to chime in after every comment.

age students to take risks, publicly speculate, ask questions, and pose arguments. Teacher listening during student discussions is challenging because we're simultaneously doing two things—we are listening *to*, and listening *for*. Listening *to* a student is the act of locating identity within her utterances. In doing so, we consider how her insights and questions in turn inform us about who she is as an individual. At the same time, we are listening *for* the turns in the conversation that signal content understandings and misconceptions. It's awfully difficult to do both, and requires self-discipline. Parker (2010) offers that a self-disciplined listener in the classroom operates under three guidelines—reciprocity, humility, and caution:

- **Reciprocity** is giving the speaker the floor in order to represent herself, rather than falling prey to the assumption that you can do it better since she is a child and you are the adult.

- **Humility** is adopting the assumption that one cannot know another's experiences and point of view, and that it may take time for this to be revealed.

- **Caution** is suppressing the urge to chime in with every thought that may be passing through your head.

Listening, of course, isn't passive. So often we listen to find the gap so we can recommence talking. Carl Rogers, of psychotherapy fame, based his model on active listening—showing clients that you had heard what they were saying. This engendered respect, showed empathy, credited clients with their personal views, allowed you to hear what they brought to the task, and—by checking you had understood correctly—was the starting point of great diagnosis and then later interventions! Providing a forum where someone can speak without interruption, using nonverbal language that communicates receptiveness, and allowing silences to happen, are all deliberate actions on the part of the teacher. These are paired with conversational moves that facilitate discussion.

> Providing a forum where someone can speak without interruption, using nonverbal language that communicates receptiveness, and allowing silences to happen, are all deliberate actions on the part of the teacher.

FACILITATE AND GUIDE DISCUSSION

Children are still children, and they have to learn how to have focused academic conversation. The prompts that propel a discussion that is lagging often need to come from the teacher. Over time, students incorporate these moves into their conversations with peers. These conversational teacher moves are intended to organize ideas and ensure productive discussion (Michaels, S., O'Connor, M. C., Hall, M. W., & Resnick, 2010, pp. 27–32):

- Marking conversation: "That's an important point."

- Keeping the channels open: "Did everyone hear what she just said?"

- Keeping everyone together: "Who can repeat . . . ?"

- Challenging students: "That's a great question, Rebecca. What do you guys think?"

- Revoicing: "So are you saying that. . . ."

- Asking students to explain or restate: "Who disagrees or agrees, and why?"

- Linking contributions: "Who can add on to what he said?"

- Pressing for accuracy: "Where can we find that?"

- Building on prior knowledge: "How does this connect . . . ?"

- Pressing for reasoning: "Why do you think that?"

- Expanding reasoning: "Take your time. Say more."

- Recapping: "What have we discovered?"

These conversational moves should be punctuated by wait time, both after posing a thought-provoking question (Wait Time 1), and again after a student responds (Wait Time 2). The first wait time allows students to process and contemplate the question, while the second wait time provides the speaker with the space to elaborate on his answer. Although it is less readily recognized, the practice of ensuring wait time allows the teacher to also process the conversation, and results in increased quality of teacher questions (Rowe, 1986). Equipped with the tools to listen carefully to children, to facilitate and guide discussion, and to provide them the space and time to think, teachers can leverage dialogic instruction to deepen knowledge.

In the next section of the chapter, we will elaborate on the first of two facets of dialogic instruction. The first are the *teacher-led approaches* that are primarily directed by the teacher, but with the intention of promoting student discussion. These are more formally structured than other aspects of dialogic instruction, and the teacher plays an active role in propelling conversation. The second facet, which is the subject of the next chapter, comprises the *student-led tools* that allow the teacher to step back further as children share the responsibility in directing these interactions (Caughlan, Juzwik, Borsheim-Black, Kelly, & Fine, 2013). While we have assigned them to one category or another, in practice these tools are used more fluidly, as teacher and students respond to one another.

The *VISIBLE LEARNER*

When teachers engage students in the type of accountable talk described in this section, students begin to use these approaches on their own. In fact, the conversation markers that teachers use can become students' self-regulation strategies. There are a number of tools that students can use to self-regulate, and the discussion markers can be some of those.

Amal, a student in fifth grade, was overheard saying to herself, "Is this accurate? I need to keep looking." When asked about this, she responded, "I found some good information but I wanted to make sure it was right. And I think that it made sense because it was connected with the other book I read, but I wanted to check for sure."

The visible learner can use self-regulation strategies.

TEACHER-LED TOOLS FOR DIALOGIC INSTRUCTION

Teachers utilize a number of tools to apprentice students into engaging in meaningful dialogue and discussion with one another. In addition, these tools activate, build, and extend knowledge, using children's thinking as the fulcrum, rather than the teacher's presentation of information. Anticipation guides, which are described in more detail in the section that follows, are a form of advance organizers specifically designed to provide students with statements that cause them to question. These can be used as an effective tool for activating prior knowledge.

EFFECT SIZE FOR BEHAVIORAL ORGANIZERS/ ADJUNCT QUESTIONS = 0.41

Anticipation Guides

An anticipation guide is a teacher-prepared list of statements based on a specific text or unit of study. The purpose is to activate prior knowledge, encourage predictions, and stimulate curiosity about a topic (Head & Readence, 1986). These guides are useful for promoting class discussion as well, because they can spark debate and foster the inevitable need to consult other sources of information. The steps to creating a guide are fairly simple:

1. **Identify the major concepts.** What are the main ideas in the passage or unit of study?

2. **Consider your students' prior knowledge.** What misconceptions are they most likely to hold?

3. **Write five or ten statements pertaining to the unit.** Don't make them all factual—be sure to create open-ended

statements as well. Look again to your major concepts to make sure you are creating statements that relate to larger concepts rather than isolated facts. For example, for a reading about Pluto, its size and distance from the sun are facts that would probably not be useful.

Heather Fields used an anticipation guide to introduce her fourth-grade students to their study of the history and geography of Pennsylvania, where they reside. Ms. Fields prepared the anticipation guide (see Figure 4.1) to encourage her students to begin thinking about the content. At the end of the unit, after the class had read about, discussed, watched videos, conducted Internet searches, and carefully examined they topic, they returned to the anticipation guide to readdress their questions.

The discussion portion of the lesson was an essential component. Although the teacher didn't provide the correct answers at the outset, she did want her students to consider what they did and did not know, and how they might have learned more to confirm or disconfirm their thinking. After completing the anticipation guide and tallying the responses for each item, they began to debate the second one in particular, concerning relations with American Indians in the state. Several students said they answered *false* because they didn't believe there were any tribes in Pennsylvania, while several others thought it was false because they thought that settlers got along well with them.

Without revealing the answer, Ms. Fields said, *"It sounds like we have some disagreement going on. What might be some ways we could find out about this? I'll keep a list of ideas for you."*

Within a few minutes, her students listed (1) reading books about American Indians, (2) looking it up on the Internet to see if there are tribes or reservations in the state, and (3) asking an American Indian for his or her perspective. From time to time, she would ask students to elaborate further on their statements, saying, *"Can you tell me more about that?"* or *"Why do you believe this is true?"*

When the class finished, she posted the list she had kept for them and said, *"Let's keep these in mind as we learn about Pennsylvania history. This will be a good reminder of our thinking."*

Later she remarked, "I also collect [their anticipation guides] as a preassessment of their knowledge, and compare it to their postunit response. It's one way I can gauge my impact on their learning."

Figure 4.1   Anticipation Guide for Pennsylvania Unit

Name: _____   Date: _____

Anticipation Guide for Pennsylvania History and Geography

Directions: Read each statement and write a "+" for true statements and a "–" for false statements.

Statement	Before Our Study	After Our Study
Pennsylvania's natural resources include wildlife, coal, oil, and gas.		
Pennsylvania American Indian tribes have always had good relations with settlers, residents, and government officials in the state.		
The Declaration of Independence was signed in Philadelphia.		
The state capital is Pittsburgh.		
The name of the state comes from a Latin phrase meaning "Penn's Woods."		
One of the great lakes, Lake Ontario, borders the state.		
The terrain of the state was formed by retreating glaciers and colliding tectonic plates.		
The Monongahela River in western Pennsylvania is one of a few rivers in the world that flows north.		
Pennsylvania is a commonwealth, like Virginia, Massachusetts, and Kentucky.		
The first zoo in America was founded by Benjamin Franklin in Philadelphia.		
Pennsylvania is home to more Amish than any other place in the world.		
The American Revolutionary War began in Philadelphia.		
The states that border Pennsylvania in south are Maryland, West Virginia, and Virginia.		

Guided Reading

Guided reading instruction has long been a hallmark of the effective literacy teacher's classroom. While it has been called various names throughout the previous century, including high/middle/low ability reading groups (Gray, 1925), directed reading activity (Betts, 1946), and three-to-five groups (Marita, 1965), the central concept has always been to teach small groups of children to read based on the skills they still need to develop. It's not tracking or ability grouping in that the groups are not formed based on assessment scores, but rather based on the needs of the students as identified on the assessments. There's a big difference.

It should also be noted that there are other small group formats, typically based on direct instruction, that build students' basic skills. These are often intervention-based, meaning that most of the class has already mastered a skill or concept, but some group of students has yet to achieve that level of learning. Again, guided reading is different. It's part of the overall structure and fabric of the elementary school classroom, and allows teachers an opportunity to observe their students reading and thinking so that they can make appropriate adjustments in instruction.

Guided reading lessons are typically between 20 and 30 minutes in length, depending on the needs and stamina of the students. Stamina is a legitimate consideration for guided reading, because this intensive instructional time may be the most cognitively demanding period of the day for students. Because the group is small and instructionally similar, the pacing of these lessons is quicker than pacing at other times of the day. Early and emergent readers in particular may tire during the first weeks of guided reading instruction.

Although guided reading lessons do not need to follow a rigid sequence of instruction, several components are generally recognized and recommended.

First and foremost, guided reading includes discussion among the teacher and the students. The small group format allows for a more focused conversation based on the text that has been read. If the whole class can engage in the reading and discussion, a close reading protocol might be more useful. Figure 4.2 gives a suggested time sequence for a 20-minute and a 30-minute small group lesson, although these times should be adjusted to meet the needs of your students. Let's look more closely at each of these components.

The Familiar Book

The guided reading lesson begins with a reading the students have seen before. For emergent and early readers, this is likely to be the book they read during their previous lesson. Transitional and self-extending readers are often reading longer texts that are not finished in one lesson. Therefore, they reread a portion from the last lesson, often the passages preceding the end of the previous stopping point. There are two key reasons for doing this:

- Engaging in repeated readings of the same text builds fluency—the ability to read smoothly, accurately, and with expression.

- Rereading aids in students' ability to recall information and in their ability to incorporate new information into their thinking—both of which are important when reentering a partially read text.

After students have warmed up in this way, the teacher transitions the group to a new book introduction.

Book Introduction

The book introduction is a time for teacher-directed instruction. Think of your book introduction as the time when your guided reading plan is the most detailed. This is your opportunity to activate prior knowledge, preview the text, and provide direct instruction about the specific strategies or skills to be highlighted in the lesson.

When using books with illustrations, the introduction is referred to as a picture walk. The purpose of a picture walk is not to tell children everything that will happen in the story. Rather, an effective picture walk prepares students for the language they will encounter in the book while giving them a sense of the theme or plot of the story. It also invites them to consider what they already know about the topic and what personal experiences they have had that are alike and different from those por-

Figure 4.2   Suggested Times for Guided Reading Lessons

	20-Minute Guided Reading Lesson	30-Minute Guided Reading Lesson
Familiar reading and discussion	3 minutes	5 minutes
Book introduction	1 minute	1 minute
Student reading	6 minutes	10 minutes
Word work	3 minutes	5 minutes
Questioning/discussing	4 minutes	4 minutes
Writing	3 minutes	5 minutes

trayed in the book. A well-crafted picture walk leaves readers with a few questions that can be answered only by reading the book. In our own practice, we rarely show children the last picture in the book so that they will have a purpose for discovering how the book ends. The written text itself is not the focus during the picture walk, although specific words or phrases may be highlighted by the teacher because they are a part of the skills being taught in the lesson. Remember that the picture walk is not a pop quiz—don't pepper students with questions about the book and its illustrations. Recognize that this is a chance for you to introduce vocabulary, themes or main ideas, and a purpose for reading. Figure 4.3 is a checklist of items to consider in completing an effective picture walk.

Books read by transitional and self-extending readers may not contain pictures or illustrations. The book introduction moves from being a picture walk to a discussion of the purpose of the reading and what the reader expects to be included in the text. Again, be careful not to disclose too much, but rather give students a taste of what to anticipate. Much like the previews for the newest Hollywood blockbuster, this introduction should prepare them for the big ideas while leaving them with questions that can be answered only by reading.

Student Reading

During this phase of the lesson, students quietly read aloud (not in unison) so that the teacher can hear them. The teacher is noticing errors or miscues that she can use instructionally. In a guided reading lesson, all of the students in the group are reading the same text and there is a clear learning intention. In advance of the reading, students should know the learning intention and the success criteria.

Word Work

Following the students' reading, there should be a time for working with words. The purpose of this time is to introduce vocabulary or word study skills necessary for more accurate reading. For emergent and early readers, word work may focus on phonics instruction and sight word development. For transitional and self-extending readers, word work may focus on spelling, word meanings, words with multiple meanings, or word families. Regardless, the teacher selects the focus words before students begin the lesson and provides instruction on those words only if there is evidence of need based on the students' reading of the text.

Questioning and Discussing the Text

Following the reading and the instruction teachers provide to individual students as they read, the teacher or students ask questions of each

Figure 4.3   Considerations for Picture Walks in Guided Reading

Teacher's Role	Examples of Questions and Prompts
Examine the cover	What do you see on the cover? Use vocabulary from the story to describe the scene. Based on this picture, what do you think the book will be about? This picture reminds me of _____. Has that happened to you?
State the theme	This book is about _____. The characters in this story learn about _____.
View illustrations	Point out important details in the pictures. State the names of the characters. Ask for personal connections. Ask questions about prior knowledge. (Remember when we learned about _____?)
Practice unfamiliar language	When _____ happens, the main character says, _____. Let's all say that together. Invite students to locate new vocabulary words on the page.
Pose a question to be answered by reading	What will _____ do to solve his problem? How do _____? I wonder how _____?

Available for download at **https://resources.corwin.com/VL-LiteracyK-5**

other about the reading. This discussion is mediated by the teacher, who guides the conversation about the text. This part of the guided reading lessons helps students focus on comprehension of texts—even from the earliest age.

Writing

Following the reading of and discussion about the text, students are asked to write in response to their reading. Since reading and writing are so closely linked, writing is incorporated into every guided reading lesson. The writing portion during guided reading is brief, so any extended writing should be completed during independent learning tasks so as not to consume instructional time intended for reading. A partial list of possible writing prompts to use before or after the reading appears below:

- Write a sentence that summarizes the text.

- Discuss your recommendation for or against reading the text.

- Predict what might happen next in a sequel to the story.

- Note the important facts in the text.

- Were the events real, imaginary, or a mixture of both?

In this first-grade classroom, we'll see Mr. Michaels teaching three readers about reading with expression. Notice in the lesson plan (Figure 4.4) that Mr. Michaels is concerned about Tony. He has included notes in the lesson to remind himself about supports Tony will need and about how to monitor Tony's success.

The *VISIBLE LEARNER*

During a small group lesson, Becky responded incorrectly to a question her teacher asked. They had been reading the poem "My Shadow" by Robert Louis Stevenson. When asked, *"What happens to the shadow in the last stanza?"* Becky said that the shadow stayed in bed because it was tired from playing too much.

In response, Sarah, another student in the group, said, *"I respectfully disagree."*

The teacher, Max Harrison became obviously excited, saying, *"So, we have an error someplace. It's not about who is right or wrong, but rather an opportunity to learn. Errors help us uncover our thinking and figure out where we went wrong. Sarah, can you tell us why you disagree?"*

Sarah responded, noting that the sun was not up and that there was dew. As she noted, *"Dew is that water on the grass on some mornings, so it was still wet out because the sun didn't come out to dry it up."* Becky said, *"Oh, I missed it. I was just thinking about the last line when he says that the shadow was still sleeping. It's really because the sun didn't come out so there couldn't really be a shadow, right?"*

Their conversation continued, with increasingly complex questions about the poem, and Mr. Harrison was pleased that errors were celebrated as opportunities to learn.

Visible learners see errors as opportunities and are comfortable saying that they don't know and/or need help.

Figure 4.4   Guided Reading Lesson Plan for *Baby Bear's Present*

Guided Reading Lesson Plan

Students: *Tony, Catrina, Maggie*   Classroom Teacher: *Mr. Michaels*   Date: *December 12*

New Book: *Baby Bear's Present (Randall, 1994)*	Level: *10*

Targeted skills for this lesson: *Fluency and expression, using short- and long-a sounds in words*

Standards: *RF.1.1.a Know the spelling-sound correspondences for common consonant digraphs. RF.1.1.b. Decode regularly spelled one-syllable words. RF.1.4 a–d: Read with sufficient accuracy and fluency to support comprehension. Read on-level text with purpose and understanding. Read on-level text orally with accuracy, appropriate rate, and expression on successive readings. Use context to confirm or self-correct word recognition and understanding, rereading as necessary.*

Book Introduction: *Picture walk using some of the pictures and discuss Baby Bear's problem when his father wants to buy him a toy he doesn't want. How will he solve it?*

Word Work: *Word sort of short- and long-a sounds in book—sort words by sounds, especially /ai/*	Writing: *Students will write a sentence describing the story in their journals.*

Student Reading: *Students whisper-read while I listen in (pay attention to Tony's reading)—look out for choral reading. Reinforce expressive voices for dialogue, especially noting the punctuation.*

Questions: *Have students retell the story by talking with partner—I pair with Tony to gauge comprehension. Ask: How did Baby Bear solve his problem? How would the story be different if Baby Bear had gotten the toy?*

Available for download at **https://resources.corwin.com/VL-LiteracyK-5**

WRITE DIALOGICALLY WITH SHARED WRITING

The teacher and students can cocreate original text using dialogic principles. In elementary education, these group writing practices include the *language experience approach* (LEA) (Ashton-Warner, 1965) and *interactive writing* (McCarrier, Pinnell, & Fountas, 2000). The teacher takes direct dictation from students, writing verbatim what is said (LEA), or guides the composition of the message as students write it on a large chart for all to see (interactive writing). In the latter form, students take turns writing the letters or words themselves on the collaborative chart. Although LEA and interactive writing differ on some key points, they have characteristics held in common. Features of these coconstructed writing lessons include

- Text is cocreated by teacher and students through rich conversation

- Language used is natural to the child

- Text is created for a purpose

- Writing occurs in full view of the students

- Text is used again for reading

Shared writing consists of two processes—the discussion that takes place in composing the message, and the procedures for recording that message on paper. An important advantage of using any shared writing is that it provides a forum for discussing any and all aspects of writing, including letter formation, planning the layout and spacing on the page, word choice, and the content of the message. The extent to which these are featured in a lesson is determined by student need. Shared writing has been found to be an effective instructional approach for teaching students how to compose and evaluate their writing.

Another benefit of these shared writing experiences is that students begin to evaluate writing (Hansen, 2001). Despite the allure of reducing all acts of writing to a linear recipe of brainstorming, drafting, editing, revising, and publishing, real writers engage in several of these processes simultaneously, often writing a few words or sentences, pausing to check for spelling or content, changing a word, continuing for a few more sentences, thinking of an idea to use later, then rereading the entire paragraph again. This ability to engage in multiple processes simultaneously is predicated on the notion that evaluation is taking place. It is analogous to the cueing systems used by readers. Real readers do not decode, then look at the syntax, then check for their semantic understanding. Instead, they consolidate these cueing systems by evaluating what they need to understand the message. Likewise, when students engage in shared writing, they see how writers continuously evaluate the writing product. The development of good writers, like that of good readers, focuses on increasing their agility at being able to engage in simultaneous processes efficiently and accurately. Skilled teachers can address key skills and strategies around composition and evaluation through shared writing.

Language Experience Approach

LEA was structured on the assumption that a person's authentic language patterns would serve as the best text with emergent readers, as they would be the easiest to read. The teacher writes down exactly what the child says. You might be tempted to correct for syntax, but remember that the point is to create text they can then read back. A common example of this is to ask young children to explain drawings they have made, scribing key descriptions under the illustration so they can read them again. The operative word is *experience,* and this is key to a successful lesson. Experiences might include a class field trip or even a simple event to discuss later.

Kindergarten teacher Eric Matsumoto did just that. He told his class he would be interviewing Marian Jefferson, the kindergarten teacher next door, in front of the class. "I wrote down my questions so I wouldn't forget to ask them." He had written on a chart:

1. How old are you?

2. What is your favorite part of teaching kindergarten?

3. Do you remember the first time you met me?

Ms. Jefferson arrived and took a seat in front of the class. Mr. Matsumoto began by asking her how old she was, and she politely told him it was none of his business. He wrote down her response and asked the next question about teaching kindergarten. She replied that five-year-olds ask interesting questions that make her think about the world in new ways. Again, Mr. Matsumoto wrote this down on the chart. He then asked his final question, and she gave a one-word response: "Yes." Again, he wrote her answer and thanked her for her time.

Having created a shared experience, he was now ready to turn the discussion over to his students. *"I have two things I would like you to help me with. Did these questions give me a lot of information about Ms. Jefferson? How can I improve them?"* he asked.

What ensued was a lively discussion about the appropriateness of the first question. Jordan volunteered, *"My dad told me it's not polite to ask ladies how old they are."* Mr. Matsumoto added that there are lots of men that don't like to answer that question, either.

The class agreed that the second question was a good one and thought that it should be kept because Ms. Jefferson's answer was an interesting one. They also agreed that the third question was not effective because he only got a one-word answer. Lynette suggested that he change the question to, *"What do you remember about the first time you met me?"*

He then invited them to suggest other questions he could use, adding five more to the list. *"When we meet in our guided reading groups, we'll use the questions we wrote together,"* he said. *"We'll get ourselves ready for the next interview tomorrow with Ms. Stevenson, who also teaches kindergarten. We'll practice reading the questions together, and this time you'll be the interviewers."*

Interactive Writing

Video 11

Interactive Writing
in Kindergarten

*https://resources.corwin.com/
VL-LiteracyK-5*

Third-grade teacher Kiara Mitchell uses an interactive writing approach to connect a book the class recently read with their math studies. The book, *How Much Is a Million?* (Schwartz, 2004), illustrates facts that have amazed her students. For instance, they learned that a goldfish bowl large enough to hold a million goldfish would also be large enough to hold a whale. She wants them to apply their mathematical thinking to solve a similar problem, and tells them they will create a mathematical investigation plan for the class to follow. She begins by rereading this section of the book, and invites discussion about what they might want to find out about.

Ms. Mitchell says, *"I've learned so much from this book about what a million of something might look like. What other things at school could we use to multiply to a million?"*

Several students offer their suggestions and Ms. Mitchell keeps track of their suggestions on a small notepad so she doesn't forget their ideas. They discuss the merits of investigating a million rulers, erasers, books, tennis balls, and whiteboard markers. The teacher continues to ask questions in order to prompt further conversation about the possibilities and challenges of each. Over the course of several minutes, the class comes to consensus—they will use tennis balls.

"Let's turn that into a math question," she says, reminding them that the task is to create a math investigation plan. After some negotiation, they agree that the precise text will read, *"How much space is needed to hold one million tennis balls?"* When Rico misspells *million* on the chart, she uses white correction tape and directs his attention to the math word wall. *"Remember to use your resources when you get stuck. It's there to help you."*

"Now we need to create a plan," Ms. Mitchell says. *"We can't count a million tennis balls. How could using a shoebox like the one I have here help us?"*

Now the class is buzzing with the possibility. *"Before we talk as a group, talk with your table group about it. How might you use a shoebox to help us with this mathematical dilemma?"*

After giving them a few minutes to discuss, she says, *"Let's hear those good ideas."* Jayden and Andre build on each other's ideas, and soon have a proposal: Fill the shoebox with tennis balls to figure out how many shoeboxes they will need to hold a million of them.

Eventually, she brings the conversation back to the plan. *"Let's write up this plan so we know exactly what to do to solve this problem."*

Guided by Ms. Mitchell, the students first formulate the exact wording of the investigation, while she prompts them as needed for word choice, spelling, and punctuation. In the afternoon, they will complete their investigation and discuss whether their plan changed as a result. (See Figure 4.5 on the next page for Ms. Mitchell's lesson plan.)

CLOSE AND CRITICAL READING

The instructional practice of close reading with elementary students has been used only in the last decade, but it has been used with older students for a century (Fisher & Frey, 2012). The purpose is to build the habit of reading closely to ascertain deeper comprehension. What is especially powerful about close reading is that it draws upon several high-impact instructional routines, typically with text that is more complex relative to the reader's independent reading level, and it is meant to stretch the student's reading comprehension through a questioning and rereading protocol. In addition, close reading requires students to annotate text. Importantly, the intent is to spur critical analysis of text using a teacher-led dialogic approach, and not simply to show or tell students what to think. For this reason, we often choose texts that have the potential to spark rich discussion.

EFFECT SIZE FOR QUESTIONING = 0.48

EFFECT SIZE FOR REPEATED READING PROGRAMS = 0.67

EFFECT SIZE FOR STUDY SKILLS = 0.63

EFFECT SIZE FOR CLASSROOM DISCUSSION = 0.82

Because the nature of close reading involves careful inspection of text, it can be time consuming if the text is too long. This is not to say that long-format novels and informational books can't be used. Rather, key passages are chosen in order to focus students on denser passages where deeper meaning might otherwise be lost. However, these insights will not be reached if we simply tell students why a passage is meaningful. We shudder to think how many books we have ruined in our own teaching careers because we were so eager to tell them why it was so meaningful, rather than providing the space for students to engage critically with the text. On the other hand, it is not sufficient to simply hand them a complex text and then hope for the best. A close reading protocol, led by the teacher, can build the mental habits needed to understand complex texts.

Edward Hurley's Year 5 students are reading a novel, *The One and Only Ivan* (Applegate, 2012), in their collaborative reading groups. The story, a work of fiction, is based on the real-life dilemma of a gorilla named Ivan, who was held for 27 years in captivity at a shopping mall and video arcade. In the novel, Ivan is the first-person narrator of the story, and Mr. Hurley knows that this story has aroused a number of discussions about animal welfare. The previous day, Mr. Hurley read aloud the

Figure 4.5   Lesson Plan for Interactive Writing

Assessed Need: I have noticed that the students need: To work on engaging in critical thinking in reading and mathematics.
Standard(s) Addressed: Writing 3.8: Students will revise and edit for correct sentence formation, grammar, capitalization, punctuation, and spelling. They will use their written communication skills across the curriculum. 3.1 CF Participate in a range of collaborative discussions building on others' ideas and clearly expressing their own (e.g., one-on-one, small group, teacher-led)
Text(s) I Will Use: How Much Is a Million? and class-composed investigation plan
Learning Intention for This Lesson: We will solve our own math mystery using materials found at school.
Success Criteria for This Lesson: Create a mathematics investigation plan based on How Much Is a Million?
Direct Instruction: Model: Strategies/skills/concepts to emphasize   Set purpose—create a mathematics investigation plan.   Reread excerpts of How Much Is a Million?   Lead discussion about possible ideas for a math mystery of our own.   Guide and Scaffold: Questions to ask   What are we curious about?   How will we find the answer to the question we ask?   Introduce shoebox as a means for solving the problem.   Coach   Students practice with partners.   Invite students to discuss with partners during interactive writing lesson.   Use mathematics word wall for vocabulary.   Assess: These are the students who will need further support   Jamal should be paired with Ashleigh, who needs further encouragement to speak in the group. Jamal is really good at doing this.
Dialogic Instruction: Teacher-Directed Tools   Use interactive writing process to jointly collaborate and compose a math investigation plan.   Students will meet in their table groups to determine possible approaches to the agreed-upon investigation.   **Student-Enacted Tools:** N/A
Feedback Opportunities: Interactive writing process will provide immediate feedback to students, especially about grammar, spelling, word choice, and conventions.
Independent Learning and Closure: Closure: Revisit the learning intention and success criteria and discuss whether we have met our goal. Reread the math investigation plan the class composed.   Independent Learning: We will continue use of this during math to create a math model and calculate results of a similar, related problem.

short passage when Ivan for the first time discloses that he witnessed the murder of his parents and sister by poachers, a memory triggered by the mistreatment of baby elephant also held in captivity. He and the class processed this difficult scene and the emotions it elicited.

Today, they are resuming the story and will read about a key turning point in the story, one that can be difficult for 10-year-olds to comprehend because of its sparse prose. Therefore, Mr. Hurley has chosen to use these two pages for a close reading lesson. (His lesson plan can be found in Figure 4.6 on the next page.) The chapter, entitled "Another Ivan," is a turning point for the gorilla, who realizes he must take action to save himself and his elephant friend. Mr. Hurley structures his questions to foster comprehension through four phases of deepening understanding (Fisher, Frey, Anderson, & Thayre, 2015):

- What does the text say? (literal)

- How does the text work? (structural)

- What does the text mean? (inferential)

- What does the text inspire you to do? (interpretive)

Mr. Hurley invites his students to read the two pages silently to themselves, and then read them a second time to make notes to themselves about questions or observations they have. (He photocopied these two pages from their books so they could annotate directly on the text.) After asking several literal questions to ensure they understood what the text said, he moves to the second phase, which focuses on organizational structures and word choice.

"Take a look at that last sentence, where he talks about the red paint on his hands. We know Ivan has always been an artist, but now what does he compare it to?" he says.

Several students immediately answer "blood" (which is right there in the sentence), and Mr. Hurley continues, *"So why is that important? The author put that in there, and we know by now she doesn't waste words."*

"I think it is because he is going to hurt someone," Belinda answers.

But one of her classmates, Yani, says, *"That could be, but maybe he's going to paint some more."*

Several students express agreement with either Belinda or Yani, citing either his past demeanor or the changes hinted at in this chapter. Mr. Hurley says, *"You've got a debate happening here, so let's make a list of the words and phrases the author uses to describe Ivan in this chapter. Then let's sort them conceptually according to like terms."* In a few minutes, they

Figure 4.6   Lesson Plan for *The One and Only Ivan*

Assessed Need: I have noticed that the students need: *Experiences analyzing the word choices in text to infer meaning.*

Standard(s) Addressed: *Language Variation and Change: Understand that patterns of language interaction vary across social contexts and types of texts and that they help to signal social roles and relationships (ACELA1501)*

Responding to Literature: Present a point of view about particular literary texts using appropriate metalanguage, and reflecting on the viewpoints of others (ACELT1609)

Text(s) I Will Use: *The One and Only Ivan (Applegate, 2012), pp. 172–173*

Learning Intention for This Lesson: *We will zoom in on the words and phrases used in this chapter to describe a character's change of perspective.*

Success Criteria for This Lesson: *I will be able to make a prediction and support it with evidence from text and discussion about changes in Ivan's attitudes and beliefs. (Use vocabulary and persuasive techniques portion of NAPLAN writing rubric to self-assess.)*

Direct Instruction:

Model: Strategies/skills/concepts to emphasize

Ask students to read the text silently, and then I will read it aloud, using expression and prosody.

Guide and Scaffold: Questions to ask

Are there any words or phrases that are confusing to you?

Assess: These are the students who will need further support

Akina and Joseph have been absent this week; give them time to catch up with the story prior to the lesson.

Dialogic Instruction:

Teacher-Directed Tools

Close reading questions for discussion:

What does the text say? (literal)

In what ways does Ivan describe who he usually is, in contrast to the hidden Ivan?

Is his image on the billboard closer to the Ivan we have known, or another Ivan? What is your evidence?

How does the text work? (structural)

What does Ivan compare the red paint on his fingers to? In what ways does this metaphor give you insight about how Ivan is changing?

What other words and phrases help you realize his change of attitude?

What does the text mean? (inferential)

The author says, "In the flicker of time it takes a snake's tongue to taste the air, he could taste revenge" (p. 172). How does this comparison to time help you to understand the depth of Ivan's reaction?

This chapter takes place at sunrise. Why is this setting meaningful in this scene? What might our author be signaling to us?

What does the text inspire you to do? (interpretive)

The last line of the chapter says, "I know how to keep my promise" (p. 173). Based on this chapter, what do you believe Ivan will do?

Student-Enacted Tools

Student partners provide peer critiques of each other's reading journal entries before they are submitted to me.

Feedback Opportunities: Provide written feedback on reading journal entries. Use NAPLAN marking criteria on 4 (persuasive devices) and 5 (vocabulary).

Independent Learning and Closure:

Closure: Remind students of learning intention and success criteria. Revisit writing criteria for vocabulary and persuasive devices before they write in their journals.

Independent Learning: Responding to literature: Writing prompt: Ivan says that he will keep his promise. What is his promise? What choices do you believe Ivan will make? Why are you making that conclusion?

Available for download at **https://resources.corwin.com/VL-LiteracyK-5**

have identified and sorted terms; they realize that only a few terms suggest the passive Ivan: *a peaceful sort* and *I think about naps*. On the other hand, there are many more that suggest a more aggressive Ivan: *angry, furrowed brow, clenched fists,* and *tear a grown man's limbs off.*

Mr. Hurley takes a few steps back from the board where he has listed them. *"Let's come back to that. We can't be certain, but it seems important."*

He transitions to the third phase (What does the text mean?) and asks about the setting, which takes place at sunrise. *"What's the symbolism of morning?"* he asks. *"What is our author signaling to us?"*

Now Berrigan enters the conversation. *"Morning's important because it's been dark all night, and now there's some light."*

"The Sun-Woman lights a torch, and that's the light. That's traditional story. But people light a torch when they set off on a journey, too," Waarrar adds.

"Did you hear that, everyone? I heard journey used in that description," says Mr. Hurley. *"Other thoughts?"* he asks the class.

"This could be Ivan's journey," Ekala observes.

Mr. Hurley signals for quiet and repeats her statement. *"This could be Ivan's journey."* He lets that linger in the air.

Yani speaks next. *"I still don't think he's going to hurt someone, but maybe he's going to use his paintings . . . I don't know, I just kind of think his paintings are going to matter."*

Mr. Hurley smiles and says, *"I can see you're all puzzling over this. Take a look at the last sentence again, when he says, 'I know how to keep my promise' (p. 173). In the last few minutes of class, write in your reading journal. What is his promise? Based on our reading and discussion of this chapter, what choices do you believe Ivan will make? Why are you making that conclusion?"* With that, his students begin to write, eager to learn how the gorilla will keep his promise.

Close reading can also be used with students in the primary grades. There are a number of similarities between close reading in the primary grades and the upper grades, namely that the text is read and reread several times; there is discussion about what the text says, how the text works, and what the text means; and the texts are more complex than students can read on their own. There are also differences between close reading in the primary and upper grades, namely in who the reader is. In most cases, close reading in the primary grades starts out as a teacher reads aloud, and the teacher is usually the one who annotates the text. Figure 4.7 includes information about the similarities and differences between close reading in K–2 and 3–5.

First-grade teacher Iman Hakim shared *Last Stop on Market Street* (de la Peña, 2015) with her students. (See Figure 4.8, starting on page 100, for her lesson plan.) She read it aloud once all the way through without telling them what to think or preteaching any of the vocabulary. Following her read-aloud, she asked students to talk about the text. In Ms. Hakim's class, every student has a partner; one of them is Gold and the other is Green (the school colors).

Ms. Hakim starts their conversation by saying, *"Green partner, please retell the story, in order, using the words* beginning, middle, *and* end. *Remember you don't have to provide all of the details, just the main points from the beginning, middle, and end."*

Immediately her students start interacting.

Peter says to his partner Sabah, *"The boy and his grandma finish church and get on the bus. They meet a lot of people on the bus, but the boy isn't really happy. Then, at the end, they get to the place where people are eating, like a restaurant."*

After several minutes, Ms. Hakim invites the other partner to talk, saying, *"Okay, thank you, Green partner. Now, Gold partner, please add two details to the beginning of the text that your partner did not include in the overview."*

Sabah responded, *"First, it was raining when they left the church and CJ got wet. And second, the bus driver does magic tricks."*

This continues for several minutes as students take turns adding details for their partner. Ms. Hakim is listening carefully to her students to ensure that they have a strong sense of the literal level of the text before moving on. When she is ready, she signals the class and begins to reread the text aloud. Her students pay close attention, putting their thumbs up when she reads something that they have shared with their partner.

Figure 4.7 Comparing Close Reading in Primary and Upper Grades

Close Reading in Primary Grades	Elements	Close Reading in Upper Grades
Text level is significantly higher than students' reading level.	*Text Selection*	Text complexity is slightly higher than in texts the student takes on during other phases of reading instruction.
The teacher is reading the text aloud to students, although they are not grasping its deeper meaning. The text may or may not be displayed.	*Initial Reading*	Students are more likely to read the text independently, although they are not fully grasping its deeper meaning.
The teacher guides annotation practices using displayed text and fosters collaboratively developed annotations.	*Annotation*	Students familiar with annotation practices are marking text independently, and adding to their annotations throughout class discussions.
The teacher reads aloud multiple times. Students may read along at the paragraph, sentence, phrase, or individual word level. A few students may read the text independently in subsequent readings due to practice effects.	*Repeated Readings*	Students are rereading independently or with minimal support. Students may also have access to audio supports (a poet reading her poem, a teacher reading dialogue, a peer reading a key sentence.)
Text-Based Discussions		
Students engage in extended discussion that is driven by text-dependent questions and dialogic teaching. Students deepen their understanding through analysis of the literal, structural, and inferential dimensions of the text.		
Students draw and write collaboratively and independently with adult support and guidance. They engage in shared investigations and debate compelling questions.	*Responding to Texts*	Students write collaboratively and independently. They investigate, research, and debate compelling questions.

Source: Fisher, D., & Frey, N. (2014a). Closely reading informational texts in the primary grades. *The Reading Teacher, 68,* 222–227. Used with permission.

 Available for download at **https://resources.corwin.com/VL-LiteracyK-5**

Figure 4.8   Lesson Plan for *Last Stop on Market Street*

Assessed Need: I have noticed that my students need: To use details to understand characters and events.
Standard(s) Addressed: RL.I.9: 9. Compare and contrast the adventures and experiences of characters in stories.
Text(s) I Will Use: Last Stop on Market Street (de la Peña, 2015)
Learning Intention for This Lesson: We will use events in a story to understand a character.
Success Criteria for This Lesson: I can explain my thinking to others using events in the book.
Direct Instruction: Model: Strategies/skills/concepts to emphasize Read the entire story aloud at least twice without interruption. Guide and Scaffold: Questions to ask (After first reading): What questions do you still have about the story? Think about them, and let's read it again. Let's see if you can answer your own questions the second time I read it to you. Turn the pages slowly as students retell to partners, to support their retelling. Assess: These are the students who will need further support I will partner with Jeremy during his retelling to make sure he understood the story.
Dialogic Instruction: Teacher-Directed Tools Close Reading questions for discussion: What does the text say? (literal) Retell the story to your partner, using *beginning*, *middle*, and *end*. Can you add two details to your partner's retelling? How does the text work? (structural) Who is telling the story? Is it CJ's nana, CJ, or someone else? What does the author mean when he says the rain "freckled CJ's shirt and dripped down his nose"? How does CJ's nana answer him when he is feeling negative? What does the text mean? (inferential) Why is CJ upset at the beginning? How does his mood change? CJ sees "familiar faces in the window." Who are those familiar faces, and how do we know? Let's look at the last two pictures together. Can you name the beautiful things in the picture?

What does the text inspire you to do? (interpretive)

Why do you believe this book won the Newbery Award?

Student-Enacted Tools

Students will meet in groups of four to talk about their opinions of the book, and give at least one reason.

Feedback Opportunities: I will provide verbal feedback to student responses during the close reading discussions, especially to prompt use of complete sentences and elaboration on details.

Independent Learning and Closure: Students will assemble picture cards depicting the major events of the story in chronological order, using the sequence words we've been learning (first, next, finally).

Available for download at **https://resources.corwin.com/VL-LiteracyK-5**

When she finishes reading the text for a second time, Ms. Hakim asks her students, *"Who is telling the story? Is it CJ's nana, CJ, or someone else? This time, the Gold partner can start."*

"I think it's a narrator because it never says 'I'. So it can't be the grandmother or CJ, right?" says Carlos, turning to his partner, Pedro.

"Yeah," Pedro responds. *"I think it's a narrator but we don't know who the narrator is. It's someone else, not grandma or CJ."*

As the lesson progresses, the students talk about specific words and phrases that the author uses and explore the pictures to figure out what some of the words mean. For example, Ms. Hakim asks, *"What does the author mean when he says 'which freckled CJ's shirt and dripped down his nose'?"*

Miguel is the first to talk in his partner, saying *"See the people with the umbrellas? It's raining so there are spots on CJ's shirt. Like freckles on your face, but water got on his shirt."*

Over time, the lesson turns to the meaning of the text. Ms. Hakim asks, *"Why is CJ upset at the beginning? How does his mood change?"* The students talk about CJ having to go someplace that he doesn't seem to want to go and having to ride the bus to get there. As Carlos says, *"The people are all really nice to him, so it puts him in a better mood. And, then, at the end, he gets to help people who are hungry."*

At the end of the lesson, Ms. Hakim asks her students, *"What made* Last Stop on Market Street *notable? Why do you think it won the Newbery Award? You can tell your partner, but then I'd like you to do some writing as well."*

Ignacio's response is, *"Even when you are sad, there are lots of things that you could look at or do to make you happy again."*

Carlos's response is, *"Broken things can still be useful, just in a different way."*

These first graders, still learning to read, have complex thoughts that are spurred by close reading of texts. Of course these students need to be taught to read, but wise teachers also use close readings to accelerate students' thinking, listening, and comprehension skills.

CONCLUSION

Discussion provides students with a chance to consider the perspectives of others. It's not the only way that students learn, but it's an important way. In this chapter, we focused on teacher-led or teacher-mediated dialogic approaches to learning. In each case, the teacher guided, facilitated, and questioned students as they engaged in literacy tasks. That doesn't mean that the students talk only with the teacher, but rather that the teacher is paying close attention to the flow of ideas in the classroom. Teacher-led dialogic approaches to learning can be used in whole class or small group settings. In the next chapter, we turn our attention to *student-led* dialogic approaches to learning, which are especially useful when the teacher is meeting with a small group of students who need targeted learning support.

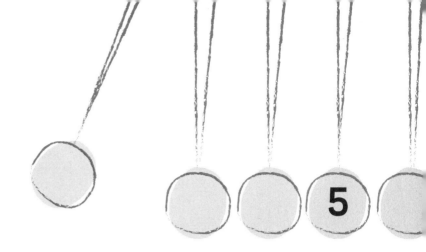

STUDENT-LED DIALOGIC LEARNING

"I would like to respectfully disagree with myself."

That was the startling (and let's be frank, amusing) statement issued by Eshan, a fourth-grade student in Gail Duryea's class. It came during a small group discussion about the merits and drawbacks of passing a new law requiring children and adults to wear bicycle helmets. The group had read two conflicting passages on the subject. One pointed out the merits, including the decreased likelihood of death in an accident when wearing one, as well as the high cost of health care for the injured. The second article

© Erin Null

argued that a study showed that cars gave less space to bicyclists wearing helmets, compared to the space allotted to bicyclists who did not. The article also stated that the safety of bicyclists increased in places where there were more of them on the road, and that mandatory helmet laws actually decrease the number of riders overall because they quit riding rather than wear a helmet.

The students in Ms. Duryea's small group discussions had been taught to engage in collaborative reasoning (Clark et al., 2003). This serves as "a forum for children to listen to one another think out loud" (p. 183). The process for collaborative reasoning is this:

1. The students, in groups of three or four, read the text(s).

2. The teacher poses a thought-provoking question for the groups to discuss.

3. Each student states his or her position using textual evidence, and then they ask one another questions that challenge the assertions their peers have made.

Eshan was in agreement with the author who argued that mandatory helmet laws further endangered riders. However, Sarai sided with the mandatory helmet laws. Using the collaborative reasoning protocol, they expanded their rationale using their own experiences as evidence. Sarai argued that parents buckle their children into seatbelts, saying, "Adults do things like that to protect children. I think there should at least be a law that if you're a kid you have to wear one." That's when Eshan decided to change his mind and disagree with himself.

THE VALUE OF STUDENT-TO-STUDENT DISCUSSION

"Out of the mouths of babes." That axiom captures a widely held belief that children can make insightful observations about big concepts. We imagine everyone reading this book has been struck silent at a profound comment made by a young student who wisely stated what should have been obvious to all, yet wasn't. To be sure, not everything they remark upon reaches this same level, but it is important to note that without a forum for speaking, the wise remark can never be heard. This is especially true when it comes to the learning that can occur through collaboration and discussion that is student-led. Children have a way of making themselves understood by their peers. The American Educational Research Association (2016) explains:

> Because their understanding is deep, based on either the underlying principles or structure of a domain or topic, expert teachers cannot always explain in a manner that allows students to integrate their explanations in a meaningful and helpful way. . . . There is a lack of correspondence between the ideas and concepts referred to by the expert teachers and the superficial concepts and entities that students refer to in their understanding.

In other words, students' thoughts and explanations can propel the learning of other children. In turn, the collaborative act of peer-assisted learning is reciprocal, with both children benefiting from the exchange (Daiute & Dalton, 1993). In student-led dialogic learning, the role of the teacher is to organize and facilitate, but it is the children who lead the discussion.

Another theoretical grounding for collaboration among children is the sociocognitive theory of Jean Piaget (1952). Zhang et al. (2016) explain that

> cognitive development is initiated by disequilibrium between a child's current understanding and unsettling new information. During collaborative interaction, a child's existing understanding is often challenged by others, which creates a state of disequilibrium. In order to restore the equilibrium, the child needs to develop a new and integrated perspective to reconcile the conflict. In other words, cognitive conflict arising from social interaction brings children's thinking to a higher level of sophistication, thus facilitating cognitive growth. (p. 200)

EFFECT SIZE
FOR PIAGETIAN
PROGRAMS = 1.28

Exposure to the knowledge, ideas, and perspectives of others, particularly when these do not align with those of a child, fosters cognitive growth when the child is given the space and tools for sense-making. Therefore, these interactions should be understood more broadly as sophisticated enactments of cognition, and not simply as a market for the trading of ideas.

Peer-assisted dialogic learning describes a constellation of instructional methods that allow learners to teach and learn from one another. The array of peer-assisted learning routines ranges from small group collaborative discussions among students to more formal structures such as whole class Socratic seminars. A specialized form of peer-assisted learning, called peer tutoring, designates one child as the tutor, and one or more as the tutees. In all cases, students assist one another in learning through completion of academic tasks. The root of collaborative learning is in an aspect of the work of Vygotsky and the zone of proximal development (1978), which posits that learning occurs through interaction with a more competent other. While in many cases this is an adult, Vygotsky and others since have argued that peer collaboration is of value for two reasons: (1) The more knowledgeable peer is better able to recall his or her own learning path and can therefore share it more ably, and (2) the interaction itself benefits the more competent peer because it reinforces and clarifies his or her own knowledge.

THE SOCIAL AND BEHAVIORAL BENEFITS OF PEER-ASSISTED LEARNING

The social and behavioral benefits of peer-assisted learning, especially for young children, are important as well. Spend time in the company of young learners, and you will witness the development of the social and language processes needed to successfully negotiate the dynamics of a group. While adults adjust their behavior and language to meet children where they are, this doesn't occur to the same degree with young peers. The ability to enter and exit conversations, take turns, pose and answer questions, and build on each other's ideas comes in part from direct experiences with peers. Consequently, if a majority of interactions are mediated by adults, gains in these communication skills are inhibited. Classroom peer interactions need to be taught of course, but students also need lots of opportunities to put these into action.

Ginsburg-Block, Rohrbeck, and Fantuzzo (2006) conducted a meta-analysis to examine the nonacademic benefits of peer-assisted learning for elementary students. They found good effect sizes related to social skills outcomes (ES = 0.39), self-concept outcomes (ES = 0.47), and positive behavior (ES = 0.65). These effects were more pronounced with students in Grades 1–3, and among students in low-income communities. This makes sense in light of the developmental trajectories of young children, who are still learning how to interact with others. This need is certainly evident in the various content standards, such as the following:

- Understand that language is used in combination with other means of communication, for example facial expressions and gestures, to interact with others. (Australia Year 1)

- Follow agreed-upon rules for discussions (e.g., gaining the floor in respectful ways, listening to others with care, speaking one at a time about the topics and texts under discussion). (California Grade 2)

- Listen attentively by making eye contact, facing the speaker, asking questions, and summarizing what is said. (Virginia Grade 3)

Kindergarten teacher Lynette Korman begins working on these communication skills on the first day of school. Over the course of the first month, her students learn how to talk to and listen to a partner, beginning with "knee to knee" conversations about favorite foods and activities. She supports their work with language frames (e.g., "My favorite _____ is _____ because _____"). Soon she has students working in triads, with each child allotted four "talking chips" to ensure that everyone participates yet no one dominates. Each time a member of the triad speaks, he or she places one chip in the cup at the center of the table.

"It gives them a visual cue for turn taking," explains Ms. Korman. To encourage listening, they play games that require careful listening. "I begin with objects that I hide in a bag, and when I make a sound they have to describe the sound and guess what the object might be," she said.

Classroom peer interactions need to be taught of course, but students also need lots of opportunities to put these into action.

EFFECT SIZE FOR SOCIAL SKILLS PROGRAMS = 0.39

EFFECT SIZE FOR SELF-CONCEPT = 0.47

EFFECT SIZE FOR POSITIVE BEHAVIOR = 0.65

Initially the objects are readily identifiable, such as a bell, but soon are much more difficult, such as a jar filled with grains of uncooked rice.

"I then have them work in small groups," she said, "with one child holding a bag with an object in it. The child has to explain what it is without naming it."

For instance, their first science unit was about animals, and Ms. Korman distributed bags filled with small plastic models of animals they were studying. "I use a modified version of 20 Questions. They get to ask 8 questions in total. This activity really stretches their listening and language skills, as the other children can ask questions of the child with the bag to figure out clues. And the student who has the hidden object has to listen carefully to answer. They begin to understand why they need each other to be successful."

FOSTERING COLLABORATIVE DISCUSSIONS

Increasing the amount of time students talk using academic language has been a priority in schools for decades. Simply said, students need practice with academic language if they are to become proficient in that language. Said another way, students must learn to speak the language of science, history, mathematics, art, and literature if they are to become thinkers in those disciplines. But the use of academic language is more than just teaching them the vocabulary of the subject. Success in using collaborative discussions requires knowing exactly how you want them to grow in their interaction skills.

Video 12

Prepping Students for Student-Led Dialogic Learning

https://resources.corwin.com/ VL-LiteracyK-5

The most obvious instructional implication relates to the use of time. Students need time every day to practice their collaborative conversations. That's not to say teachers should simply turn over their classrooms for students to talk, but rather that there are expectations established for student-to-student interaction and that students are held accountable for these interactions. An easy way to do this is to use a conversation roundtable. Students can simply fold a piece of paper like the one in Figure 5.1 on the next page. As students read a selected text, they take notes in the upper left quadrant of their own paper. Then they take turns discussing the text and recording the content that their peers share in the other quadrants. At the end of the conversation they summarize their understanding of the text, identify the theme, or ask questions (depending on the task assigned by the teacher) in the area in the center.

It's also important to provide students with instruction in how to engage in a collaborative conversation. They may need sentence starters at first to

Figure 5.1   Template for Notes for Conversation Roundtable

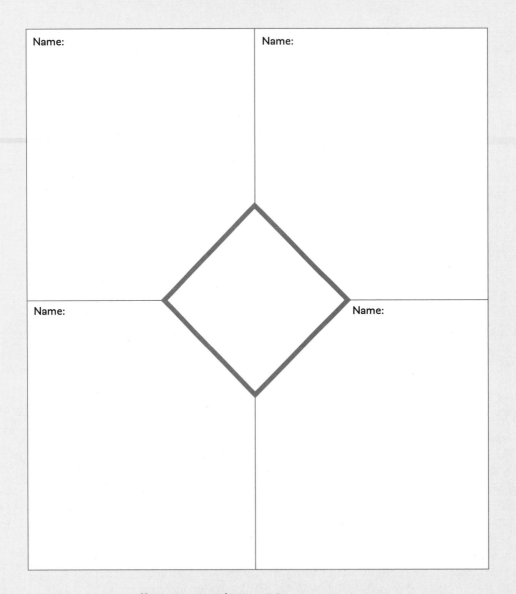

begin using argumentation in their discussions. For example, fourth-grade teacher Karen Jessop provided her students with the following frames when they wanted to offer a counter claim:

- I disagree with _____ because _____.
- The reason I believe _____ is _____.
- The facts that support my idea are _____.
- In my opinion _____.
- One difference between my idea and yours is _____.

In addition, students need to be taught the rules of a conversation, so Ms. Jessop teaches her students the following (Blyth, 2009):

1. Avoid unnecessary details.
2. Don't ask another question before the first one has been answered.
3. Do not interrupt another while he or she is speaking.
4. Do not contradict, especially if it's not important.
5. Do not do all the talking.
6. Don't always be the hero of your story (but have a hero).
7. Choose a subject of mutual interest.
8. Be a good listener.
9. Have a conversation that is in harmony with the surroundings.
10. Do not exaggerate.
11. Do not misquote.
12. Cultivate tact.

"I like using these rules just as they are, because the vocabulary is a bit high for them," said Ms. Jessop. "By the time they get to this age, most of them seem to think this is old hat for them, and they don't really listen. But because I've got more challenging vocabulary, it gives us an authentic reason to talk about them," she explained.

She said that *being in harmony with the surroundings* is a good challenge for them. "We talk about choosing appropriate times based on the context," she said. "For instance, if groups are supposed to be discussing a character's motivation in a book we're reading, that's not a good time to be telling jokes."

Another one is *cultivating tact*. "This one is especially important when they are critiquing each other's work. We talk about giving meaningful feedback, without being mean."

TEACH CHILDREN TO DEVELOP THEIR OWN QUESTIONS

The peer-assisted learning that can come from collaborative discussions will fall short of your expectations if attention is not given to the development of student questions. While most children know how to obtain information, it is more challenging to pose questions that move the conversation forward. Since many of the student-led dialogic learning is centered on text, we make sure to teach older students (third grade and above) a simple frame for seeing the relationship between questions, texts, and themselves. The question-answer relationship (QAR) strategy describes four types of questions: Right There, Think and Search, Author and You, and On Your Own (Raphael, 1986). It is based on the three categories of questions described by Pearson and Johnson (1978):

- *text explicit* (the answer is a direct quote from the text)

- *text implicit* (the answer must be implied from several passages in the book)

- *script implicit* (requires both the text and prior knowledge and experiences)

See Figure 5.2 for a table linking these question types.

Students use QAR to generate their own questions about a text. For example, students can write Right There and Think and Search questions for one another to check on their understanding of the facts of the passage. This inquiry interaction promotes more personal involvement than using only teacher-generated questions. As well, Author and You and On My Own questions invite the reader to integrate personal experiences and prior knowledge into their responses. These inferential and evaluative questions require the reader to make connections between concepts and ideas. As they generate Author and You and On My Own questions, readers deduce, infer, connect, and evaluate.

> The peer-assisted learning that can come from collaborative discussions will fall short of your expectations if attention is not given to the development of student questions.

Figure 5.2   Question-Answer Relationship Comparison Chart

QAR Strategy	Category	Description
Right There	Text explicit	The question is asked using words from the text, and the answer is directly stated in the reading.
Think and Search	Text implicit	The questions are derived from the text and require the reader to look for the answer in several places and to combine the information.
Author and You	Script and text implicit	The question has the language of the text, but in order to answer it, readers must use what they understand about the topic. The answer cannot be found directly in the text, but the text can provide some information for formulating an answer. The information is implied, and the reader infers what the author meant by examining clues in the text.
On My Own	Script implicit	The question elicits an answer to come from the reader's own prior knowledge and experiences. The text may or may not be needed to answer the question.

Available For download at **https://resources.corwin.com/VL-LiteracyK-5**

To initially introduce QAR, we advise the teacher to do a think-aloud process:

1. Read aloud a small segment of text.

2. Ask a question about what was read.

3. Reflect aloud on the selection and answer the question, using a think-aloud process in front of the class.

4. Identify the *type* of question and the *source* of the answer (e.g., *Think and Search, in the text*)

When students learn to classify questions and locate answers, they learn to recognize that comprehension is influenced by both the reader and the text. Eventually, students are ready to formulate original questions in response to text.

The use of QAR, applying the strategy in real time as students read, can be reinforced during small group discussions. For example, after a small group of Hailey Donovan's fifth-grade students read a chapter of *Hatchet* (Paulsen, 1987), the students asked one another a series of questions about the chapter they had just finished. When asked a question, the respondent first indicated which type of question it was and then provided the answer with evidence. At one point in the conversation, Maggie asked Joe, *"Could this really happen? Could a boy live alone after a plane crash?"*

Joe responded, *"I think this is an Author and You question, because the author really doesn't tell you if this could , and I have to think about this in my own brain and there are clues in the book. But, I think it could happen. Kids know things and they can live. Brian knows a lot because he learned things from his father and from his teachers. So, I think it really could happen."*

STUDENT-LED TOOLS FOR DIALOGIC LEARNING

The flow from direct instruction to teacher-led dialogic teaching to student enactments of learning is always recursive, as students' conceptual knowledge, communication skills, and capacity to think critically are continually under construction. So in no way do we mean to suggest that direct instruction happens during the first part of the school year and is replaced by teacher-led dialogic instruction at the midpoint, and that only during the latter part of the school year do students ever get to lead discussions. Although there is always going to be a period during which children learn about the structure of such activities, the goal is to move them forward in taking steps toward becoming their own teachers. Some of the ways teachers can do this are discussed next.

> The flow from direct instruction to teacher-led dialogic teaching to student enactments of learning is always recursive.

Fishbowl

Students benefit from bearing witness to quality student-led discussions. One method for doing so is the fishbowl. Here's how it works:

1. The teacher hosts a small group of students in the center of the room for a discussion, while the other students observe the interaction.

2. After introducing the purpose and the topic, the teacher is primarily an observer, interjecting only as needed to forward the discussion, usually by posing a new question.

3. The inner circle of participants (those in the fishbowl) debates the topic, while those in the outer circle listen.

4. A member of the outer circle can temporarily join the inner circle to comment, occupying an empty chair placed in the inner circle.

5. After the first round of discussion, members of the outer circle exchange places with those in the inner circle, and the discussion continues.

6. After all the students have participated in the inner circle, the teacher takes a more overt role in the discussion, asking questions that encourage students to synthesize their thinking.

7. The teacher asks students to comment on the process and their own learning.

8. Teachers can take a smaller role or eliminate themselves from the process when students become used to participating in fishbowl.

Third-grade teacher Kiara Mitchell is midway through a unit on fairy tales. "This unit is important because it provides some cultural knowledge that some of my students may not be familiar with," she explained. "But I also want them to think critically about what we are reading, and to question texts and ideas."

She paired two fairy tales from the Western tradition because they offered a platform for discussing ethical decision making. Her school has adopted a character education program that includes responsible decisions and taking care of others as well as the importance of adherence to rules.

"*Puss in Boots* and *Jack and the Beanstalk* are well-known fairytales, but the messages they convey are not commonly questioned," said Ms. Mitchell. "These are two stories where the heroes lie and steal. In fairy tales, the villain who does similar things is punished, but in these two stories, the heroes commit these acts, yet are rewarded. I want my kids to get underneath that idea and pick it apart." Her lesson plan can be found in Figure 5.3.

Ms. Mitchell's students have participated in two fishbowl discussions in the last month, so she is now ready to turn more of the responsibility for leading them over to students. Janette and Darius are moderators, and they will regulate the discussions; this includes timekeeping (each fishbowl group will have 5 minutes) and asking follow-up questions. Ms. Mitchell has given them clipboards with suggested prompts, such as "Can you tell us more about your idea?" and "Why do you think that?"

> **Teaching Takeaway**
>
> Display accountable talk prompts prominently in the classroom so that students can use them in many other lessons.

Figure 5.3   Lesson Plan for Third Grade Using a Fishbowl Technique

Assessed Need: I have noticed that my students need: Extended discussion experiences to synthesize information.
Standard(s) Addressed: Oral Language 3.1: The student will use effective communication skills in group activities. Reading 3.7: The student will demonstrate comprehension of information from a variety of print and electronic sources.
Text(s) I Will Use: Puss in Boots and Jack and the Beanstalk
Learning Intention for This Lesson: We will state our opinions and furnish evidence to support them. We will consider the opinions of others to make ethical decisions.
Success Criteria for This Lesson: After listening and participating in the fishbowl, I will write my opinion and use evidence to support it
Direct Instruction: Model: Strategies/skills/concepts to emphasize Set the purpose: Form an opinion and supply evidence to address the question: Is it ever okay to lie and steal? Provide a review of the fishbowl technique, modeling active listening and discussion behaviors. Inside circle and outside circle will be used, and everyone will have a turn in the inside circle. Review how to tap in / tap out of the inner circle to join and exit the discussion. Demonstrate listening behaviors (track the speaker, don't interrupt, use a friendly facial expression). Demonstrate discussion behaviors, and remind students of sentence frames we have been using. (For example, I agree/disagree with _____ because _____. I would like to add on to _____'s idea _____. Can you tell us more about your idea?) Guide and Scaffold: Questions to ask Central question: The heroes in these two fairytales lied and stole. Is it ever okay to lie and steal? Why or why not? Are there times when rules should be broken? Is a good intention enough? Assess: These are the students who will need further support D'Andre, Rachel, Rico, and Ashleigh will have modified text versions of these stories.
Dialogic Instruction: Teacher-Directed Tools I'm going to use this carefully, as I want the students to take a lead on the discussion. However, if a misconception arises that they can't resolve on their own, I will ask focusing questions to come to an understanding of the concept or idea Student-Led Tools: Fishbowl discussion: Is it ever okay to lie and steal? Janette and Darius are the moderators for this discussion. Make sure they have a list of possible clarifying questions to ask when needed. They will keep time (5 minutes per circle session) until all students have participated in the inner circle. I will sit with the outer circle to encourage student leadership of this discussion. Assess: These are the students who will need further support Listen and watch for any students who are having difficulty in explaining their opinion, and prompt the moderators if needed to pose additional questions.

Feedback Opportunities: Keep track of the number of times each student contributes to the discussion. Share this individually with students after the session. If there are students who have not yet contributed near the end of their fishbowl, share the data with them and prompt them to participate.

Independent Learning and Closure:

Closure: Moderators Janette and Darius will summarize the fishbowl discussion at the end and provide a list of points, pro and con, that were discussed. I will then review the learning intention and success criteria for the lesson, and move students back to their tables for independent writing.

Independent Learning: Now that you have read <u>Puss in Boots</u> and <u>Jack and the Beanstalk</u> and have participated in the fishbowl discussion, write a 100-word essay that (1) explains your opinion, (2) provides evidence to support your opinion from your experiences, and (3) uses at least one other example that came from another student.

Available for download at **https://resources.corwin.com/VL-LiteracyK-5**

Ms. Mitchell begins by explaining the learning intentions and success criteria for the lesson; then she reviews the fishbowl discussion process with her students, and takes the time to model active listening and discussion. While these ideas are not new to her students, "my explicit use of them keeps them on their front burners," she said. Ms. Mitchell then joins the outer circle, further signaling that her role is more participatory and directive in nature.

The moderators begin by referring to the two fairy tales, which they read earlier in the week. All the children have their annotated copies of the two on their laps. *"Our discussion question for today is, 'The heroes in these two fairy tales lied and stole. Is it ever okay to lie and steal? Why or why not?'"* says Janette.

Darius invites five students to join in the inner circle to begin the discussion. (A sixth chair is empty so that members of the outer circle may temporarily join to add to the discussion.) The first group relies more heavily on examples from the two texts, such as when Jack steals the harp and the goose from the giant, or when Puss in Boots tricks the king into believing his master is a marquis, rather than a penniless miller. Soon Darius calls time and invites a second group to the inner circle, and he reminds them of the central question about lying and stealing in general. By now the class is warming to the topic.

"Sometimes you have to lie," Jacy says, *"'cause it might be for a good reason."* Janette invites her to elaborate, saying, *"Keep going, Jacy."*

"Well, I told my momma a lie 'bout my little brother, 'cause I knew he would get in trouble if I told. He broke the lamp 'cause we was roughhousing in the living room. I knew it was on accident. I didn't want to get him in trouble."

"Hmm, that's a big one," says Ms. Mitchell.

The other children looked at one another, and then Kenneth quietly said, *"I told a lie like that, too. I said I didn't see a kid steal a bike, but I did."*

Janette called time, and by now nearly all the remaining students were vying to join the inner circle. What ensued was a deeper discussion about ethical dilemmas faced by Jacy and Kenneth. Is it okay to lie when you know it will keep yourself out of trouble, too? What about when you think someone might be hurt you if you tell?

"It was really interesting that we ended up spending a good deal of time discussing being a 'snitch' and how that is understood in our community," Ms. Mitchell said. "To think we started with a discussion about the storyline of *Puss in Boots*."

When the fishbowl discussions concluded, the moderators shared a t-chart they had been constructing. On one side were listed some of the arguments explaining that certain circumstances warranted lying and stealing; on the other were examples given to support the opinion that it was never okay to do so. Ms. Mitchell continued with the closure, returning her students' attention back to the learning intention and success criteria.

"Now's your time to write. You've read these stories and listened to your classmates. I'd like you to write about 100 words, and include three parts." She pointed at the success criteria displayed on the document camera:

1. Explain your opinion.

2. Provide evidence from your experiences to support your opinion.

3. Use at least one other example that came from another student.

For the next 20 minutes, her students wrote quietly, rarely breaking the silence as everyone worked. Ms. Mitchell provided further guided instruction as needed for individuals, and reported the number of times each student participated during the fishbowl discussion. "There's a lot happening this morning academically, like writing and discussion. But I'm even more impressed with how they're wrestling with these ethical issues," she said. "They need to develop a sense of self, not just report on what others think."

Collaborative Reasoning

While a fishbowl discussion involves a large group of students, collaborative reasoning is used with smaller groups. In each case, the goal is to deepen students' knowledge and comprehension through discussion and argumentation.

Although the teacher is present, his or her role is limited to that of facilitator and moderator, and the goal is to say as little as possible in order for students to assume the dominant role in learning. Rather than a recitation of facts and details in the text, the central question invites broader consideration of the dilemmas the text raises. Importantly, this line of discussion contributes to the students' overall comprehension of the text as well as to their growing ability to use more formal reasoning (Clark et al., 2003). Figure 5.4 shows a side-by-side comparison of two illustrative discussions. Note that the one on the left, a traditional recitation discussion, features more teacher talk and less sophisticated student responses. In the collaborative reasoning discussion on the right, students talk more and use advanced reasoning skills, and the teacher's input is minimal.

Collaborative reasoning discussions follow seven basic steps (Clark et al., 2003, p. 184):

1. After the class reads the text, small groups come together for a discussion. (The teacher reviews the rules listed below.)

2. The teacher poses a central question concerning a dilemma faced by a character in the story.

3. Students freely explain their positions on the central question to the members of their group.

4. They expand on their ideas, adding reasons and supporting evidence from the story and everyday experience.

5. They challenge each other's thinking and ways of reasoning.

6. At the end of the discussion, a final poll is taken to see where everyone stands.

7. Finally, the teacher and students review the discussion and make suggestions on how to improve future discussions.

Of course, children need to be instructed in collaborative reasoning; simply locating four students and a text at a table is not going to be sufficient. But when children are regularly involved in the use of accountable

Figure 5.4   Comparing Quantity and Quality of Student Response in Two Types of Discussions

Traditional Recitation Discussion[a]	Collaborative Reasoning Discussion[b]
T: Who is the main character of this story?[c]	*T:* The big question is, "Should the coach let Ronald play?"
S: Ronald.	*S:* I don't think so, because he couldn't do anything right.
T: Yes, and what was the problem he faced in this story?	*L:* Yeah, if he was on a team he would make people lose.
S: He couldn't do anything right.	*R:* Nobody would want to pick him.
T: No, what was he trying to do?	*J:* I think he should have a chance to be on the team, because then he might have a chance to get better.
S: He was trying to play baseball.	
T: Yes, so, our stories usually *have a problem* and a solution. Remember? We talked about that yesterday. So what was the problem in this story?	*B:* That wouldn't be fair, because he would make everybody lose in the meantime.
	A: Winning isn't everything.
S: (no response)	*T:* So. What do you think? "Should the coach let Ronald play?"
T: Okay, B. Can you help S out?	*A:* Maybe the coach could get his dad to practice with him.
B: He wanted to play, but he ran the bases backward and closed his eyes so he couldn't hit the ball.	*G:* When I first started playing baseball, I was scared I'd get hit by the ball so I wasn't very good at first, but then after a few practices I got better.
T: Okay, J, what else did he do wrong?	
J: He drew letters in the mud with a stick?	*K:* How would you feel if nobody wanted you to play and called you "four eyes" just because you wore glasses? I think they ought to let him play.
T: Why is that a problem?	
B: He wasn't paying attention to what his coach was telling him?	*B:* But the rest of the team would have to suffer until he got better. Wouldn't that make him feel pretty bad? It would me!
T: Okay, so the problem in the story was that he couldn't do the things he was supposed to be able to do to play ball, he couldn't hit, he couldn't run, and he didn't pay attention. Is that a problem when you want to play ball?	*A:* I think he deserves a chance.
	B: I disagree, because no one would like him then.
Class: (in unison) yeeeeesss.	
T: So the problem Ronald faced in this story was he kept making mistakes every time he tried to play ball. What happened next?	

Source: Clark, A. M., Anderson, R. C., Kuo, L., Kim, I. H., Archodidou, A., & Nguyen-Jahiel, K. (2003). Collaborative reasoning: Expanding ways for children to talk and think in school. *Educational Psychology Review, 15*(2), 181–198. Reproduced with permission of Springer New York LLC in the format Book via Copyright Clearance Center.

[a]Traditional Recitation Discussion: nine teacher turns, seven student turns (three different students), one whole-class response.

[b]Collaborative Reasoning Discussion: two teacher turns, twelve student turns (eight different students).

[c]T = Teacher; B, S, J, G, K = Students.

Available for download at **https://resources.corwin.com/VL-LiteracyK-5**

talk, and their teacher uses conversational moves to model reasoning and argumentation, they begin to internalize this type of thinking. Jonathan Gates's second-grade students have been regularly using collaborative reasoning since the beginning of the school year.

"We're reading and discussing more complex texts, and when you couple that with their growing curiosity about the world, it's a powerful combination," he said. The teacher began the school year with Jerry Pallota's series of picture books entitled *Who Would Win?* (*Lion vs. Tiger, Tarantula vs. Scorpion,* etc.). "These were a good platform for figuring out their opinions. There's a checklist to help you decide, so it's a tangible way to figure out their reasoning," Mr. Gates explained.

As the year progressed, they considered other big questions for books they read collaboratively or as shared readings:

- Should the tree be angry with the boy? (Silverstein, *The Giving Tree,* 1964)

- Does the big bad wolf have a point when he talks about how awful the three little pigs really are? (Scieszka, *The True Story of the Three Little Pigs,* 1996)

- Should Matilda have stayed with her parents, or moved in with Miss Honey? (Dahl, *Matilda,* 1988)

"I'm really looking for them to build the habit of reading critically, and not just to get information. I need them to notice their thinking, and I want them to experience other people's thinking, too. How can they learn to explain their thinking if they don't get chances to talk about their ideas?" Mr. Gates said.

> When children are regularly involved in the use of accountable talk, and their teacher uses conversational moves to model reasoning and argumentation, they begin to internalize this type of thinking.

Gallery Walks

Student-led dialogic learning routines such as fishbowl discussions and collaborative reasoning still have an adult presence, albeit one that takes a backseat as children direct the experience. Other routines, like gallery walks, are performed away from the company of an adult. Collaborative discussions of this nature, done in small groups or pairs, tend to be a bit more informal, and the structure of the talk is left a bit more in the hands of students. Gallery walks are one example, and the purpose is to elicit knowledge in a shared environment such that

Figure 5.5   Lesson Plan for First Grade Using a Gallery Walk in Science

Assessed Need: I have noticed that my students need: To sharpen their powers of observation using visual clues.
Standard(s) Addressed: RI.1.7: Use the illustrations and details in a text to describe its key ideas. SL.I. 2: 2. Ask and answer questions about key details in a text read aloud or information presented orally or through other media.
Text(s) I Will Use: Guess Whose Shadow?
Learning Intention for This Lesson: We will use words and illustrations to make logical predictions.
Success Criteria for This Lesson: My partner and I can correctly identify at least five shadows using clues.
Direct Instruction: Model: Strategies/skills/concepts to emphasize Set the purpose: Review the learning intention and success criteria, and explain how partners will write their predictions on the Guess Whose Shadow? worksheet. Model how to ask questions of one another ("What do you think this shadow is?"), ask for evidence ("What clues are you using?"), and respond to similar questions. Guide and Scaffold: Questions to ask When partners appear to be stuck, I will ask them to look at the questions to ask that are written on their worksheets. Assess: These are the students who will need further support Pair Jeremy with Gabriela, who will be able to scribe for him.
Dialogic Instruction: Teacher-Directed Tools N/A Student-Led Tools Gallery Walk: students will visit seven stations with photographs of shadows, ask each other questions about their guesses and clues, and record their opinions on the worksheet. Assess: These are the students who will need further support Check for understanding: monitor groups as they work through each station, and assist as needed.
Feedback Opportunities: They will compare their written predictions to pairs of photographs, with each pair showing an object casting a shadow, and the shadow the object casts.

Independent Learning and Closure:

Closure: Summarize the learning intentions and success criteria. After they complete the independent task, ask partners to give a thumbs-up sign if they were able to complete the task. Follow up with any partners who indicate they have not completed the task.

Independent Learning: Ask pairs to choose one photograph pair of a shadow and its object, and draw and write an explanation using the words surface, object, shadow, and light.

students can build on the observations of one another. Here's how gallery walks work:

1. Three-dimensional items, photographs, or language charts are placed at stations throughout the room.

2. Small groups of students rotate to each station and discuss what they are seeing and observing. Their talk is much like the conversations that occur in museums as one travels from one object to the next (hence the name *gallery walk*).

3. These stations often include posted questions or multiple texts for students to ponder.

First-grade teacher Iman Hakim uses gallery walks to spark shared knowledge about a topic under study. Her students are currently learning about light and shadow in science, and they are learning that opaque objects can cast a shadow onto a surface when in the presence of a bright light. She uses pages from *Guess Whose Shadow?* (Swinburne, 1999) and places them in clear vinyl sleeves at various numbered locations throughout the classroom. After she reads the foreword aloud to the children, they discuss the properties of light and the necessary conditions for creating shadow. She reminds the students that the biggest shadow they see is night, which is when the sun shines on the other side of the earth. She reviews the learning intention for the lesson (discussing clues in photographs and text) and the success criteria for the lesson (to correctly identify the source of at least five shadows in the photographs), and explains the gallery walk. See Figure 5.5 for her lesson.

"You and your partner will use this sheet to record your predictions for the source of the shadows in the photographs," Ms. Hakim explained. *"There are*

seven of them at different stations. Look for the clues and explain them to your partner. Be sure to ask your partner questions, like 'What do you think this shadow could be?' and 'What clues are you using?' When you've visited all seven stations, come back to the carpet and we'll check our answers."

The students travel as partners through each station. Ignacio and Alfonso begin at a photograph of the shadow of what appears to be a long-legged animal. It's upside down, and cast on a grassy lawn. *"We're supposed to ask questions,"* says Alfonso, *"I'll go first. What do you think this could be?"*

Ignacio studies the image, turning in around. *"I think it's a camel,"* he says. *"What's a clue?"* asks Alfonso. Ignacio points out the long neck, the legs, and a hump on the back of the shadow.

"Okay," says Alfonso, *"now it's my turn."* He squints at the photograph. *"I think it's a bird with a long neck."*

"How come? What's your clue?" asks Ignacio. *"Well, it's on grass, and I don't think a camel would be standing on grass. I think he would be in the desert."* Now they have to agree on an answer. In the end, Alfonso is able to persuade his friend that it might be a bird, given the context. The boys travel to each of the gallery stations and then return to the carpet to find out the answers.

Ms. Hakim displays each photograph of a shadow and the object that cast it, and the children check to see how many of their answers were correct. The boys are glad to learn that their prediction that one of the shadows was cast by a bird is indeed correct. Each pair of students had at least one incorrectly identified, but all met the success criteria. The teacher closes this part of the lesson by reviewing the learning intention, and invites the pairs to continue their collaborative work.

"Please select one photograph and make a diagram of it, using the object and the shadow," she says. *"Please label your diagram with our science target vocabulary:* light, shadow, object, *and* surface."

Ignacio and Alfonso choose the photograph of a boy tossing a baseball in the air, his shadow falling on the street surface behind him. "Let's do this one," says Alfonso. "It's like when we practice on our baseball team. But now I'm going to look for shadows when we're on the field!"

Literature Circles

Perhaps the most popular way to organize student-led dialogic learning in literacy is through literature circles (Daniels, 2002). Literature circles are organized around a large theme, with each group of students in a classroom choosing a book within a set of texts that express this theme or related themes. Small groups of students form based on their interest in a particular book, and remain together until the book is finished. This also allows the teacher to differentiate reading levels while building a common set of understandings. Students function within their literature circle somewhat autonomously. They make agreements about what will be read in advance of each meeting, and fulfill roles for the collective good of the group.

These skills are especially important for the fourth graders in William Trang's class. The skills they are working on include arriving at discussions already prepared and making decisions about deadlines. For a unit on the lives of children long ago, Mr. Trang organized his class into literature circles reading one of three books:

- *The Door in the Wall* (De Angeli, 1990)

- *Catherine, Called Birdy* (Cushman, 1995)

- *Crispin: The Cross of Lead* (Avi, 2003)

Each literature circle consisted of four to six students, and each of the titles was read and discussed by two groups.

"I used to have a unique book for every group, but I had a hard time monitoring six different titles. This keeps us all more focused," said Mr. Trang.

Each book is a fictional account of the life of a young person during the Middle Ages in Europe; this commonality provides the teacher with common ground for building background knowledge with his students. Mr. Trang previewed the titles for students, and shared an excerpt from each of the books with them so they could get a taste of the author's writing style. Students rank-ordered the titles, and Mr. Trang constructed groups based on student preferences.

"Choice is really important," he explained. "I used to think I needed to put them into a different book if I thought their choices were too easy or too hard, but I learned that kids are pretty great about picking the right book for them. "It's rare that I get a student who's in over his head with the book. The collaboration is the secret," he smiled.

The literature circle groups meet twice per week for discussion and planning. At the beginning of the school year, Mr. Trang assigned specific roles for each student: Illustrator, Connector, Word Wizard, Literary Luminary, and Discussion Director (Daniels, 2002).

"I had them rotate these roles each time they met during the first book we read, so that everyone had a feel for the role," the teacher explained. By midway through the second book, Mr. Trang had phased out use of the formal roles entirely. "They caught on to the fact that good readers do all of these things, not one in isolation."

The students in the literature circles meet initially with Mr. Trang to discuss deadlines for the book to be completed, as well as the tasks they will complete during the three weeks set aside for this unit. Mr. Trang brings a calendar with him so that each group can plot out their pacing for the book they have selected, as well as the interim due dates for the response logs the students submit to him. By making students active decision makers in the planning, he increases the level of engagement and responsibility (Daniels, 2006).

Once the planning has been completed, students are now free to read, meet, discuss, and write about their reading. Mr. Trang designates times for formal literature circle meetings twice a week, and it is during these times that student-led dialogic learning takes place. Students meet to discuss the chapters they read in advance of the meeting, first discussing the major events that took place in the story to make sure each member understood the plot. Since this unit has a particular emphasis on character development, the groups also talk about the direct characterizations, such as descriptions, and the indirect characterizations, such as actions, and the reactions of other characters, which contribute to their understanding. Next, students talk about "golden lines"—powerful sentences in a chapter—and why these sentences had an effect on them.

Video 13

Visible Learners: "What do you do when you get stuck?"

https://resources.corwin.com/ VL-LiteracyK-5

The *VISIBLE LEARNER*

In a literature discussion group about *A Wrinkle in Time* (L'Engle, 1962), all of the students are stuck. None of them can understand why the children were repeatedly told to stay together. The group members have been talking about this for some time when James says, "We need a different strategy. Nobody really knows, right?"

In response, Holly says, "We could look on the Internet. They probably have an answer."

Amber counters, "I'm not sure that I'm ready to give up and look on the Internet. I think that there are other things we can do. We could each write three reasons why it's better to stay together and then see if any of our ideas make sense to the story."

James said, "I like that. And if that doesn't work, we can call over Ms. Arthur and ask for more advice. Or we could look on the Internet to see if we are right."

Visible learners know what to do when they don't know what to do.

After each meeting has concluded, students return to their desks to write independent responses in their journals. "I've learned over the years not to try to control these conversations too much," said Mr. Trang. "I used to rely a lot more on protocols and role sheets. But that seems to stifle conversation."

Instead, he spends time on teaching about discussion, accountable talk, and the norms for the classroom. "As they develop these skills, the discussions get stronger, whether we're using literature circles or any other collaborative learning arrangement. But they need lots of opportunities to use these skills. Otherwise, the skills wither away."

Readers Theatre

Readers Theatre is a choral reading strategy that that uses scripts of poems, plays, and children's literature to create a performance piece. Unlike traditional school plays, the performers do not utilize costumes, staging, lighting, or even gestures. Instead, they use their voices to convey the appropriate meaning of the text. As well, they do not memorize their parts, instead using the script to read. Readers Theatre is considered a fluency-building activity because students engage in repeated readings while perfecting their parts. Struggling readers in particular may resist reading anything more than once, but the accountability of performance in front of peers can eliminate such hesitancies (Tyler & Chard, 2000). Poems, picture books, and other texts can be easily adapted for use as Readers Theatre scripts. There are a number of books and Internet resources for scripts available as well.

Beyond fluency building, Readers Theatre can be an excellent platform for student-enacted discussion. Martinez, Roser, and Strecker (1998) propose a five-day instructional plan for managing multiple Readers Theatre groups. Here's how it works:

1. Day 1. On the first day, during shared reading, discussing meaning, building background knowledge, and teaching vocabulary, the teacher introduces to the entire class the stories that will be performed. Students are put in groups and assigned to perform a script later in the week.

2. Days 2, 3, 4. On each of the subsequent days, the groups reread their script, discuss roles, and rehearse. It is within this space that students must figure out how they will resolve problems.

3. Day 5. Each group performs for the class.

A summary of the five-day instructional plan appears in Figure 5.6.

Figure 5.6   Five-Day Instructional Plan for Readers Theatre

Day 1	Teacher • Models fluency by reading aloud the stories on which the week's scripts are based • Provides direct instruction that presents explicit explanation of some aspect of fluency • Discusses each of the stories • Distributes scripts for students to read independently
Day 2	Students • Gather in collaborative groups using scripts with parts highlighted • Read the script several times, taking a different part with each reading Teacher • Circulates and coaches, providing feedback
Day 3	Procedures are the same as on Day 2. During final 5 minutes, students within each group negotiate and assign roles. Students are encouraged to practice their part at home.
Day 4	Students read and reread their parts with their collaborative group. During final 10 minutes, each group makes character labels and decides where each member will stand during the performance.
Day 5	Collaborative groups perform, reading before the audience.

Source: Adapted from Martinez, M., Roser, N. L., & Strecker, S. (1998). "I never thought I could be a star": A Readers Theatre ticket to fluency. *The Reading Teacher, 52,* 326–334.

 Available for download at **https://resources.corwin.com/VL-LiteracyK-5**

Reciprocal Teaching

Developed by Palincsar and Brown (1986) as a reading comprehension strategy, reciprocal teaching involves student-directed groups of four working together with a piece of informational text that has been segmented into smaller chunks. These stopping points (chunks) allow students to discuss the text more deeply throughout the reading. This is accomplished through a discussion format and is repeated several times until the reading is complete. The teacher may create stopping points in advance, although more experienced groups can decide on their own how best to break up the text. At each stopping point, students apply four kinds of reading comprehension strategies to understand the text:

- **Questioning the text passage** by asking text-explicit (literal) and text-implicit (inferential) questions of one another

- **Clarifying understandings** through discussion of any confusions that might need to be cleared up (for example, using the glossary, consulting another source, asking the teacher)

- **Summarizing** the main points contained in the passage

- **Predicting** what the writer will discuss next, based on what is known thus far

A strength of reciprocal teaching is that it fosters consolidation of knowledge and comprehension. Once learned, the four strategies do not need to be performed in a strict order, and all members are encouraged to use these freely in their discussions.

Mr. Hurley's Year 5 students are seated at tables of four to engage in the familiar practice of reciprocal teaching. They have been reading and discussing *Papunya School Book of Country and History* (Papunya School, 2001) as part of a larger unit on Aboriginal and Torres Strait Islander histories and cultures. This book, written collectively by the school community of the title, conveys information through both visual and text-based modalities, and the book emphasizes the importance of two-way learning (using both Western and indigenous peoples' funds of knowledge) to, in the words of one contributor,

> EFFECT SIZE FOR RECIPROCAL TEACHING = 0.74

> see the children, after being educated at Papunya School, coming out like honey ants full of honey—nice and healthy honey—not poison inside. We want to see the children learning both ways, and coming out bright orange and yellow together, like honey ants. (p. 45)

Discussion of the book has raised many questions about race. In response to his students' queries, Mr. Hurley has selected a brief informational reading on facts and misconceptions about race for his students to read collaboratively. This one-page informational text presents facts in a list format. Fred, Yani, Berrigan, and Akina have used reciprocal teaching a number of times and quickly begin to chunk the text into manageable sections. They also utilize a discussion notes guide to capture their ideas, and it further serves to remind them about the comprehension strategies they will employ during their discussion (see Figure 5.7).

"It makes sense to read it a couple bullets at a time. They probably have a lot to do with each other," says Yani. The others nod in agreement and draw lines under the third, sixth, and tenth items on the list, and then read the title and opening statement silently.

Figure 5.7   Reciprocal Teaching Note-Taking Guide

Members: Date: Text:	Learning Intention:
During Reading	**After Reading**
Your Predictions: Section 1: Section 2: Section 3:	Were your predictions accurate? Why or why not?
Your Questions: Section 1: Section 2: Section 3:	Do you have unanswered questions?
Your Clarifications: Section 1: Section 2: Section 3:	What tools did you use to clarify your understanding?
Summary Statement of Complete Reading:	

Noting that the paragraph contains several rhetorical questions, Berrigan says, *"The person who wrote this made my job easy to predict. The answers to the questions will be in the list."*

After the students read the first statement about race as a modern, European concept, the conversation picks up. Akina says, *"I was surprised that the word* race *didn't exist in English until the 1500s. How can that be?"*

EFFECT SIZE FOR QUESTIONING = 0.48

"I think it's because of what it says in the third fact—'human subspecies don't exist.' I never thought of that before. It's not like when we divided up the plants we're studying in science," says Fred. *"Like when Whites came here and saw people who looked different from them. They brought that idea with them. They thought we were a subspecies, not like them."*

"I wonder what happened. Why it got changed around all of a sudden?" speculates Yani. *"What happened to make people think about race?"*

"We still got to summarize," says Fred. *"How 'bout this? 'Race is an idea that started with Whites long ago, before Whites came to Australia. There's no difference in our genes.' How does that sound?"*

"That's good. Write that down for us. Let's read the next three so we can get finished," says Akina.

Ten minutes later, they have cocreated some summary sentences that their group will use when Mr. Hurley leads the entire class in a discussion of the article and its connections to *Papunya School Book of Country and History*. His lesson can be found in Figure 5.8 on the next page.

Peer Tutoring

A final example of student-led dialogic learning is peer tutoring. These partnerships can be same-age peers, or cross-age, with an older student tutoring a younger one. Peer tutoring is best accomplished in pairs, as it can be difficult for children to manage the learning of a group of peers. Tutors and tutees can be of similar ability, or may be partnered because one is more skilled than the other. As with other forms of peer-assisted learning discussed in this chapter, peer tutoring works because it leverages the social dynamics present in relationships. There are intrinsic rewards, including friendship and motivation to perform well academically and behaviorally (Ginsburg-Block et al., 2008).

EFFECT SIZE FOR PEER TUTORING = 0.55

It is important to support both tutors and tutees in this endeavor. Sandra Moscowitz presents peer-tutoring arrangements to the entire class together, in order to provide directions to all of her second graders at the same time.

Figure 5.8   Lesson Plan for Year 5 Using Reciprocal Teaching

Assessed Need: I have noticed that my students need: *To use their voices to inform, explain, question, and narrate.*

Standard(s) Addressed: *Literacy: Listening and speaking interactions: Clarify understanding of content as it unfolds in formal and informal situations, connecting ideas to students' own experiences, and present and justify a point of view (ACELY1699)*

Literature: How texts reflect the context of culture and situation in which they are created: Identify aspects of literary texts that convey details or information about particular social, cultural and historical contexts (ACELT1608)

Text(s) I Will Use: *Papunya School Book of Country and History, and informational text on misconceptions about race*

Learning Intention for This Lesson: *Learning by becoming: We will use knowledge about race to understand the history of Aboriginal peoples in Australia.*

Success Criteria for This Lesson: *I will discuss ideas about our readings with classmates to develop notes for use in our discussions.*

Direct Instruction:

Model: Strategies/skills/concepts to emphasize

Review reciprocal teaching protocol with class. Since they are familiar with it, spend more time on errors to avoid (e.g., no one takes notes, leaving the group unprepared for the discussion; forgetting to invite others into the conversation when they have not yet participated.)

Guide and Scaffold: Questions to ask

As tables work through the process of reciprocal teaching, ask students reflective questions about their learning: How are the questions and explanations helping you understand the text? What are you being mindful of as a participant in this discussion?

Assess: These are the students who will need further support

Check in early with Berrigan to make sure he's off to a good start. The last time we did this, he didn't provide much information to his group.

Dialogic Instruction:

Teacher-Directed Tools

When the students have finished the reciprocal teaching activity, but before they record their responses, ask them to debrief their own contributions to the discussion and offer positive feedback to peers.

Student-Led Tools

Reciprocal teaching groups of four students will read and discuss the list of misconceptions about race to prepare for a class discussion about our understanding of the target text.

We will conduct a learning circle discussion on the effects of misconceptions about race on the lives of Aboriginal peoples both historically and today. Ekala and Getano will lead the discussion. Opening question to begin discussion: "What happens when belief systems of different societies collide?" Closing question: "Can stories, such as the _Papunya School_ book, change people's beliefs?"

Assess: These are the students who will need further support

Join Belinda's reciprocal teaching group because she has had limited experiences with reciprocal teaching since moving here last month.

Feedback Opportunities: Use guided instruction as needed with Belinda; debrief with Koorine's group after reciprocal teaching to see what they have concluded.

Independent Learning and Closure: Students will make audiovisual recordings of their own responses to the question: If our school wrote a book about our community, what story would I want to tell? (These will be edited and played at our open house next month.)

"I pair the kids up to read to one another, using a paired reading format," said the teacher. Paired reading is a form of peer tutoring developed by Topping (2001), in which mixed ability students read to one another to develop fluency and comprehension. "I use the terms *coach* and *player* because they are more understandable," she said. Each child will in turn play both roles, but it is the stronger reader who is the initial player."

Jonah and Hunter are two students who have been paired today. Jonah is the stronger of the two readers, so he will assume the initial role of the player. The boys have copies of the same text, which is about community helpers, and Jonah begins by reading the entire passage aloud, while Hunter follows silently in his text. Hunter's role as coach is to correct any errors Jonah makes. Of course, what's really occurring is that the stronger reader is modeling prosody, accuracy, and fluency. After the initial reading is completed, the boys switch roles, and now Hunter is the player. He rereads the same passage to Jonah, who is now serving as coach, and who makes similar corrections as needed.

After the passage has been read a second time, the students discuss the content of the text and write a joint summary of the piece. "We do this twice a week," explained Ms. Moscowitz. "I couldn't possibly meet with all my students individually to work them, but paired reading provides the kind of assistance they need." Importantly, the passages have another life beyond paired reading. "I actually use this as a warm-up for close readings, because it's a great way to have them do some initial rereading before we move into an extended lesson."

CONCLUSION

There is a role for the teacher in much of the learning that students do. Having said that, this chapter focuses on learning that students do in the presence of their peers. Of course, the teacher has a hand in organizing the learning environment and monitoring the impact on students' learning, but the differences in the lessons contained within this chapter related to the role of peer-mediated learning. Some of what we all know was mediated by our peers. In the world of work, most of us engage with others, trying to get our point across and recognizing that other people have good ideas. The same processes can be used in the classroom to create learners who make their own learning visible.

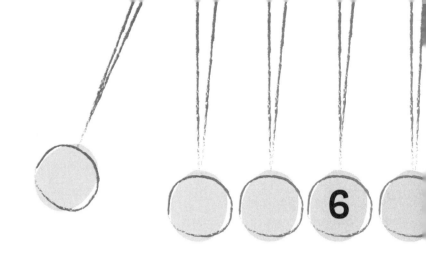

INDEPENDENT LEARNING

Finishing her third individual conference of the day, fourth-grade teacher Yessenia Torres asks her students to pause their reading and update their vocabulary journals.

"Remember," she says, *"today is Stump the Teacher, so you're looking for words that you don't think that I'm familiar with."*

As they read, Ms. Torres's students are aware of the words the author is using, including words that they are not sure that they know. Every few

© Richard Hutchings/PhotoEdit

days, Ms. Torres invites her students to quiz her using the words they've been reading. The conversation is lively as Ms. Torres tries to provide definitions and examples of the words her students find. She knows that other students in the room benefit from her explanations, but she is mostly interested in the words that her students recognize as confusing.

The class has been studying the lives of native peoples (American Indians, Native Alaskans, and Native Hawaiians) and there are a lot of confusing words in the books they have been reading. Ms. Torres uses independent reading in her classroom to build students' reading habits. She knows that exposure to reading, from her read-alouds to students independent reading, is important practice. Students are encouraged to select books to read from a collection she has assembled. Each of the books in the independent reading box focuses on the social studies or science theme. Independent reading builds students' background knowledge and their vocabulary, and develops their reading habits.

Ellery wants Ms. Torres to talk about the word *leggings,* and she says, *"Oh, those are tight pants that really hug your legs. I wear leggings when I go to my yoga class. I think in older times, leggings were extra clothing that people wore on their legs to keep them warm. It's kind of like an extra pair of pants, but just from the knee to the ankle. Sometimes these were decorated. When we go to the Museum of Man, you'll see a pair of leggings that have walnut shells sewn on them so that they make noise. Let's remember to see those when we go."*

Hailey asked about the word *toboggan,* and Ms. Torres said, *"I'm not really sure. Can you use it in a sentence?"* Hailey responds, *"Let me find it. Okay, here it is. 'As he balances the toboggan on the crest of the hill. . . . ' Does that help?"* Ms. Torres responds, *"Kind of. So it's something that he carried. Let's Google Image it. [She displays the search results.] Well, that looks like a sled to me. I wonder if they used a different word? Interesting. We'll have to see if they have any of these toboggans at the museum when we visit next week. Thank you Hailey for stumping me. I learned something new. Are we ready to read some more? I have a couple more conferences scheduled. Could I see Marco?"*

The goal of a reading conference is to engage a student in a conversation about the book he or she is reading. The purpose of the conference is determined by the teacher and student together, because the conversation should be a give-and-take of questions and ideas. However, there are several suggested topics a reading conference may focus on. In any case, the student and teacher should use both the book and the student's reading journal during the conversation. Useful activities for a reading conference include these:

- Listen to the student read aloud.
- Discuss something in the story.
- Ask the student if there is something he or she didn't understand.
- Refer to the focus lesson taught that day.
- Discuss the content of the book.
- Discuss the writer's craft.
- Review the student's list of books read or list of reading interests.
- Set goals together.
- Discuss recent journal entries. (Fountas & Pinnell, 2001, p. 139)

> Independent reading builds students' background knowledge and their vocabulary, and develops their reading habits.

Marco joins Ms. Torres at the table, opening his book. The rest of the class has returned to their independent reading books. Ms. Torres asks Marco to read the second paragraph of the open page, saying, "I like to hear you read. I know that you mostly read in your head, but when you read to me, it helps me think about your progress toward our success criteria."

Marco reads fluently, and when he finishes Ms. Torres says, *"I'm interested in your gems from this text. What do you love about these couple of paragraphs?"*

Marco: *"I really like the descriptions. The author helps me see it in my mind. I can picture the people living on the plains."*

Ms. Torres: *"I'm pleased that you're able to do that. Remember when reading informational texts was really hard? And I'm thrilled that you're self-monitoring. Do you want a bit more advice?"*

Marco: *"Yes, sure."*

Ms. Torres: *"Your reading has developed really well and now I'm thinking about your fluency and flow. Sometimes your reading sounds more like you are talking with friends. Other times it is stilted. Remember when we talked about that word?* [Marco nods.] *Is that just when you read out loud or does that also happen in your mind?"*

Marco: *"It happens in my mind more. When you're listening I'm more careful and I can hear myself so I try to make it sound like talking."*

Ms. Torres: *"Fluency, not how fast you read, but the way is sounds in your mind, could be an area for your next focus. Thoughts?"* [Marco agrees.]

The conference continues for a couple of minutes as Ms. Torres continues to talk with Marco about ways he can practice silently and orally to improve his fluency. In the meantime, the rest of the students are reading widely, building their background knowledge and vocabulary. These independent learning tasks complement the direct and dialogic instruction that she provides her students.

During the block of time allocated to literacy learning, students read and write every day and spend time working with their teacher, collaborating with peers, and working independently. As we have noted, some of this time is used for direct instruction and other time is used for dialogic instruction. But teaching is not a simple dichotomy

There are instructional times when independent learning is valuable. And there are also ways to bore students to tears with independent tasks.

Teaching Takeaway

Effective conferences allow students to focus on accomplishments before they are introduced to a new area to work on.

EFFECT SIZE
FOR WIDE READING
= 0.42

between these two. There are instructional times when independent learning is valuable. And there are also ways to bore students to tears with independent tasks.

As we noted in Chapter 2, teacher clarity includes relevance. Applied to independent learning, this means that students understand why they are asked to complete certain tasks or they have a goal that directs their own independent learning. Relevance matters throughout the literacy instructional period, but it is highlighted in independent learning because so many students see these tasks as busy work that they are required to complete. In part, this is because teachers have not communicated the value of independent tasks and the ways in which these tasks can contribute to their learning. And in part, students see independent learning as the busy work that it unfortunately sometimes is. Far too many students are required to complete worksheet page after worksheet page of skills and concepts that they have already mastered. We call these "shut-up sheets," because they keep students quiet and busy, despite the fact that they are not learning much.

The remainder of this chapter focuses on independent learning tasks that are not boring or repetitive. Rather, they allow students to practice and apply what they have learned, or gain new information that they can use later. Unlike direct and dialogic instruction, independent learning tasks require that students develop habits of learning. They need to remain focused on the task at hand. They need to persevere in the face of challenge. And they need to recognize their successes and celebrate them. Ideally, students enter a state of flow when they are engaged in independent learning, as many of Ms. Torres's students did during their reading.

FINDING FLOW

Mihaly Csikszentmihalyi (1990) believes that the optimal state for humans is a balance between skill and challenge. When we have sufficient skills (especially at the surface level) and the challenge is appropriate, we fall into a state of flow in which we are cognitively engaged, often losing track of time. When our skills exceed the challenge, we are bored. This is too often the case in school. Students expect school to be challenging and appreciate when it is. Having said that, when the challenge far exceeds our skill level, we become frustrated or anxious. Who hasn't seen students become so frustrated that they act out? Flow is the careful balance between skills and challenge, as noted in Figure 6.1.

Figure 6.1   Flow

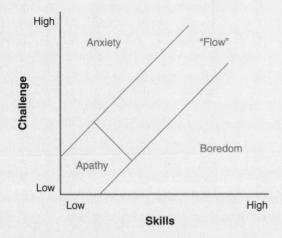

When the teacher is present, the challenge level can increase. That's what happens during direct and dialogic approaches to instruction. But when students work independently, the challenge has to be reduced a bit to ensure that they enter the state of flow. If the challenge is reduced too much, boredom ensues.

Yes, it's challenging. If creating flow with and for students was easy, everyone would be a teacher. Expert teachers know their students well, know their content well, have formative evaluation data that identify learning gaps, and then plan assignments and tasks to close the gap between students' current performance and their expected performance. And it bears repeating, independent learning is not the only tool that teachers have to close the gap! Students move from surface to deep to transfer when teachers use a combination of direct, dialogic, and independent tasks. The remainder of this chapter focuses on tasks that teachers can use to help students enter the state of flow such that they are responsible for their own learning. Since we already noted students' use of vocabulary journals in Ms. Torres's class, we'll start there.

> When students work independently, the challenge has to be reduced a bit to ensure that they enter the state of flow. If the challenge is reduced too much, boredom ensues.

LEARNING WORDS INDEPENDENTLY

An important part of literacy learning is instilling a love for words. One way to do this is for teachers to model their interest in words and their word-solving strategies. This direct instruction approach was discussed in Chapter 3. Another way to instill a love of words is to engage students in collaborative conversations, which was discussed in Chapters 4 and 5 as dialogic approaches to learning. Having said that, we recognize that a majority of words that students learn come from their reading. As such, teachers must ensure that their students engage in significant amounts of wide reading. As noted in Figure 6.2, there is a correlation between students' achievement and their reading volume (Anderson, Wilson, & Fielding, 1988). In a large part, this is because of the vocabulary knowledge that develops through reading.

Of course there are other ways that teachers can develop students' independent word learning. We will highlight a few approaches here, but it's important to consider what they have in common:

- First, they directly involve students, who notice that they need to learn a word.

Figure 6.2 Relationship Between Achievement and Outside Reading

Percentile Rank	Minutes of Reading per Day (Books)	Words Read per Year
98	65.0	4,358,000
90	21.1	1,823,000
80	14.2	1,146,000
70	9.6	622,000
60	6.5	432,000
50	4.6	282,000
40	3.2	200,000
30	1.8	106,000
20	0.7	21,000
10	0.1	8,000
2	0.0	0

Source: Adapted from Anderson, R. C., Wilson, P. T., & Fielding, L. G. (1988). Growth in reading and how children spend their time outside of school. *Reading Research Quarterly, 23,* 285–303. Used with permission.

 Available for download at **https://resources.corwin.com/VL-LiteracyK-5**

- Second, students keep records of the words they want to learn.

- Third, students share their ideas with others so that their peers can choose to add new words to their learning goals. Here are three effective approaches:

  o **Vocabulary Self-Awareness.** Teaching vocabulary is complicated by the varying word knowledge levels of individual students. Even when the text is held in common, students bring a range of word knowledge to the reading. Rather than apply a one-size-fits-all approach to vocabulary instruction, it is wise to assess students before the reading. The assessment is valuable for the student as well, because it highlights their understanding of what they know as well as what they still need to learn in order to comprehend the reading. One method for accomplishing this is through vocabulary self-awareness (Goodman, 2001). Words are introduced at the beginning of the reading or unit, and students complete a self-assessment of their knowledge of the words, resulting in a personalized vocabulary chart. An excerpt of a third-grade student's vocabulary chart for *High Tide in Hawaii* (Osborne, 2003) can be found in Figure 6.3. Notice that this student identified her understanding of key words with dates to match the codes. As the unit of study progresses, she will update her self-awareness chart, adding new dates when she masters a new level of understanding.

> EFFECT SIZE FOR VOCABULARY PROGRAMS = 0.67

Figure 6.3   Vocabulary Self-Awareness Chart

Directions:

Put the date in the "+" column when you can can write an example and definition of the word.

Put the date in the "✓" column when you can either write a definition or an example, but not both.

Put the date in the "−" column for words that are new to you.

Word	−	✓	+	Example	Definition
tidal wave		9/15			A really big wave
volcano			9/15	Mt. St. Helen	A mountain that explodes
tsunami	9/15				
paradise		9/15			A very beautiful place

Available for download at **https://resources.corwin.com/VL-LiteracyK-5**

○ **Vocabulary Self-Selection (VSS).** Students identify words they believe are important for themselves and the class to learn. These words can occur in their readings, their independent research, or their interactions with others. Students independently record how they located the word (for example, heard it on television or read it on the Internet) and why they believe it is important. When developing VSS with her second graders, Marla O'Campo read the book *Donavan's Word Jar* (DeGross, 1994). This story of a boy who is fascinated with words resonates with emergent and early readers. Like Donavan, Ms. O'Campo's students are encouraged to write down words they enjoy to be added to the class word jar. The word jar is opened periodically and students get to share their words with others, who can add them to their vocabulary journals when the words interest them.

○ **Scavenger Hunts and Realia.** Like VSS, scavenger hunts challenge students to locate representations of new vocabulary. Students are given a list of words, both new and familiar, that are related conceptually. They have one week to find either visual examples (e.g., magazine clippings), realia (the object itself), or evidence of the use of the word in something other than their textbooks. For instance, kindergartners can be given a list of vocabulary words like the ones in Figure 6.4. While many of these words are familiar, others will be new to most kindergartners.

Figure 6.4   Vocabulary Scavenger Hunt for Kindergarteners

Fruits and Vegetables	
Apple	Orange
Blueberry	Pear
Broccoli	Peas
Corn	Tomato
Cucumber	Watermelon

Available for download at **https://resources.corwin.com/VL-LiteracyK-5**

INDEPENDENTLY WORKING WITH WORDS

For students to deepen their understanding of vocabulary, they need to engage with those words both collaboratively and independently. Dialogic approaches to instruction provide students with opportunities to use words and clarify meanings. If we want students to develop their academic language, they have to use that language. We don't get good at things we don't do. Having said that, it's important to recognize that students also have to engage with the words (and the concepts behind those words) individually. There are a number of ways to ensure that students work with words individually; word sorts and vocabulary cards are two of those ways.

Open and Closed Concept Word Sorts

Concept word sorts are a means for encouraging students to create classification systems based on word meaning. Students can also sort words to build phonics knowledge through the use of word families. Sorts can either be closed (categories are furnished by the teacher) or open (students develop their own categories). Because concept word sorts, especially open ones, are rarely identical among students, the independent task can end with a collaborative conversation about each student's respective understandings of word meanings.

Like word sorts for phonics development, concept word sorts typically feature words on slips of paper or index cards (recommended for younger students). Younger students find it easier to sort words using a mat made of construction paper or tag board to create a defined field for placing the word cards. For example, a group of first-grade students in Iman Hakim's class sorted the vocabulary words in Figure 6.5 using a closed sorting system provided by their teacher. You'll notice that there are a number of correct variations possible with these categories of the seasons.

The next example is an open sort from the same first-grade classroom. One group labeled their categories as *breakfast, lunch, dinner,* and *snacks* and sorted accordingly (see Figure 6.6). At the same time, another collaborative group with the same words created two categories: *we're allowed to have* and *we're not allowed to have*! Ms. Hakim's lesson plan can be found in Figure 6.7 on page 144.

Vocabulary Cards

Another way to encourage students to engage with word learning individually is to assign them the task of creating vocabulary cards. Students are

Figure 6.5   Closed Word Sort in First Grade

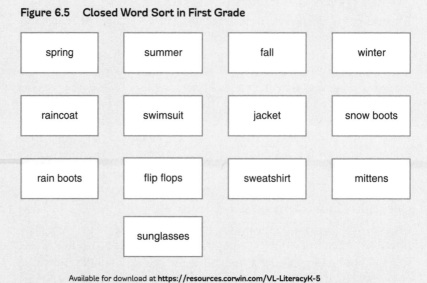

spring	summer	fall	winter
raincoat	swimsuit	jacket	snow boots
rain boots	flip flops	sweatshirt	mittens
	sunglasses		

Available for download at **https://resources.corwin.com/VL-LiteracyK-5**

Figure 6.6   Open Vocabulary Word Sort

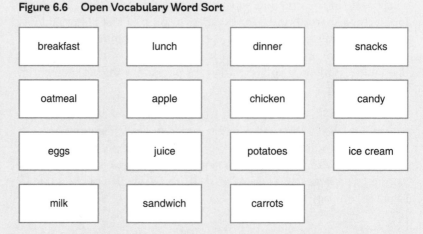

breakfast	lunch	dinner	snacks
oatmeal	apple	chicken	candy
eggs	juice	potatoes	ice cream
milk	sandwich	carrots	

Available for download at **https://resources.corwin.com/VL-LiteracyK-5**

given a set of 4″ × 6″ index cards and instructed to divide each into quadrants (see Figure 6.8 on page 146). Depending on the content and focus, specific terms are selected. For example, fifth-grade teacher Debra Geary selected terms related to the Latin root word *manu-* meaning "to make." Students created their vocabulary word cards for *manufacture*, *manuscript*, and *manual*. The target word is written in the top left quadrant, and the definition, after class instruction, is recorded in the student's own words in the upper right quadrant of the card. An antonym or something that the word does not mean is written in the lower right quadrant and an illustration or graphic symbol representing the term is drawn in the lower left quadrant.

Constructing vocabulary cards serves several uses. First, when placed on a binder ring the cards become an easily accessible reference for the student. The time involved in creating each card also provides an opportunity for students to spend an extended period of time concentrating on the meaning, use, and representation of the term, thereby increasing the likelihood that the term will become a part of their permanent vocabulary.

SPELLING WORDS

It is a common misconception that entry into school represents an introduction to language. To the contrary, children entering school have been drenched by the sounds of language since their birth. During the first five years of life, English speakers have learned to sort out the 44 phonemes of the English language in order to make sense of the jumble of sounds coming at them.

For many children, kindergarten represents an introduction to the formal operations of the language. During the primary years, they will learn the speech-to-print connection that lies at the heart of reading and writing. Stated simply, these students will become skilled at recognizing how spoken words can be represented through graphs (symbols). Phonics is the process of bolting the sounds of the language onto the symbols of the language.

EFFECT SIZE
FOR PHONICS
INSTRUCTION = 0.54

Understanding the speech-to-print connection comprises three elements:

- **Phonemic Awareness.** The ability to manipulate sounds, for instance, segmenting the sounds in *cat* and converting it into /c/ /a/ /t/.

- **Letter Knowledge.** Recognizing the names and shapes of the letters of the alphabet.

- **Sound/Symbol Relationships.** Matching the sounds of the language to the letters and letter combinations.

Figure 6.7   Lesson Plan for First Grade Using Concept Sorts

Assessed Need: I have noticed that my students need: To organize word knowledge in order to build schema.
Standard(s) Addressed: L.1.5a: With guidance and support from adults, demonstrate understanding of word relationships and nuances in word meanings. a. Sort words into categories (e.g., colors, clothing) to gain a sense of the concepts the categories represent.
Text(s) I Will Use: Word cards in envelopes
Learning Intention for This Lesson: We will sort words that are similar and put them in categories to show relationships.
Success Criteria for This Lesson: I can explain why I have grouped words into categories.
Direct Instruction: Model: Strategies/skills/concepts to emphasize Review how words are sorted into categories. Name the strategy, state its purpose, explain its use: I am going to model how I sort words into categories. I have done this before, but it helps when I remind myself about how to complete this independent task. Analogy: A word sort reminds me of when I sort the laundry at home. I group the clothing by colors. All the whites go in one basket, and the dark clothes go in another. The words are like the clothes I sort, and the categories are like the baskets. Demonstration: First I take all the words out of the envelope. Some envelopes have category cards, and others don't. If there aren't any category cards in the envelope, then I get to make my own. Next, I spread them out so I can read them. I straighten up the ones that are upside down. Now I am going to start moving them on the desk, putting similar ones together. I see one of my cards says shoes and the other says socks. Those two words might go together in the same category. I have category cards, so I will read them again. Here's one that says, "Things that go on your feet." Yes, shoes and socks go on my feet, so I will move these word cards to this category. Errors to avoid: I know that one mistake is not taking all the cards out and reading each one of them before I begin. When I tried that before, it took longer to sort the word cards. Assess the skill: When I think I am finished, I will explain my thinking to my teacher. That means I need to study these for a few minutes so I know what I will say. Guide and Scaffold: Questions to ask Can one of you repeat the directions in your own words? Assess: These are the students who will need further support Sometimes Alyssa is slow to start because she doesn't want to be wrong. I will sit with her to get her started.

Dialogic Instruction:

Teacher-Directed Tools

N/A

Student-Led Tools

After they have sorted the words, table partners will examine each other's work, and engage in informal peer tutoring as needed.

Assess: These are the students who will need further support

Valeria is an English learner, so her cards will also have a picture cue to reinforce vocabulary.

Feedback Opportunities: I will meet with each student to hear their thinking about why they grouped words as they did.

Independent Learning and Closure:

Closure: Before moving them to independent work, I want to revisit the learning intention and success criteria so they don't lose sight of the purpose for learning.

Independent Learning: I have prepared one closed sort and one open sort for students to complete during their centers rotations.

Available for download at **https://resources.corwin.com/VL-LiteracyK-5**

As students master these constrained skill systems, they become better spellers. Over time, they realize that some words are spelled based on the meaning of the word rather than sound/symbol relationships and that some words are borrowed from other languages that have different rules. Now the unconstrained skill of vocabulary knowledge comes to the forefront. In general, strong spellers have a good command of language, and their spelling develops as their overall literacy learning progresses.

As you likely recall from your own school days, cramming for a spelling test does not result in long-term retention of the words. Students cannot simply pass through the spelling lists and be expected to remember the words when the time comes to use them. Fearn and Farnan (2001) identify a three-phase process required for students to authentically learn how to spell: acquisition, retention, and automaticity. In other words, we're moving students through surface to deep learning, and to transfer their knowledge to new and novel situations. Let's take each of these in turn and examine their application. Note the value of independent learning time required for students to become strong spellers.

Figure 6.8   Vocabulary Cards in Fifth Grade

Template	
Vocabulary word	Definition in student's own words
Graphic or picture	Antonym or reminder of what the word does not mean

Example	
manufacture	make a large amount of things on an assembly line
	We don't manufacture oranges because they grow on trees.

Image source: Courtesy of clipart.com.

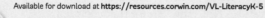

Acquisition

This first component of spelling concerns students learning to spell words correctly. Students must pay attention to the words they can and cannot spell. One way to focus students' attention is through a self-corrected spelling test. However, these tests should not occur only on Friday after students have "studied" the words for a week. Students should participate in regular testing situations and receive immediate feedback via self-corrections. When students are invited to correct their own spelling tests, they begin to notice where they make errors.

> EFFECT SIZE FOR SPACED VERSUS MASS PRACTICE = **0.71**

The *VISIBLE LEARNER*

John and Sarah had finished their independent learning tasks. John had selected to create a presentation and Sarah had elected to engage in research. Their fourth-grade class was involved in the study of resources, natural, human, and capital. Noticing that she was finished, John approached Sarah and asked if she had time to review his presentation, saying "You could look at my presentation and tell me if you think it's excellent. I think it's good, but I want it to be excellent and I'm not sure what to change. I have all of the parts that Ms. Henderson told us to have, but it needs to be better. And, can you check to see if my ideas go in a good order?"

Sarah responded affirmatively and said, "I completed my research project and wrote about three pages. Can you read it? Don't check spelling and stuff. Can you focus on the ideas to make sure that they make sense? I will check the spelling and grammar after that."

The visible learner actively seeks feedback.

For example, Kiara Mitchell's third-grade students were focused on the spelling pattern that included words with *sc-*, including *score, scared, scarf, scanner,* and *disc.* They had other spelling patterns on their weekly list. Ms. Mitchell does not simply tell students to go home to study the words and then hope for the best. Rather, they take short quizzes on the words each day. Ms. Mitchell gives the words in random order and students attempt to write them correctly. When the list has been exhausted, the teacher goes back to the words and tells students how to spell them. The students circle each error they've made on their own papers; these could include a missing letter, an extra letter, or letters transposed. In other words, they don't circle an incorrect word, but rather the places within the word were the errors occurred. "This is immediate feedback for them," said Ms. Mitchell. "Noticing where they make the errors, and which words they have already learned, focuses their studying for the next day." Ms. Mitchell's weekly spelling lesson plan can be found in Figure 6.9.

> EFFECT SIZE FOR FEEDBACK = **0.75**

Figure 6.9   Third-Grade Weekly Lesson Plan for Self-Corrected Spelling

Assessed Need: I have noticed that my students need: Spaced practice to develop accurate spelling of new words.
Standard(s) Addressed: 3.10: The student will edit writing for correct grammar, capitalization, punctuation, and spelling.   f) Use correct spelling for frequently used sight words, including irregular plurals.
Text(s) I Will Use: Weekly spelling program words, and common errors in their writing
Learning Intention for This Lesson: We will use what we know about phonics, affixes, and meaning to learn to correctly spell identified words.
Success Criteria for This Lesson: 100% accuracy by the end of the week!
Direct Instruction: Model: Strategies/skills/concepts to emphasize Monday only   Name the strategy, state its purpose, explain its use: The words I selected this week have a similar pattern: they have sc- in them. When I see sc- at the beginning or end of a word, I know it makes the sound of /sk/. I chose this pattern because it's close to Halloween and Day of the Dead, and some of you are using words like scary in your stories.   Analogy: It's like the first and last car on a train. When s and c together are the first two or last two letters in the word, it makes the sound of /sk/.   Demonstration: Take each word, and use sound and word part strategies to spell words.   Errors to Avoid: When sc- is in the middle of a word, the pattern doesn't work any more.   Assess the skill: I will use my spelling self-correction strategy to practice words.   Guide and Scaffold: Questions to ask   Tuesday: Brainstorm with class: What other words use the same pattern?   Wednesday: Look-say-cover-write practice.   Thursday: Compose generative sentences with the class using the spelling words.   Assess: These are the students who will need further support   Monday: Preassess to determine which words they will need to study. Have a second word bank for students to select from in cases where they already know the correct spelling on Monday. Customize student word lists as needed based on preassessment results.
Dialogic Instruction: Teacher-Directed Tools   N/A   Student-Led Tools   After they complete their self-corrected spelling, groups of four will meet and use a conversation roundtable to compose notes and then discuss strategies they are using to learn spelling words (e.g., how they are practicing, what words are tricky, where they are seeing progress).   Assess: These are the students who will need further support   Alberto is new to the class and has not done this before. I will scaffold instruction as he completes this.
Feedback Opportunities: Students receive feedback each day by scoring their work.

Independent Learning and Closure:

Closure: Restate the learning intention and success criteria before each day's quiz.

Independent Learning:

Monday: Preassessment of spelling words. Students take a quiz, then circle each error within the word. They grade each word. (0–1 errors in a word is an A; 2 errors is a B; 3 or more errors is a C.) Next, they rewrite the missed words with correct spelling and turn in their entire quiz.

Tuesday: Spelling quiz and self-correction grading.

Wednesday: Spelling quiz and self-correction grading.

Thursday: Spelling quiz and self-correction grading of any words that have not yet been mastered. Write a silly story that includes this week's words. Highlight the spelling words in the story.

Friday: Pair students, who read each other's story aloud. The reader pauses after each highlighted word, while the listener writes the spelling word on a separate paper. Students then switch roles, score their tests, and staple their spelling tests and stories together.

Available for download at **https://resources.corwin.com/VL-LiteracyK-5**

In addition to self-corrected spelling tests, students learn to spell words during direct and dialogic instructional time. Teachers can focus students' attention to words as they find them in reading assignments and as they work on successive versions of their writing. A short, small group or individualized session focused on spelling in which the student is really paying attention can pay big dividends in learning. It is important to remember, however, that these times should be used to focus on spelling words that are part of a system, and not on isolated words.

Retention

Once students have learned a set of words in a given lesson, there is a risk that the words will be forgotten. Retention requires remembering the spelling of words once they have been acquired. As Fearn and Farnan (2001) note, "Learning depends not only on attention, but also on the ability to hold information in active memory long enough for it to be recorded in long-term memory" (p. 431). One way that teachers can provide students some practice with retention is to include some old favorites on the self-corrected spelling lists. This provides students an opportunity to draw words from memory. Teachers can also use word activities and games that provide students with an opportunity to use the words they have learned. Finally, teachers can ensure that students have multiple opportunities to write during the day. This provides young writers with authentic opportunities to use, and spell, words in contexts in which they need them.

Automaticity

Interestingly, accurate spelling on a test does not mean the student can use a word in his or her writing. In a study of their second-grade students, Beckham-Hungler and Williams (2003) discovered that the children consistently misspelled words in their writing that they had successfully spelled on pretests. They speculated that "the cognitive demands of the pretest situation were much less than the demands of journal writing" (p. 304).

Successful spelling in connected writing signals automaticity. This means that students can spell, or write, a chosen word automatically and without thinking about it. This is especially important during writing. If a writer has to stop continually to think about how words are spelled, he or she will not be able to focus on the ideas to be written. Writers need a host of words to draw from as they write. Understanding the developmental nature of spelling, a teacher would not expect a first grader to automatically spell *playground*. The student will likely slow down when he or she comes to that word. However, the teacher can and should expect the student to have a number of words flow automatically, and without conscious effort, from the student's fingers.

Word Games

Games are an excellent method for creating opportunities for rehearsal and practice, which facilitate retention. Because games are engaging, they also are chosen frequently by students during collaborative learning time. These include board games like Scrabble, Concentration, and Boggle. In addition, there are other easy word game activities that students can do independently:

- **Spellamadoodle.** This is a fun activity whose only purpose is to invite students to focus on the spelling of a word for a few minutes. Students create designs using spelling words in order to convey the meaning as well as to practice spelling the word. For example, they write the word *vacuum* several times in the shape of a vacuum cleaner.

- **Word Pyramids.** Students begin with one letter and then write a two-letter word that begins with the same letter. This is followed by a three-letter word, then a four-letter word, and so on. The goal is to build a pyramid of words that extends to ten letters or beyond. When students can go no further, they write a sentence for each word in the pyramid.

- **Endless Words.** Beginning with a three- or four-letter word, the student creates a list by changing only one letter at a time to create new words. For example, a sequence might look like this:

  pat rat sat Sam Pam tam Tim tin tan tap

BUILDING FLUENT READERS

Fluency—to be fluent—has many connotations in education. One focuses on the skills in learning language, as in "she is a fluent speaker." Another focuses on learning additional languages, as in "she is newly fluent in Spanish." However, the one we use in this book concerns the rate and accuracy at which students process text. "Reading fluency is the ability to read quickly and accurately, with appropriate and meaningful expression" (Rasinski, 2003, p. 16). In other words, reading fast is not the true goal of fluency. Readers must understand what they are reading and add expressiveness to their oral reading. Comparing fluency with music, Worthy and Broaddus (2001/2002) note that fluency "consists not only of rate, accuracy, and automaticity, but also of phrasing, smoothness, and expressiveness. Fluency gives language its musical quality, its rhythm and flow, and makes reading sound effortless" (p. 334).

Reading fast is not the true goal of fluency.

Let's define some of those terms that were just mentioned. Rate is the speed at which the learner reads. If the reader's rate is too slow (less than 50 words per minute), it will interfere with comprehension, because the reading becomes choppy and disconnected from other ideas in the sentences and paragraphs. If it is too fast, especially in oral reading, it may also interfere with comprehension, as the reader rushes too quickly past the details that make the passage meaningful. Reading too fast may also indicate that the learner lacks prosody—the ability to adjust tone, pitch, and rate to read with expression appropriate to the meaning of the words. After all, a reader can only use expression when the meaning of the message is understood. Finally, accuracy refers to the ability to read the words correctly. Remember that relative accuracy reflects text difficulty. Automaticity is the ability to recognize words with a minimum of attention, allowing the reader to direct most of his or her attention to matters of comprehension. Not surprisingly, automaticity is closely associated with decoding and spelling.

Expanding on this connection, it is worthwhile to note that fluency is the bridge between decoding and comprehension. Students learn to decode words by matching sounds and symbols. This ability is related to their oral language development and early phonemic awareness. Children use more than just decoding to read. Some English words are difficult to decode and are learned as sight words. Fluent oral readers should be able to read orally with speed, accuracy, and appropriate expression. The National Reading Panel report cautions, "If text is read in a laborious and inefficient manner, it will be difficult for the child to remember what has been read and to relate the ideas expressed in the text to his or her background knowledge" (National Institute of Child Health and Human Development, 2000, ¶ 29). The ability to remember what has been read and relate it to background information is critical for reading comprehension.

In addition to being fluent in oral reading, students must also be fluent in silent reading. While much less attention has been given to this area, the goal of reading is that students read independently for both enjoyment and information. Again, they must read fast enough to make sense of the information and accurately enough to gain information.

As Rasinski (2010) notes, slow, inefficient, and disfluent reading should be taken seriously. These readers will likely have reading difficulties for their entire school experience if nothing is done. Therefore it is useful to attend to both silent and oral fluency rates throughout the academic year to monitor progress. Figure 6.10, on pages 154–155, offers a chart of silent and oral fluency rates by grade level.

As we noted in the direct and dialogic instruction chapters, there are many things that teachers can do to build students' fluency. Readers Theatre, for example, provides students with opportunities to practice their oral fluency, both rate and prosody. At the independent task level, teachers can have students audio-record themselves reading and then rerecord themselves at a later time, checking for improved fluency. As they get older, students can monitor their own fluency levels, setting goals for their growth. These goals can include improvements in rate or prosody. A sample self-assessment for prosody is included in Figure 6.11 on pages 156–157. This requires that students have data to analyze; these are easy to acquire using the audio-recording devices available on most tablets and smart phones.

Reading Into Recorder

This oral fluency exercise is predicated on the value of repeated readings. Many children like to hear the sound of their voice on an audio recording, and reading into an electronic device capitalizes on this motivation. The student selects a brief reading (50–100 words) and records his or her voice while reading aloud. After stopping the recorder, the student reads the same passage three more times aloud. For the fifth reading, the student records himself again and then plays the entire recording. Students are often astounded at how the quality of their oral reading has improved.

> EFFECT SIZE FOR
> REPEATED READING
> PROGRAMS = **0.67**

Neurological Impress Model

In 1966, Heckelman developed a process of "imprinting" words into children's minds called the neurological impress model or NIM. As he noted, this is an economical and time-saving method of helping individual students become fluent and proficient readers. In general, the teacher and student sit side by side (also known as "at the elbow"), reading the same text. Together, the teacher and student read aloud. The teacher directs his or her voice directly into the reader's ear. The student follows along, reading at the normal reading rate of the teacher. The teacher does not stop to correct the student's oral reading mistakes. Instead, the teacher focuses on having the student duplicate the appropriate reading rate. In the beginning, it may be necessary for the student to repeat sentences and/or paragraphs several times to perform at normal speed. Over time, the student reads faster, as does the teacher. The research evidence for NIM is fairly specific (e. g., Gibbs & Proctor, 1977; Heckelman, 1986; Henk, 1983). Students typically require a total of 12 hours of instruction and need to participate in NIM on a regular basis, several times each week, until they can read fluently.

Independent Reading

Although this may seem like an oversimplification, developing fluency in any skill—whether it is reading or writing or making free throws—requires time to practice. There is an oft-repeated story about basketball player Michael Jordan, who holds the NBA record for the most career points scored (5,987), and his penchant for daily practice. Similarly, even good readers benefit from daily practice through the act of reading. Wide, independent reading increases reading volume, the overall amount of reading a student engages. In turn, reading volume is correlated with reading achievement (Stanovich, 1986). Thus, teachers should provide students time to engage in wide, independent reading not only to build

> EFFECT SIZE FOR
> SPACED VERSUS MASS
> PRACTICE = **0.71**

Figure 6.10   Norms for Reading Fluency (in words correct per minute)

Oral Reading Fluency Norms, Grades 1–8

WCPM: Words correct per minute

SD: Standard deviation

Count: Number of student scores

Grade	Percentile	Fall WCPM	Winter WCPM	Spring WCPM
1	90		81	111
	75		47	82
	50		23	53
	25		12	28
	10		6	15
	SD		32	39
	Count		16,950	19,434
2	90	106	125	142
	75	79	100	117
	50	51	72	89
	25	25	42	61
	10	11	18	31
	SD	37	41	42
	Count	15,896	18,229	20,128
3	90	128	146	162
	75	99	120	137
	50	71	92	107
	25	44	62	78
	10	21	36	48
	SD	40	43	44
	Count	16,988	17,383	18,372
4	90	145	166	180
	75	119	139	152
	50	94	112	123
	25	68	87	98
	10	45	61	72
	SD	40	41	43
	Count	16,523	14,572	16,269
5	90	166	182	194
	75	139	156	168
	50	110	127	139
	25	85	99	109
	10	61	74	83
	SD	45	44	45
	Count	16,212	13,331	15,292

6	90	177	195	204
	75	153	167	177
	50	127	140	150
	25	98	111	122
	10	68	82	93
	SD	42	45	44
	Count	10,520	9,218	11,920
7	90	180	192	202
	75	156	165	177
	50	128	136	150
	25	102	109	123
	10	79	88	98
	SD	40	43	41
	Count	6,482	4,058	5,998
8	90	185	199	199
	75	161	173	177
	50	133	146	151
	25	106	115	124
	10	77	84	97
	SD	43	45	41
	Count	5,546	3,496	5,335

Source: Hasbrouck, J., & Tindal, G. A. (2006). Oral reading fluency norms: A valuable assessment tool for reading teachers. *Reading Teacher, 59*(7), 636–644. Used with permission.

 Available for download at **https://resources.corwin.com/VL-LiteracyK-5**

their background knowledge and vocabulary, but also to provide spaced practice for developing fluency.

INDEPENDENT WRITING

Students should write every day in class. Some of the writing they do will be brief, and sometimes they will write longer pieces, with the writing extended over several days. Writing requires thinking, and often students clarify their thinking as they write. Writing provides teachers with glimpses into students' thinking and allows for additional instruction based on that thinking. Writing requires that students put pen to paper or fingers to keyboard and flow their ideas. As is the case with many other things, you don't get good at something you don't do. Students need regular writing practice if they are going to get better. But writing independently, in and of itself, does not necessarily result in

EFFECT SIZE
FOR WRITING
PROGRAMS = 0.44

Figure 6.11   Sample Self-Assessment for Prosody

I can read with fluency. I put my words together so my reading sounds right and makes sense. This means that I am paying attention to my phrasing.

PHRASING:

1	2	3	4
I read word-by-word, or one word at a time, like a robot.	I am trying to read the way the author wrote the words. Sometimes I read 2 or 3 words at a time. Sometimes I read word by word, like a robot.	I am really close to reading the words the way the author wrote them. I usually read in 3 or 4 word groups.	I put the words together the way the author wrote them. I put the words together so that it makes sense.
I - like - to - read. - It - is - fun.	I like - to - read. It - is fun.	I like to - read. It - is fun.	I like to read. It is fun!

I can read with fluency. I read at the correct rate. Not too quickly, and not too slowly. My reading sounds right and makes sense.

RATE:

1	2	3	4
I am really slow and have to figure out each word on the page. I read so slowly that it really does not make sense.	I can be slow because I have to read word-by-word when I don't know the words. I take breaks, pause too much, and repeat words when I read.	I try to read like I talk. Sometimes I go too fast, or too slow. I might slow down when I am trying to figure out a tricky word. Sometimes I pause or stop when it doesn't make sense.	I read like I talk. I only slow down, stop, or repeat words when it make sense and sounds right.

I can read fluently. I use the punctuation to help me know how to read the story, so that it sounds right and makes sense.

PUNCTUATION:

1	2	3	4
I don't pay attention to periods, commas, exclamation points, question marks, and quotation marks when I read. My reading doesn't sound right or make sense.	Sometimes I use the punctuation, but I might use it the wrong way.	I usually pay attention to the punctuation. I may make a mistake every once in a while.	I always pay attention to the punctuation. My reading sounds right and makes sense.

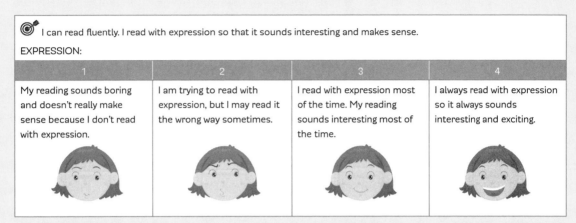

	1	2	3	4

 I can read fluently. I read with expression so that it sounds interesting and makes sense.

EXPRESSION:

1	2	3	4
My reading sounds boring and doesn't really make sense because I don't read with expression.	I am trying to read with expression, but I may read it the wrong way sometimes.	I read with expression most of the time. My reading sounds interesting most of the time.	I always read with expression so it always sounds interesting and exciting.

Source: Adapted from Kristin Houser (www.mshouser.com) and from Houser, K. (n. d.). *Tracking my progress: Fluency.* Retrieved from http://www.mshouser.com/instructional-coaching/tracking-my-progress-fluency

Image sources: Boy on the phone image courtesy of iStock/ia_64; Bentley car image courtesy of Pixabay/Karen Arnold; all other images courtesy of clipart.com.

Available for download at **https://resources.corwin.com/VL-LiteracyK-5**

improvement. Students need robust instruction in writing that includes both direct and dialogic approaches, and time to practice. Practice does not make perfect, but it does make permanent.

Power Writing

To increase writing fluency, students should be provided opportunities to engage in timed writings on a regular, nearly daily, basis. Fearn and Farnan (2001) called this process *power writing* and recommended that students write for 1 minute as fast as they can and as much as they can, and then repeat this two more times per day. The topic changes for each round. Following each timed minute, students are asked to count the number of words they have written, circling any errors they notice as they reread what they have written. The goal is to increase volume while decreasing errors. When any of us write fast enough, we make errors. If we notice our own errors, we don't need instruction. When readers don't notice their own errors, they likely need additional instruction.

For example, students in Michelle Arce's third-grade class were learning about the solar system. On a given day, Ms. Arce used single words to get students writing about what they knew. The first minute, students wrote

> Writing independently does not necessarily result in improvement. Students need robust instruction in writing that includes both direct and dialogic approaches, and time to practice.

about *rotation*. The second minute, they wrote about *meteors*. And during the third minute, they wrote about *asteroids*. Marlo did not use the correct version of *their* but had accurate information about the solar system. Isaac confused meteors and asteroids and did not notice that his answers were inaccurate. Augustin noticed several errors that he made, including lack of some capitalizations and missing commas. Each of these errors, missed by the student or not, provided Ms. Arce a glimpse into students' thinking and provided her with information about what she needed to think about in terms of their literacy development and content knowledge. As an added benefit, power writing topics or prompts can activate students' background knowledge on a given topic. Ms. Arce's students were ready for their solar system lesson because of the writing and thinking that they did.

As part of the power writing process, about every three weeks students set goals for themselves. These goals tend to focus on increasing fluency or decreasing errors. Ms. Arce has her students individually graph the highest number of words they write each day on a histogram that students keep in their writer's notebooks. On the first page of their notebooks, they keep track of their goals and progress toward each goal they set for themselves.

EFFECT SIZE FOR GOALS = 0.50

Importantly, power writing builds fluency but is not a comprehensive writing curriculum. Students need examples, modeling, mentor texts, time to talk with others about their writing, and feedback from readers to become strong writers who can influence the world with their words. Having said that, it's important to note that it's hard to edit and revise when you don't have anything written. Fluency in writing is just as important as fluency in reading; it's fodder for understanding.

Extended Writing Prompts

In addition to high-quality instruction and time to develop their writing fluency, students need to practice writing longer and longer pieces. To facilitate their writing, teachers (and test-makers) design writing prompts. A good writing prompt has the following components:

- **Topic.** What the writing is to be about

- **Audience.** Who is reading this piece of writing

- **Format.** Rhetorical structure, text type, or genre to be produced

- **Texts.** Source from which ideas are used

- **Demands.** Additional writing and cognitive challenges that increase complexity

Students should not have to guess what their teacher wants them to write. The prompt should be clear enough to actually guide students in thinking about their responses. Here's an example of an all-too-common prompt:

> Who motivates you? What did that person do?

This prompt is certainly motivating for some students, but how will they know what the teacher is looking for? Are they supposed to include only their experiences, or should they make connections with the text they are reading? Consider a better prompt on the same topic, written for a fifth-grade class following a discussion about heroes and people who make a difference:

> After viewing the Singapore Ministry of Education video about the difference a teacher can make, write an opinion-based essay in which you identify your "Mrs. Chong" and make a case for why this person has made a positive difference in your life. Make sure that you inform your reader (the person who made a difference or another person of your choice) about the video itself and how Mrs. Chong impacted her student. Compare the actions of Mrs. Chong to the influential person you have identified, and provide specific evidence of his or her actions and their impact on you.

If we analyze this prompt, we notice the following:

- **Topic.** Difference a teacher can make

- **Audience.** The person who made a difference or another person of your choice

- **Format.** Opinion-based essay

- **Texts.** Singapore Ministry of Education video

- **Demands.** Compare the actions of the two, provide specific evidence of the actions, and note the impact on you

Teaching Takeaway

The prompt makes a difference! A good place to get help writing prompts for students is the Literacy Design Collaborative. They provide templates for creating writing prompts (they call them *task templates*), and they can be found at www.ldc.org.

BIG IDEAS ABOUT INDEPENDENT LEARNING

Across the examples we have provided, there are three indicators of quality opportunities to deepen learning in the independent phase of instruction: thinking metacognitively, setting goals, and developing self-regulatory skills. To ensure that students continue learning while they engage in tasks, assignments, or activities on their own, teachers should consider the following questions:

- Does it promote metacognition?

- Does it promote goal-setting?

- Does it promote self-regulation?

Does It Promote Metacognition?

The first question to pose of an independent task is whether or not it promotes metacognition. Awareness of one's own learning evolves over a lifetime, and this habit is developed through opportunities to think about one's own thinking. Metacognitive questions embedded in the task can provide these opportunities. It is common to ask reflective questions at the end of a complex task, and to be sure, their regular use encourages the habit of post-hoc analysis. But metacognition should also occur *during* a task. Year 5 teacher Edward Hurley uses four questions designed by Anderson (2002). Before his students begin an independent task, he reminds them to think through the tasks as they work:

1. **"What am I trying to accomplish?"** This first question encourages students to locate the purpose. In Mr. Hurley's case, it causes his learners to think about what the task or assignment is asking of them.

2. **"What strategies am I using?"** The second question requires students to determine what will be required of them to support their learning, such as making a decision about whether to keep notes in a journal or annotate directly on the text.

3. **"How well am I using the strategies?"** Students need to monitor a complex task in order to see if it is working, which means they must pause to see if they are headed in the right direction. The ability to make a midcourse correction is an important factor in developing procedural knowledge. Mr. Hurley promotes this by setting a 2-minute timer to remind students to stop and evaluate their progress.

4. **"What else could I do?"** We expect students to get stuck; if that doesn't occur from time to time, then the work is too easy. But we also need to promote resilience and flexible thinking. This last question reminds Mr. Hurley's students that thinking critically involves reasoning, synthesizing information, and exploring alternative solutions and perspectives. Mr. Hurley's lesson plan can be found in Figure 6.12 on the next page.

The *VISIBLE LEARNER*

Marla looks up to the poster in her classroom, repeating each question to herself. She has just finished a writing task and is engaged in thinking about her thinking. When asked to explain her thinking about her thinking, Marla responded as follows:

- *What are you trying to accomplish?* I am trying to write an opinion paper. And it has to include reasons for my opinions, not just say what I think. And some of my opinions should come from the things we've been reading.

- *What strategies are you using?* I used my annotations and my journal. I also wrote out my opinion about the topic and then did an outline.

- *How well are you using the strategies?* They are starting to work for me. I changed my opinion when I was doing this, so I had to change my opinion paper a little. I mean I didn't change everything, but I think it is better now. And I have good reasons for my opinion.

- *What else could I do?* I could read more to see if there are other things that I have missed. And I could ask someone else to read my paper to see if I have good reasons for my opinion.

The visible learner has metacognitive skills and can talk about these (systematic planning, memory, abstract thinking, critical thinking, problem solving, etc.).

Does It Promote Goal-Setting?

A second indicator of quality concerns goal setting by the student. A student should understand how this task advances his or her goals, as this is the basis of intrinsic motivation. Students' motivators vary, but they are likely to include some mix of performance (grades and recognition), mastery (acquiring knowledge), and work-avoidance (conserving effort) goals. While "work avoidance" may not sound like something positive, it is something that all of us consider in our own decisions. For example, we may weigh an opportunity by thinking about the possible reward and the chance to advance our learning, but these are always considered within the context of the amount of effort it will require.

EFFECT SIZE FOR
GOALS = 0.50

Figure 6.12   Lesson Plan for Year 5 Using Metacognitive Strategies

Assessed Need: I have noticed that my students need: *To make their learning visible to themselves.*
Standard(s) Addressed: *Reflect on learning to propose personal and/or collective action in response to an issue or challenge, and predict the probable effects (ACHASSI04, ACHASSI132)*
Text(s) I Will Use: *Classroom poster of metacognitive questions for independent learning.*
Learning Intention for This Lesson: *To acquire tools for reflecting on learning and making a plan of action.*
Success Criteria for This Lesson: *I use these questions before I begin a task, and to check in with myself to gauge my own progress toward goals.*

Direct Instruction:

Model: Strategies/skills/concepts to emphasize

Introduce and model the use of four questions for checking in with myself. Explain to students that I use these same questions when I've got a complicated job in front of me.

"What am I trying to accomplish?" This first question reminds me to check in with the purpose. The learning intention is a good place to start.

"What strategies am I using?" When I cook, I get out the ingredients and tools I need before I begin. When I've got a classroom task, I do the same. I might need to make notes for myself, or maybe I'm reading something I have need to pause to summarize in my head before tackling a new section of the book.

"How well am I using the strategies?" I don't want to get too far down the path only to realize I've gone the wrong way. I set a timer to check in about 5 minutes after I've started to ask myself how I'm doing.

"What else could I do?" When I do realize I'm struck, I have to sit back for a bit to see if there's something else I could do. Sometimes it helps to retrace my steps. If I'm still stuck, I've got other resources, like asking someone else for some help.

Guide and Scaffold: Questions to ask

Did these questions help me to resolve my problem?

Where else in my life could I use these questions to help myself?

Assess: These are the students who will need further support

Check in with Patrick, as he is quick to give up on himself. Keep an eye on Camira, because she sometimes works too fast to get the job done, without being reflective.

Dialogic Instruction:

Teacher-Directed Tools

N/A

Student-Led Tools

After students have applied these metacognitive strategies in independent work and filled out their checklists, meet as a fishbowl group (inside/outside circles) to discuss, first, what worked and why. The second group will discuss difficulties, and how they can get better at using these strategies to solve problems.

Assess: These are the students who will need further support

Getano and Patrick should be in the first fishbowl, so they can be encouraged to discuss positives of the approach.

Feedback Opportunities: *Provide written feedback about their thinking processes on the checklist for each student.*

Independent Learning and Closure:

Closure: Revisit the learning intentions and success criteria, and remind students to consistently use them when they are in independent learning.

Independent Learning: Include these same four questions on a checklist for students to report on and include with completed major tasks.

Our students are no different. Written essays and research papers require quite a bit of effort, but there are performance and mastery elements at stake as well. Fifth-grade teacher Alison Gallegos builds goal setting into such assignments. After discussing the writing project at hand, she asks each student to set a performance goal (the grade they want to achieve), a mastery goal (what they propose to learn during the process), and their planned effort (how many hours they will invest). They submit their goals to her in advance, and she uses these during writing conferences. At the time of submission of the writing project, they also rate themselves on attainment of their goals: the expected grade, evidence of achievement of the learning goal, and the amount of time actually spent on the assignment. "I have found these to be among the most valuable conversations I've had this year," she said. "Conferences about their progress toward their goals can jumpstart less-than-diligent students. And when it comes to grading, they can see how their efforts played an active role in the result."

Does It Promote Self-Regulation?

A third indicator for independent learning concerns the ability to assume autonomy and develop a sense of efficacy. Self-regulation doesn't stand apart from the first two quality indicators; in fact metacognition and goal setting are necessary in order to self-regulate one's learning. Choice is critical for developing a sense of autonomy. We don't mean that an independent learning task should be an "anything goes," freewheeling assignment. However, students should have the freedom to explore and customize their learning. Independent reading is one example of how the principles of self-regulation can be developed. Teachers often assign texts to be read independently. For example, third graders are told to read Chapter 5 of *Shiloh* at home for a discussion the next day. When learners are presented with a theme or an essential question, and then choose books that will help them address the theme or answer the question, they get the opportunity to formulate a reading plan. In fact, choice is a cornerstone of literature circles, a student-led dialogic strategy profiled in Chapter 5. This is far superior to the usual "read this for tomorrow" assignments that are usually given.

A final aspect of self-regulation is providing students with opportunities to explore and expand their own learning. This can be accomplished by allowing time for students to research and write about a topic of their own choosing. Called "genius hour" by many, it is inspired by Google's practice of releasing engineers for 20% of their work time to explore their own learning. Genius hour at school encourages students to ask questions, find answers, and share what they have learned with others.

For example, the students in Suzanne Clark's third-grade class had time each week to work on a project of their own choosing. Each student had to identity a topic and a course of study. Imagine how much surface and deep learning was required for students to do this. Oscar chose to learn about cars. As he said, he would like to invent the next type of car. He read widely, print and digital texts, interviewed people—including a sales person from a car dealership and a mechanic—and visited the automotive museum on a free admission day after school one afternoon with his family. His research extended beyond the genius hour, and Oscar was ready for the world café that his teacher organized. On a special day, the   classroom was transformed into a café, and students were each assigned a time to host a table discussion about their learning. During their unassigned times, they were free to visit other tables and learn about topics of interest to their peers. Ms. Clark created a note-taking tool that her students could use to record information and provide feedback to their peers.

EFFECT SIZE FOR
STUDENT-CENTERED
TEACHING = 0.54

CONCLUSION

Learning shouldn't stop when independent work begins. This seems obvious, but in too many cases, the tasks and the thinking required to complete independent tasks are limited to regurgitation of knowledge. The work itself doesn't forward students' learning; it is simply assigned to determine how closely their factual knowledge pairs with what the teacher has taught. We use the phrase *independent learning* intentionally, as it is more than *independent practice*. The term *practice* suggests recitation and rehearsal. Practice is a necessary intermediate step in the knowledge-building process. But *independent learning* conveys an expectation that knowledge acquisition continues; it doesn't cease in order for the brain dump to begin. Importantly, independent learning should be combined with direct and dialogic approaches to instruction. Teachers have to identify the level of learning students need to accomplish (surface, deep, or transfer) and then design experiences for them that work. These practices are likely a combination of direct, dialogic, and independent approaches. Knowing what level students need for their learning requires assessment. And understanding if the direct, dialogic, or independent approach worked requires using assessment information to determine impact.

TOOLS TO USE IN DETERMINING LITERACY IMPACT

© Michael Newman/PhotoEdit

"I think it worked!" Karen Abernathy said, looking up from her computer.

These excited words were shared at a third-grade team meeting following the administration of a spelling inventory. Yes, teachers do get excited about their students' literacy learning. The team of teachers had been working hard to impact their students' word knowledge and had tried several things, to no avail. They had monitored the impact that they had on students' literacy development, using spelling as a proxy for overall literacy learning. As Templeton and Morris (1999) noted, "Spelling is so visible, so obvious, that it often assumes the role of a proxy for literacy and in that role is bound to generate controversy" (p. 102).

Controversy aside, the teachers on this team understood the value of monitoring students' spelling. They had implemented a number of classroom routines, not directly related to spelling, to improve students' literacy. They were not simply drilling students to learn isolated words, but rather using a spelling inventory to determine if students' understanding of language was progressing. The teachers met weekly, and included spelling data in their conversations once a month. For the first several months of the year, spelling achievement data were flat. Although other areas might have been progressing, students' were not developing their understanding of English orthography.

Starting in late November and running through December, the teachers had refocused their energy on writing. They engaged students in lessons about word choice, voice, and organization. They taught students how to give effective feedback to their peers, and they organized small group, needs-based instruction that aligned with the patterns of errors they noticed in students' writing. And their January data suggested that students' spelling performance had improved.

In response to Ms. Abernathy's comment, April Baker said, "I can't wait for you to run the numbers. Hurry! Let's see if we really did have an impact!"

DO YOU KNOW YOUR IMPACT?

A foundational assumption in education is that what we do has a positive impact on the learning lives of our students. But how do we know what our impact truly is? We can't rely solely on grades and state test scores, which serve as decontextualized data points because often there is nothing to compare them to. And waiting until high-stakes test results are returned and students have moved to a new teacher seems unwise and unproductive. These end-of-unit exams and state test scores are mere snapshots; without preassessment measures of where students actually began, there's no real way to understand how your teaching influenced their learning. And here's why that's important: How can you make wise adjustments to your teaching when you don't know what worked and what didn't work?

Assessment is assessment. Any assessment can be used formatively or summatively. In other words, there's nothing magical in the tool itself; it's what you do with it (or don't do with it) that matters. Using assessments for the purpose of formative evaluation casts a light on our teaching practices. It has the potential to be eye-opening—to help us consider what worked and what didn't as we carefully examine the evidence of student progress. Unfortunately, it has more often been used as an isolated measure of a given student's achievement at one point in time than it has as a nuanced consideration of the overall trajectory of his or her learning experience.

As you have read throughout this book, John's work has focused on calculating the effect size of instructional and curricular approaches to identify those that have a high impact—at least a year's worth of growth for a year in school. But what if you could determine your own effect sizes about your own practice? He maintains that teachers should be able to determine their

> EFFECT SIZE
> FOR WRITING
> PROGRAMS = 0.44

> A foundational assumption in education is that what we do has a positive impact on the learning lives of our students. But how do we know what our impact truly is?

impact. The same statistical tool used to examine the results of 500,000,000 learners—effect size—can be used to determine the impact that a given influence has on your students' learning. To calculate an effect size, first determine your students' average score for the posttest and the average for the pretest. It's easy to do this in an Excel spreadsheet. Here's how:

- Type the students' names in one column.

- Type their scores for the pre- and postassessments in other columns.

- Highlight the column with the preassessment scores, select the "average" tool, and place the average at the bottom of that column.

- Do the same for the postassessment column.

However, this portion of the calculation only gets you so far. Let's say you are using a writing rubric as your assessment instrument, and after a semester of writing instruction, your class has made an average gain of one point on a seven-point rubric. Is that a worthy impact? It's hard to judge, because one point average growth isn't a meaningful metric; you need to calculate the effect size. The next step in determining the effect size is to calculate standard deviation. Excel will do this as well[1]:

1. Type = STDEV.P and then select the student scores in the preassessment. column again.

2. Do the same in the postassessment column.

Excel will use these two sets of scores to calculate and display the standard deviation.

3. Next, subtract the preassessment average from the postassessment average, and then divide by the standard deviation. Here's the formula:

$$\text{Effect size} = \frac{\text{Average (postassessment)} - \text{Average (preassessment)}}{\text{Average standard deviation or SD}}$$

As a note of caution, effect sizes do not establish causation. No teacher can say with confidence that her specific actions caused her

---

[1] You can also quickly calculate standard deviation using a number of websites, such as graphpad.com/quickcalcs/CImean1.cfm.

students' writing to be better, but she should be encouraged to share her approach with others so that they can determine the impact her teaching strategy might have on their students. You may have noticed that the value she calculated for effect size is an average value for the group, so really the teacher should say that the efforts to improve writing worked on average. That's why we suggest that teachers calculate effect sizes for individual students. It's pretty simple to do: Subtract an individual student's preassessment score from his or her postassessment score, and divide by the average standard deviation. The formula looks like this:

$$\text{Effect size} = \frac{\text{Individual score (postassessment)} - \text{Individual score (preassessment)}}{\text{Average standard deviation or SD for the class}}$$

By drilling down to the individual level, you gain a clearer picture of what worked or didn't work for a targeted student. Although you may not choose to calculate the effect size of your instruction for every student in your class, it should be a priority for those working above or below expected levels, as well as for students who are new to your class.

DO YOU KNOW YOUR COLLECTIVE IMPACT?

Now let's take another step forward. You will recall that of the 195 effect sizes John has calculated, one of the top influences on student learning is collective teacher efficacy. Collective teacher efficacy describes a constellation of attitudes and beliefs about the efforts of a school to affect student learning (Goddard, Hoy, & Hoy, 2000). But the day-to-day demands make it difficult for most teachers to know what their colleagues are doing, and this lack of knowledge about their work undermines collective teacher efficacy. Instead, we begin to think, "Am I the only one doing this?" Schools must take deliberate actions to ensure that teachers have regular opportunities to collaborate with one another. We're not calling for more grade-level meetings to discuss the next field trip, but we hold firm in the belief that without meaningful teacher collaboration, the learning of children is harmed.

One common structure for fostering teacher collaboration to improve the quality of learning has been the formation of professional learning communities (PLCs). PLCs usually involve small groups of educators who have come together to support each other's learning for the purpose of improving student achievement. These are not book clubs or professional development sessions. The use of these four PLC questions keeps

> **Teaching Takeaway**
>
> Teachers can calculate effect sizes for their classes and individual students to determine the impact their instruction and intervention have had.

> EFFECT SIZE FOR COLLECTIVE TEACHER EFFICACY = 1.57

the focus relentlessly on the learning of children, and explains why the impact of PLCs is powerful (DuFour, DuFour, & Eaker, 2008):

Video 14

Collective Teacher Efficacy

*https://resources.corwin.com/
VL-LiteracyK-5*

- What is it we expect our students to learn?

- How will we know when they have learned it?

- How will we respond when some students do not learn?

- How will we respond when some students already know it?

These discussions have resulted in improved instruction as well as better outcomes for students (e.g., Lai, Wilson, McNaughton, & Hsiao, 2014). In collaborative teams, teachers identify learning targets and discuss ideas for instruction. They met to review student work and figure out if their efforts have been fruitful.

The challenge in the PLC process is the second question. As educators, we have to continually ask ourselves, how will I know if students have learned what they were supposed to learn? Obviously, the answer is "through assessment," which implies that teachers need to know how to assess students and then work collaboratively with their peers to respond when students do, or do not, learn. But what if students already knew the information before the lesson? What if we used the effect size method to answer the second PLC question? In doing so, teachers could understand their impact on students' learning. That understanding, in turn, would guide improvements in instruction and intervention, especially for those students who either already know the content, or who continue to struggle in literacy.

Lots of books have a chapter on assessment, and in this regard we are no different. But we hope that you will see the added value in two essential elements:

- The first, which we have already discussed, is how to calculate your impact on your class and on individual students, and how to then use that information to leverage professional learning with your colleagues to build efficacy.

- The second is to know the wide range of tools available to help you engage in formative evaluation. In addition to your own teacher-created assessments, we believe you will find these to be of value, especially given the developmental nature of literacy learning at the elementary level. Best of all, most of these tools are in the compendiums at the end of this book.

ASSESSING READING

Thus far in this chapter, we have focused on specific ways for teachers to determine impact. As we noted, this is dependent on having appropriate assessment tools that teachers can use at the outset of a unit and then again as the unit ends, and even at various points during the lesson. Here, we provide a list of tools that teachers can use to determine students' literacy learning, specifically in reading, writing, and English language development. We have further divided reading assessments into two subsections:

Video 15
Determining Impact

- The first are tools that are especially useful for assessing emergent and early readers, who are found primarily in Grades K–3. These tools target some of the more salient aspects of early reading development, especially for decoding and early comprehension.

- The second section in the assessing reading portion of this chapter is dedicated to tools that are helpful when working with developing readers, most commonly found in Grades 3–5.

Video 16
Visible Learners: "How do you know what you're supposed to learn?"

https://resources.corwin.com/ VL-LiteracyK-5

We recognize this is a somewhat artificial organizational structure, and that the reading development of an individual child rarely falls neatly into one category. Having said that, it is important to note that assessments have to be shared with students. Yes, the data collected during assessment should be used to plan instruction moving forward, but visible learners are assessment capable. In other words, they understand

The *VISIBLE LEARNER*

Anthony reviewed his writing and compared it with the descriptions of writing development that were posted on the wall in his first-grade classroom. When asked about his progress, he said, "I used to be at Level 6 because I didn't always have spaces between the words and I didn't stay on the lines and other things. But now I am a 9. Look. I have spaces between the words and I have the words in the lines and I indented. I spelled almost all of the words right and I answered the question and didn't add other things not about the question. But I'm going to the 10 place. That's the next place for me. I just need to make the letters more neatly and spell the words a little better. And I have to keep the topic so that it doesn't confuse the reader."

Visible learners are assessment capable—they understand the assessment tools being used and what their results mean, and they can self-assess to answer the key questions: Where am I in my learning? Where am I going? and What do I need to do to get there?

the assessments being used and what their results mean. In the classrooms described in this chapter, you'll see which students know what they are learning and where they are in the learning progression.

ASSESSING EMERGENT AND EARLY READERS

Teachers of emergent and early readers use a range of assessments that profile a child's growing sense of sounds, letters, words, and stories. Therefore, even the earliest emergent reader can be assessed in many aspects of literacy learning, which all contribute to reading comprehension. If children face difficulty with either language comprehension (understanding spoken language), or decoding (transforming written words into language), they will have difficulty reading.

Language Comprehension

The ability to process spoken language is key to early reading development. Closely related to language comprehension are these skills:

- **Background Knowledge.** The amount of information a child has about a topic, usually gained through experience and exposure.

- **Linguistic Knowledge.** An understanding of the rules that govern language. These fundamentals of linguistics are
  - ○ **Phonology.** The ability to discern the phonemes (individual units of sound) in a language. The English language has 44 phonemes; other languages differ. For instance, Spanish has 24.
  - ○ **Syntax.** The grammatical rules of the language.
  - ○ **Semantics.** The meaning of the words and concepts represented.

Decoding

Decoding is the ability to translate the squiggly black shapes on the page (for this is what print looks like to young children) to letters and combinations of letters representing sounds. As is the case with language comprehension, there are a number of elements of knowledge that must consolidate in order for a reader to successfully decode:

- **Cipher Knowledge.** The relationship between how the word sounds and how it is spelled in phonetically regular words like *cat* and *book*.

- **Lexical Knowledge.** The ability to decode phonetically irregular words like *laugh* and *write*. Both cipher and lexical knowledge are in turn influenced by four sets of skills:
    - **Letter Knowledge.** Recognition of the shapes and names of each of the 26 letters in the English language.
    - **Alphabetic Principle.** Understanding that letters and combinations of letters in words are associated with the sounds (phonemes) of spoken language.
    - **Phonemic Awareness.** The ability to manipulate the sounds of the language. Rhyming is one type of phonemic awareness.
    - **Concepts About Print.** Understanding the way print works on the page. For example, knowing that the words are read from left to right is one element of concepts about print.

These fundamental emergent and early reading skills are necessary for students to master, and therefore these skills become the focus of assessment. The first category, language comprehension, is assessed using inventories that invite students to demonstrate their knowledge of phonemes and use language to explain stories. A database of preK–3 reading assessments can be found at http://www.sedl.org/reading/rad.

EARLY LANGUAGE LEARNING ASSESSMENTS

A large portion of instructional time for emergent and early readers is devoted to language learning—fostering each child's ability to process and produce spoken language in order to develop fundamental reading comprehension skills. Students also learn how print works and to recognize some words by sight. To determine impact, assessments of these abilities should be given before and after instruction.

Concepts About Print

As young readers master the alphabetic code, they also learn how print works on the page. In particular, they learn that books have an expected format that includes a front and back cover and a title with the author's name. They learn about book handling skills like turning pages and orienting the book so that the print is not upside down. These students also discover that print must be read from left to right across the page, progressing line by line from top to bottom. This collection of skills is called *concepts about print* (Clay, 1979). Mastery of concepts about print represents important benchmarks in a child's reading development. A checklist of concepts about print appears in Compendium 1.

Kindergarten teacher Eric Matsumoto uses an early concepts about print checklist to determine his students' adeptness at handling books. "I use it early on to get a sense of what their experiences have been with books," he said. Initially he focuses on their knowledge of the front of the book, the location of the title, and whether they can turn the page. "I can tell if they've had books read aloud to them a lot or not," said Mr. Matsumoto. When students don't have these early behaviors yet in place, he puts them in charge of introducing books to the class. "I try to create more experiences for them, like retrieving the book, putting it on the easel, and announcing it to the class." These opportunities add up, as Mr. Matsumoto typically reads two books to the class every day. "I do the [concepts about print] checklist every month or so. It's quick. But the ones I'm really checking in on are the ones I've targeted for these book introductions. I need to get them up to speed as quickly as I can, so they don't lose ground."

Yopp-Singer Test of Phoneme Segmentation

The Yopp-Singer (Yopp, 1995) is a 22-item assessment of a child's ability to repeat the phonemes of one-syllable words. This assessment is administered individually and takes about 10 minutes to complete. Phonemic awareness is considered to be a predictor of later reading success (e.g., Nation & Hulme, 1997). A copy of the test and administration directions can be found in Compendium 2.

Kindergarten teacher Saul Romero uses this language comprehension assessment periodically throughout the school year. "The Yopp-Singer is one that our entire grade level administers three times a year to gauge student progress, and to identify those students who are falling behind," he said. "We then get together and plot their progress on a graph, so we can track the progress of each student. Those who aren't making expected gains can be identified to get more support. It's not just intervention," explained Mr. Romero, "it's knowing which students need more repetition and practice. It helps me to know who I need to call on more."

He went on to explain that based on the last administration a few weeks earlier, he has four students who are not making gains. "Three of them are getting tangled up with diagraphs and aren't segmenting them properly. The other student, who's new, was only able to correctly segment a few, and all of them began with hard consonant sounds." Mr. Romero continued, "When I am reading with these students, I pause to make sure they can segment the word, not by looking at it, but by hearing it. We all get hung up on breaking words apart, and this reminds me that if they can't hear the sounds when I say the word, that's going to interrupt their ability to decode written words."

Sight Words

There are many words we want young readers to decode using their knowledge of alphabetic principles; other words are more efficiently learned using recognition skills. Called *sight words,* these represent some of the most frequently used words in the English language and are typically taught in the primary grades. Edward Dolch identified a list of 220 of the most commonly used words, and collected them into what is now called the Dolch sight word list (Dolch, 1948). Some of these words are irregular in letter-sound correspondence and are therefore more easily learned by sight (e.g., *the, one*). Others are phonetically regular but so frequently used that they can be processed more quickly when learned through sight recognition (e.g., *I, a, for*). These five lists appear in Compendiums 3 through 7.

Second-grade teacher Darnell James uses the Dolch sight word lists to monitor the progress of his students. "At this point in the game, my students are learning these words within connected text, not only in isolation," he said. "They're encountering these words all the time, and when they can't recognize them right away, it gets in the way of their comprehension." Mr. James plays "My Pile, Your Pile" with students to increase their practice with the words. "Spaced practice, right?" he laughs. Each of his students has a customized pile of Dolch words they are working to master, based on progress on interim assessments. "So here's the game," he said. "The student takes out his own personal set of flashcards, and I show them one at a time. If he's correct, in goes in his pile. If it's incorrect, it goes in mine. My pile gets used again and again until the student's got all the cards back."

Using flashcards in this way isn't anything new, but what Mr. James does with the information is innovative. "I'm always looking to see what works best for individual kids, especially those who aren't moving forward as quickly as I like. So I have to look at the impact I'm having with playing skills games like this. It doesn't matter at the end of the day if I think something's a good idea, but the kid didn't learn. That's on me. If one technique doesn't work for that kid, it's up to me to switch it up and figure out what works better."

Retellings

Retellings are used for a variety of purposes, including fostering listening comprehension, oral composition, sequencing ability, attention, and memory. For younger children, retellings allow teachers to determine whether or not a child can process language when the burden of reading a text is removed. One of the easiest ways to do this is to read a short text to a student and then invite her to retell the story. A retelling rubric for narrative texts can be found in Compendium 8, and one for informational texts can be found in Compendium 9. As students begin to read, they can also retell the story based on their reading comprehension.

Did he or she understand the story? What about characters and setting? Prompting students to retell the story they have just listened to can provide insight into how much the reader understands the text. To assess a story retelling, make notes about the level of detail and breadth of knowledge about the key parts of the story. The retelling can include prompts or questions to promote further detail.

It should be noted that retelling should be used cautiously. Retelling can devolve into a test of memory rather than understanding; for this reason we usually encourage students to return to the text to support their retelling. As well, successful retellings should not be seen as the ultimate measure of comprehension. As teachers, we want readers to respond on a personal level to the book. This means that they formulate opinions, make connections to themselves and the world, and analyze the text. Rather, retellings should be viewed as a basic measure of a student's understanding of the text.

First-grade teacher Iman Hakim uses retelling of narrative and informational text rubrics regularly to determine the understanding of her students. After an interactive read-aloud and discussion of *Moonbear's Shadow* (Asch, 2014), Ms. Hakim met with several students individually to elicit a retelling of the story. She made the text available to each child, noting how each used knowledge of story grammar (e.g., character, setting, plot) to tell the story. "I selected these students because I'm trying to improve my ability to utilize story elements," she said. "At a collaborative planning meeting with the other teachers at my grade level, we looked at whether our students had improved at retelling since we had assessed them last quarter. My students didn't perform as well compared to the other classes, so I am looking at how I can strengthen my instruction."

She was especially interested in how her students would do in terms of problem and solution. "The problem is really obvious—the bear keeps seeing his shadow and tries to get rid of it. Most of the book is about all of his failed attempts. But the solution is a lot subtler, and has to be inferred," she explained. Equipped with the knowledge that her previous instruction had not led to desired results, Ms. Hakim spent time discussing what Moonbear did and did not understand about light and shadow, even at the end of the book. Later, when she met with a sampling of

> Retelling should be used cautiously. Retelling can devolve into a test of memory rather than understanding; for this reason we usually encourage students to return to the text to support their retelling.

her students, she listened for whether they could explain the problem and solution. "It's hard with a retelling, because you're not supposed to prompt them. I have to resist that urge," she smiled. "But getting to hear from them about what they know and don't know helps me in the end."

DECODING ASSESSMENTS

Just as children need to be able to understand sounds and meaning of the spoken language around them, they also need to accurately and efficiently process the printed word. Decoding is an essential component of reading. As described earlier, decoding is made up of several dimensions, including letter and alphabetic knowledge. There are several useful tools that collectively assess these aspects of decoding.

Letter Identification

One of the most basic skills needed for decoding is the ability to recognize both lowercase and uppercase letters. This assessment is typically administered individually to students who look at a student form (Compendium 10) and identify the letter or the sound of the letter. Although it may seem unnecessary to have a student form for the alphabet, the consistency of the presentation ensures that other cues are not inadvertently interfering (e.g., familiar flashcards with pictures). The student form also includes alternative representations of the letter *a* and *g,* which can confound young children who are still new to these symbols. A recording sheet to accompany the assessment is in Compendium 11. It should be noted that this assessment can be administered in more than one sitting.

Kindergarten teacher Lynette Korman and her grade-level colleagues consider measures of their students' alphabet knowledge to be a core element of the first semester. "Of course we work on isolated letters and their sounds," she explained, "but we've also learned to get much more strategic about pointing out letters that occur in medial positions." One of her students, Jayson, arrived at kindergarten already knowing all of his letters, both lowercase and uppercase. "I don't need to teach him these, since he knows them. It keeps me realistic about what my impact really is." Because he knew them before kindergarten began, she takes him out of the effect size analyses she calculates every few weeks. "If I pretend that Jayson's knowing his letters is due to the fact that I'm a great teacher, I'm deluding myself. But that's exactly what I used to do," said Ms. Korman. "I used to turn a blind eye to the fact that some kids arrive at my classroom door with a lot of prior knowledge, and not because I taught them. So my goals with Jayson have to be different. I have to gauge his progress using other measures. I've assessed him on the first set of sight words, and he knows a few of them, so I'm starting there with him."

Phonics

Phonics is the term used to describe the relationship between sounds and their symbols (letters). It differs from phonemic awareness, which focuses only on the ability to distinguish sounds. These sound-symbol relationships are essential in order for students to effectively and efficiently decode texts. The first step is letter identification, and the next is the ability to chunk clusters of letters together to read more fluently. In the primary grades, rimes are taught to assist students in rapidly expanding their knowledge of many words. A rime is the cluster of letters in a one-syllable word following the beginning consonant or consonants, called the onset. A rime always begins with a vowel. For example, in the word *sink*, /s/ is the onset and /ink/ is the rime.

These rimes are an efficient way to teach a large bank of words to young readers. Wylie and Durrell (1970) estimated that the 37 most common rimes could be used to make more than 500 words. Because these rimes can form clusters of words, they are sometimes called word families.

Rimes are one aspect of phonics knowledge that can be assessed to determine if students are learning. There are a variety of other phonics assessments that are too extensive for this book. We recommend using a phonics battery to assess students; for instance, the CORE Phonics Survey (http://www.scholastic.com/dodea/Module_2/resources/dodea_m2_tr_core.pdf).

Third-grade teacher Kiara Mitchell and her grade-level team members administer a phonics survey at the beginning of the year, and again each quarter, to help students set goals for themselves. "We actually use a host of assessments, and then we confer with each student individually, so all our students can get a sense of where they currently are and where they need to go," said Ms. Mitchell. Her school has developed a dashboard of sorts for each student on the school's learning management system, so all students can see where they currently stand. "I meet with them to figure out their interim goals, and when I reassess, we plug in the new numbers," she said. "I don't know why we didn't think to do this in years past," she remarked. "I've been able to have great conversations with students because they get to set goals."

She also noted that it isn't sufficient to just tell children where they should be by the end of the year. "The finish line is going to be a little different from student to student," she said. "Some are already halfway down the track, while others aren't even close to the starting line. My goal is for every child in my classroom to make a year of progress for a year in school." Her team meets twice a month, and each teacher presents the data for a student with whom they are struggling to close the gap. "It's like a medical review board," she said. "We bring our toughest cases and put them on the table. We can't get caught up in blaming kids. We're in this together to find solutions, not admire problems."

ASSESSING READING OF MEANINGFUL TEXT

Many of the assessments discussed in the previous section on assessing decoding are designed to record progress at the letter or word level. However, it is equally important that teachers assess even the youngest readers as they read meaningful text—books, stories, and poems. In other words, we don't wait until the foundational skills develop to assess student comprehension. Emergent and early readers are taught language comprehension, decoding, and reading comprehension strategies from the beginning. Therefore, these aspects of literacy development are assessed from the start of school. By creating a permanent record of a child's oral reading development, we can analyze her growing understanding of the phonological, syntactic, semantic, and pragmatic strategies she is using to comprehend text.

> Many assessments of decoding are designed to record progress at the letter or word level. However, it is equally important that teachers assess even the youngest readers as they read meaningful text.

Miscue Analysis

Why do young children make the reading errors they do, and how can we leverage this knowledge to forward learning? Miscue analysis (Goodman & Burke, 1972) is an error analysis technique that gives the teacher insight into the types of strategies that children use as they read.

A coded form of notation is used to describe an emergent or early reader's oral reading performance, typically on readings of less than 100 words. The performance is then analyzed for miscues, or errors the child makes in an attempt to solve the problems posed by the text. In this stance toward literacy, miscues are viewed as a window into the reader's command of problem-solving strategies related to the cueing system (Goodman & Burke, 1972). The types of miscues recorded include these:

- **Substitutions.** Replacing one word for another; for instance reading "horse" when the print says "house."

- **Omissions.** Skipping a word in a sentence.

- **Insertions.** Adding a word to a sentence that is not in print.

- **Appeals.** Student asks the teacher for help, either verbally or nonverbally.

- **Teacher Told.** Teacher furnishes word for student. This may or may not be proceeded by an appeal for help.

- **Self-Correction.** Student makes a miscue and then fixes it independently.

- **Reruns.** Student rereads a word, phrase, or the entire sentence.

A consistent coding system is essential for miscue analysis to be understood and interpreted later. A coding system based on the work of Clay (1979) and Goodman and Burke (1972) appears in Compendium 12. A few basic guidelines make coding easy to learn with a little practice:

1. Only the coding is recorded. The title of the text is identified at the top of the page so that it can be consulted later if needed. However, the only words of the text that are written are those involved in a miscue.

2. The correct word in the text always appears below the line; the miscue appears above the line.

3. Multiple codes can be used to record an event. For instance, when a reader asks for help (*appeal*) and then is told the correct word (*teacher told*), both miscues are recorded as *ATT*.

4. A miscue analysis is intended as a means of notating the performance of a child reading aloud. It can be difficult to capture every nuance of the oral reading. Don't worry—the goal is to get down as much as you can. If you feel you have missed something important, make a note of it. It can be helpful to record the reading on your smartphone or tablet to consult again later.

We recommend placing a copy of the coding system inside a clear sheet protector for easy reference while you collect oral reading records.

At a later time, the miscues are analyzed in order to make instructional decisions. Note that self-corrections and reruns are not counted as miscues (although an error within a rerun is). The next step is to analyze the elements present and absent in the miscue. Keep in mind that learners use what they know to resolve problems. Therefore, the analysis involves the three cueing systems employed by young readers: graphophonics, syntactic knowledge, and semantic knowledge. To analyze the miscues, examine each one and ask yourself the following questions:

1. Is the miscue graphically similar to the correct word? (e.g., saying *cup* instead of *cut*.)

2. Does the miscue make sense syntactically? That is, does the sentence work grammatically?

3. Does the miscue make sense semantically? In other words, does the sentence work in terms of preserving its meaning?

Once the results of the analysis are calculated, the teacher can review them and make decisions about future instruction. Instructional questions for consideration include the following:

- Does the student need more instruction in vocabulary?

- Does the student need more instruction at the letter or word level?

- Does the student need more instruction in the syntax of the language?

- Is the student using early reading strategies, including making predictions, monitoring understanding, and applying problem-solving strategies to decode unknown words?

Third-grade teacher Kiara Mitchell uses miscue analysis with some of her students who are not making expected progress. "By the time they're eight years old, some of them have more complicated profiles, especially those who are reading below grade level. I can't rely on a single number, like a Lexile, to tell me what's up," she said. Ms. Mitchell used one of her reading groups as an example. "I put Kenneth, Ashleigh, and Jayden together with me for a few weeks because they have one thing in common," she said "They are not using semantic cues efficently." She explained that while their reading scores represented a 75-point range on a quantitative measure, she believed what held all of them back was a lack of self-monitoring.

"I've done some miscue analyses with them, and the results make me think they're not hearing themselves internally as they read. They're just barking at print," she said. "So I grouped them together to build the habit of paying attention to whether it makes sense. As they read, I hold up a card every time they make a semantic error. The card says, 'Hold up! Did that make sense to me?' I'm trying to get them to be more conscious about the habit of self-monitoring." She went on to explain that she'll follow up with another round of miscue analyses in a few weeks. "That's when I'll know whether my instruction is working," she said, "or if I need to try something else."

The assessments profiled thus far represent a broad cross section of the types of instruments available for teachers of emergent and early readers. As students progress in their literacy development, the types of assessments needed change as well. The next section of this chapter addresses the needs of developing readers, typically those in Grades 3–5.

ASSESSING DEVELOPING READERS

Like primary-grade teachers, educators of older readers require assessment tools that provide a portrait of each student's strengths and areas of need. As students master reading, they come to possess more background knowledge and prior experience, and they become more sophisticated in their ability to access these during their reading. These readers also have more stamina and can read longer, more complex passages of text. Because they have read more widely, they can make connections between texts. Some of the tools discussed in the previous section are also useful for students in upper elementary classrooms. For instance, the retelling rubrics are not bound by age or developmental reading level. However, most assessment instruments used in intermediate classrooms (Grades 3–5) are designed to focus on the areas of comprehension, fluency, and reading attitude.

ASSESSING READING COMPREHENSION

Reading comprehension is embedded in many of the other aspects of literacy already discussed. A student's knowledge of how letters and words work is woven into the ability to formulate those words into meaningful sentences and paragraphs. Meaning is further influenced by the reader's background knowledge and experiences. Therefore, reading comprehension is a measure of a student's ability to consolidate of all these elements.

Arrasmith and Dwyer (2001) described six traits of effective readers, which were further developed by the Northwest Regional Educational Laboratory (NWREL) as a means of assessment. NWREL (now called Education Northwest) is one of ten federally funded information networks across the nation that serve as clearinghouses for resources and research for teachers, parents, administrators, and policy makers. They describe efficient and effective readers as being able to use

- Decoding conventions to read new or unfamiliar words

- Comprehension strategies to determine meaning

- Context to determine setting or time period

- Synthesis of information to make connections

- Interpretations to formulate opinions

- Evaluation to support those opinions

The assessments used by teachers of older students focus on the above named aspects of reading. This is accomplished through informal reading inventories, cloze procedures, attitude surveys, self-assessments, and metacomprehension assessments.

Informal Reading Inventories

One of the most useful ways of assessing reading comprehension with older readers is with a criterion-referenced assessment called an *informal reading inventory,* or IRI. An IRI uses a series of passages written at various grade levels. These are used to measure students' accuracy as well as their ability to answer literal and inferential questions about a text at a specific level of difficulty. The most popular ones are commercially prepared narrative and expository passages of 100–150 words. The student first reads the passage silently, then aloud. During the oral reading, miscues are coded using a system similar to the one presented earlier. However, the words of the passage are already provided on the form, so that only coding of miscues is necessary. Postreading questions probe the student's understanding of the text. Each IRI comes with an extensive set of directions for administering and scoring the reading. Figure 7.1 features a list of some of the most widely available IRIs in schools.

Figure 7.1   Informal Reading Inventories

IRI	Grades	Special Features
Basic Reading Inventory (Johns)	K–8	• Graded word lists • CD-ROM for administration guidance
Burns/Roe Informal Reading Inventory (Burns & Roe)	PreK–12	• Graded word lists • Silent and oral reading measures • Expository and narrative passages
Critical Reading Inventory (Applegate, Quinn, & Applegate)	K–12	• Evaluates critical literacy skills • Expository and narrative passages • Includes case study examples
Flynt-Cooter Comprehensive Reading Inventory–2 (Flynt, Cooter, & Flynt)	K–12	• Uses sentences for passage selection • Expository and narrative passages
Qualitative Reading Inventory (Leslie & Caldwell)	K–8	• Questions for prior knowledge • Graded word lists • Expository and narrative passages

The third-grade teachers at Kiara Mitchell's school track reading compre-hension progress using a commercially prepared IRI. These are adminis-tered three times a year across the district, and are used as a metric for the benchmarks reported to schools. Ms. Mitchell previously taught in another district that did not offer such a system. "I began my teaching career [in another district] where no one did IRIs. I didn't even know they existed until I enrolled in a reading specialist credential program at the university. Once I learned about IRIs, I started doing them in my classroom. But it was a big relief when I moved to this district and we do them routinely."

Ms. Mitchell explained how the data are used in her PLC. "We bring our results to the meeting and start talking about patterns we're seeing. Like I noticed, or rather my teammates noticed, I had a large number of kids that were clustering in the midrange of expected progress, but very few that were higher. So we looked at the results of those midrange kids, and figured out that a lot of them were getting stuck on the inferential questions after the reading. No surprise. That draws on a higher level of reading comprehension," she said. "But it was the chance to drill down in my data that was so valuable. I mean, I'm a reading specialist, and I know what I'm doing. But it's invaluable to have others look at your data and draw your attention to something you've overlooked because it's right in front of you."

Cloze Procedure

The cloze procedure is an assessment used to gauge a reader's comprehen-sion by omitting every fifth word from a passage. The entire first sentence and last sentence of the passage are typically preserved in their entirety to assist the reader in gaining context. The reader fills in the missing words using context clues and syntactic strategies to complete the pas-sage accurately. The words the student supplies must match those of the original text exactly to be considered accurate. Although some will argue that synonyms should be counted as an accurate response, research on this scoring procedure has found that too many variables are introduced when synonyms are allowed (Henk & Selders, 1984). Cloze procedure passages are easily constructed using online tools, and can be admin-istered either individually or to an entire class. A teacher-constructed cloze passage for use in a fifth-grade classroom has been adapted from the opening of *Alice's Adventures in Wonderland* (Carroll, 1865/2008). The passage and answer sheet appear in Compendiums 13 and 14.

Edward Hurley uses a cloze procedure as a preassessment of student knowledge at the beginning of units of instruction. "I like to use them in science and social sciences," he said, explaining that the cloze procedure results give him a good sense of how much they already know going in. "I had to make sure they understood that this wasn't for a grade," Mr. Hurley explained. "They freaked out a bit the first time because they thought they were getting tested on things they had never been taught." The teacher explained that the results help him figure out what he doesn't need to teach, so he can instead devote time to what they still need to learn. "I'll give an example of how I use it," he continued. "Last week we began a unit on the solar system. I used the summary paragraph at the end of the unit in their textbook and turned it into a cloze. I like those conclusions in the textbook because they touch on the main concepts of the unit."

Mr. Hurley asks his students to do their best in filling in the blanks, reminding them once again that this is so he can better plan on their behalf. "No word boxes, of course. Just use what you know to make the passage make sense." Although he has constructed the cloze using conventional methods (first and last sentence intact, and deleting every fifth word), he has also constructed a modified one for two students in his class with special education needs. "I deleted every seventh word, rather than every fifth, so they could draw on some additional contextual and grammatical clues." He used the conventional scoring system to evaluate the results. These figures indicate the percentage of missing words that his students were able to fill in correctly:

- 60% and above indicates an independent level

- 40–59% indicates an instructional level

- 39% or below indicates this is at the frustration level

"For my purposes, even if kids are scoring at the frustration level, that's okay. It just means I might need to spend more time building background information," he said. Based on the results, he learned that six of his students scored below the 39% threshold. "I had to examine those results more closely. What I discovered was that four of them made errors that were related to syntax and language, but not necessarily their content knowledge. They are also speakers of Aboriginal English, and the text is written in Standard Australian English." However, the two other students made more content errors than the other students in the class. "I've beefed up the texts they're reading independently to build their background knowledge. Those two students have some easier texts about planets so they can use that knowledge to access what we're learning about in science."

Mr. Hurley noted that his postassessment is already constructed. "I administer the same cloze passage again at the end of the unit to measure my impact on their learning. It's a simple and convenient way for me to figure out what they know and need to learn before the unit begins, and then posttest at the end for impact."

Reading Fluency

Fluency is a measure of the rate and accuracy a student is able to achieve during silent or oral reading. You will recall that Chapter 6 features normed grade-level expectations (Grades 1–8) for assessing oral reading fluency. A more fluent reader is able to free up cognitive space for comprehending text through increasing automaticity in recognizing words in running text. But equally important is the student's ability to read fluently; that is, with the correct prosody, emphasis, and expression. These are important qualitative indicators of the reader's comprehension, as he or she is unlikely to exhibit these reading behaviors without understanding the content of the text. Hudson, Lane, and Pullen (2005, p. 707) provide a detailed checklist of a student's prosody:

- Student placed vocal emphasis on appropriate words.

- Student's voice tone rose and fell at appropriate points in the text.

- Student's inflection reflected the punctuation in the text (e.g., voice tone rose near the end of a question).

- In narrative text with dialogue, student used appropriate vocal tone to represent characters' mental states, such as excitement, sadness, fear, or confidence.

- Student used punctuation to pause appropriately at phrase boundaries.

- Student used prepositional phrases to pause appropriately at phrase boundaries.

- Student used subject-verb divisions to pause appropriately at phrase boundaries.

- Student used conjunctions to pause appropriately at phrase boundaries.

A more fluent reader is able to free up cognitive space for comprehending text through increasing automaticity in recognizing words in running text. But equally important is the student's ability to read fluently; that is, with the correct prosody, emphasis, and expression.

Fourth-grade teachers Gloria Hansen and Diane Lincoln use the normed grade-level expectations found in Chapter 6 as a means for their students to formulate goals for themselves. "We share the table of norms for fourth grade at the beginning of the year so that students get an idea of where they are headed," explained Ms. Lincoln. "We teach them how they can help each other in assessing their oral reading fluency, and then set realistic goals for themselves on how they want to improve." Ms. Hansen added, "We'll get goals for them like, 'I want to improve my WCPM [words correct per minute] from 70 to 90 by December 15.'"

The teachers themselves complete the prosody checklist. "It's easy to complete the checklist while they're working in their Readers Theatre groups," said Ms. Hansen. "It's a natural setting for doing this, because the students are already focused on developing their prosody. They call it 'acting' but we call it prosody," she said with a laugh. "The point with this is that the purpose of this assessment is as authentic as you can possibly get, because prosody is the name of the game in Readers Theatre."

Metacomprehension Strategies Index

Another measure of reading comprehension is the MSI, a 25-item questionnaire that asks elementary students about their use of comprehension strategies during the reading of narrative texts (Schmitt, 1990). This tool can be administered either individually to students in an interview format, or to the entire group as an independent task. Many teachers like to preview this assessment by first telling students about the purpose (to find out about the way they use strategies in their reading), and then giving them a short independent reading. Students are invited to pay attention to how they read and understand. After the reading, they complete the MSI. Compendium 15 is the entire MSI.

Scoring of the MSI is straightforward; an answer key and categorization chart are included in Compendium 16. Responses are regrouped into six categories:

- **Predicting and Verifying.** Good readers make predictions about a reading, and then check and adjust their predictions as they read.

- **Previewing.** Good readers scan the text to foster predictions.

- **Purpose Setting.** Good readers understand the purpose for reading (they gain knowledge, etc.).

- **Self-Questioning.** Good readers generate questions as they read and search for answers to these questions.

- **Drawing From Background Knowledge.** Good readers use prior experiences and knowledge to understand the text.

- **Summarizing and Applying Fix-Up Strategies.** Good readers summarize as they read and know what to do when they are having difficulty understanding what they are reading.

Fifth-grade teacher Hailey Donovan uses the MSI as a way to guide her own planning and instruction. "I understand the value of teacher modeling and thinking aloud, but I'm not always sure if what I'm choosing to model is on target with my students' needs. The results of the MSI help me make decisions about what I model." Ms. Donovan explains that she administers it twice a year—at the beginning of the school year, and then at the midpoint. "Because the emphasis is on the comprehension strategies readers apply or don't apply, I find out what they are doing well or not at all."

After analyzing the results of the first administration, Ms. Donovan discovered that many of her students didn't do particularly well at setting a purpose for reading or at verifying predictions as they read. "That alerted me to the fact that I needed to be cognizant of doing this more frequently when I modeled while reading. We have worked on other aspects of comprehension, too, but purpose setting and verification became my mantra for the first semester."

Her attention to these elements paid off when she readministered the MSI at the semester break. "I saw some impressive gains for many of the students," she said. "I also saw who didn't make as much progress. I'm developing some additional small group lessons to work with these students. I'm thinking that I'll be previewing more of the texts we use in a small group first, before I introduce the reading to the rest of the group."

ASSESSING ATTITUDES TOWARD READING

> Motivation to read and interest in reading plays are important factors in reading acquisition.

Motivation to read and interest in reading are important factors in reading acquisition. After all, if a student is not interested in reading, this is likely to inhibit his exposure to texts and thereby limit time spent practicing the strategies needed to comprehend text. A decline in attitudes toward reading occurs throughout the elementary years, precisely at the time when reading as a vehicle for learning content begins to rise (Kush & Watkins, 1996). The impact of negative reading attitude persists for many into adulthood, where those who perceive reading negatively continue to engage in less reading than their peers who enjoy reading (Pew Research Center, 2013).

Elementary Reading Attitude Survey

A useful instrument for assessing attitude toward reading is the Elementary Reading Attitude Survey (McKenna & Kear, 1990). This 20-item survey for students in Grades 1–6 can be administered to an entire group or conducted as an interview with individual students. This survey uses four Garfield the Cat cartoon figures, with Garfield exhibiting expressions that range from very happy to quite displeased. Students circle the appropriate Garfield in response to questions like "How do you feel about reading for fun at home?" and "How do you feel about reading your school books?" Scoring is completed for two aspects—recreational and academic—and a table of normed results collected on over 18,000 students across the country can be used to measure your students' individual scores against expected ones. A copy of the survey and scoring sheet appear in Compendium 17.

Second-grade teacher Francisco Reynoso used the Elementary Reading Attitude Survey to acquire more information about several students in his class. "It really got started this winter," explained Mr. Reynoso, "especially among a group of boys in my class. They were definitely voicing opinions about how much they didn't like reading, that it was boring. Stuff like that." Mr. Reynoso wanted to find out more about their perspectives. "I had the whole class take it, because it's good information. And I didn't want to single these students out. But I was mostly interested in their responses." What he discovered didn't necessarily surprise him, but it did confirm his suspicions. "They were already viewing reading as something that you did for school, but not elsewhere. Their attitudes toward recreational reading were really poor."

Armed with these results, Mr. Reynoso equipped his classroom with some new tools. "I introduced the class to a website called Guys Read (http://www.guysread.com) which is run by Jon Scieszka, the guy who wrote *The Stinky Cheese Man and Other Fairly Stupid Tales* (Scieszka & Smith, 1992). "We liked that book," he chuckled. "Some of my students found books on that website that appealed to their sense of humor." He pointed out that this wasn't solely a gendered issue. "I realized that I needed to get more families and community members involved. This semester I've been hosting community readers who I've invited to come in and share why reading matters to them," he said. "Then they read aloud a favorite story of theirs." Mr. Reynoso said that the firefighter who came in was especially popular. "She lives here in the neighborhood. Grew up here, too. She told them about why reading is important for her job, like keeping up on new techniques for fighting fires. And then she shared her favorite book, *Martina the Beautiful Cockroach* (Deedy, 2014) and talked about listening to Martina folktales as a child from her Cuban grandmother."

"I know it's hard to change attitudes," he continued, "but I'm curious to learn about whether my reading attitudes campaign is resulting in meaningful changes. I plan to administer the attitude survey again to everyone in the last few weeks of school to inform me about next year, too."

ASSESSING WRITING

Like the reading assessments used daily by classroom teachers, writing assessments are used to make instructional decisions about the class and about individual learners. These decisions may include grouping, introduction of new skills, or reteaching. Effective writing assessment requires examination of multiple aspects of writing. Some assessments target particular subskills of writing like spelling and fluency. Other assessments look at the overall quality of the writing using a holistic rubric to articulate how well the student is progressing in becoming a more competent writer. In this section, we will look at useful tools for assessing spelling and fluency, and then examine holistic scoring of writing. Finally, we will return to the notion of attitude and motivation in writing.

ASSESSING SPELLING

Typically, receptive language exceeds expressive language. Therefore, students are likely to be able to read more words than they can write. This does not mean that spelling should be ignored until students are reading—to the contrary, spelling instruction begins in kindergarten. At the earliest emergent levels, this takes the form of interactive writing instruction, an instructional practice of collaborative writing between student and teacher.

Spelling is a developmental process. Therefore, students are assessed and taught developmentally. These developmental stages have been described by Henderson (1990) as follows:

- **Emergent.** Uses few or no sound-letter associations.

- **Letter Name.** Spells by sound.

- **Within Word Pattern.** Uses familiar patterns to spell one-syllable words.

- **Syllable Juncture.** Uses syllables and double consonants to arrive at spellings.

- **Derivational Constancy.** Uses word origins to spell new words.

The table in Figure 7.2 demonstrates how spelling changes over time as the speller advances through these stages.

It is useful to assess students at the beginning of the year to determine what developmental spelling stage they are currently working in. This

Figure 7.2   Stages of Spelling Development

Ages: Grades:	Emergent Prephonetic 1–7 PreK to Mid-1	Emergent Semiphonetic 1–7 PreK to Mid-1	Letter Name 4–9 1–2	Within Word Pattern 6–12 2–4	Syllable Juncture 8–12 3–8	Derivational Constancy 10+ 5–8+
pan	b∃igt	n	pan	pan	pan	pan
stem	132tb	cm	sam	stem	stem	stem
bike	erl88i	k	bik	biek	bike	bike
chart	abge	ht	crt	chrat	chart	chart
dotted	∃a23	dd	didt	dotid	doted	dotted
drizzle	iabtt	z	jrezl	drizul	drizzel	drizzle
criticize	bbegba	k	cretsiz	critusize	critasize	critisize
majority	8bgre	m	mgrt	mujortea	mejoraty	mejority

Source: Ganske, K. (1999). The developmental spelling analysis: A measure of orthographic knowledge. *Educational Assessment, 6*(1), 41–70.

can be accomplished through the use of the Developmental Spelling Analysis Screening Inventory featured in Compendium 18 (Ganske, 2000). This screening inventory is administered to determine a student's developmental spelling level; subsequent assessment is accomplished through the use of this and other tools of analysis such as those discussed in Chapter 6 on self-correction in spelling.

Administration and scoring of the screening inventory can be completed quickly. The inventory is divided into four sets of five words. The first set is administered, and subsequent sets are used only if the student gets at least two correct answers in a set. When a child gets only one or none of the words correct, the assessment ends. Each correct spelling earns one point, and the total number of correct answers is compared to the chart in Compendium 19 to determine the student's developmental spelling level.

"One of the things we do on the first day of school is write about our name," said third-grade teacher Kiara Mitchell. "It's a great way for me to introduce myself to the class and for my students to introduce themselves to me. I explain how I got my name. I tell them that in Italian it means 'bright' and that my mom grew up in New York City in a predominantly Italian neighborhood. She always liked the name, so she called me that when I was born." Ms. Mitchell continued, "I have ulterior motives, right? I also get a first writing sample from them."

The teacher explained that this gives her a first glimpse at their control of ideas, conventions, and spelling. "As a follow up, I have all of them do a developmental spelling inventory so I can group them according to their needs and strengths," she said. "All the groups have some words in common, but each group also has their personal words that are targeted toward their development needs." She uses subsequent administrations to regroup students. "I need to be careful not to let these groups stagnate. Not let them go on for months at a time. So I have to look for movement, and who's growing, and how much. When I know where they are, I can assess my own teaching. It's like GPS, right? The spelling inventory tells me where they are on the map, but I always have to think about who's driving the car, and make adjustments. The driver is me."

ASSESSING WRITING FLUENCY

Accurate spelling contributes to the overall quality of writing. As well, writers need to write smoothly and quickly in order to compose meaningful text. This aspect of writing is referred to as *fluency,* and it is assessed through timed writing sessions. There are not set benchmarks for writing fluency expectations by grade level, and of course a writer's fluency is impacted by a number of factors, including topic, background knowledge, and motivation. However, timed writing samples should be collected each grading period to track student progress as they become more proficient and fluent writers. This can be easily accomplished by administering a 5-minute timed writing prompt. These writing prompts should be general in nature so that background knowledge does not confound performance. Useful topics for collected timed writing samples include the following:

- Describe a time when you were surprised.

- Tell about a time when you tasted a new food.

- If you could travel to any place in the world, where would it be and why?

Students are encouraged to write as much as they can and as well as they can and to write continuously for the entire period. At the end of 5 minutes, the papers are collected and analyzed to yield several measures of student success. First, the overall number of words is counted. All words are counted whether they are spelled correctly or not, and numbers, regardless of digits, count as one word. Next, the piece is read and each error in spelling, punctuation, or grammar is underlined, yielding a total number of errors. Finally, the overall number of sentences is counted. Based on these numbers, the average number of errors per sentence, mean sentence length, and total number of words can be recorded. This quantitative measure can serve as a way of reporting the overall fluency of each student. A classroom log of writing fluency can be found in Compendium 20.

A fourth-grade teacher, Ms. Duryea, tracks the writing fluency of her students throughout the year. Several times a week, she leads her students through three rounds of power writing, in which she encourages them to "write as much as you can, as well as you can." They keep track of their best effort each time on graphs inside their writer's notebooks.

"The thing is, I had been doing power writing for years, but I didn't link it back to student goals," she said. "When I started to do the longer 5-minute time samples quarterly, it opened up a whole new line of discussion with students in their individual writing conferences. Now they not only look at their daily power writing graphs, but they can also compare these to their quarterly performance. I help them set goals. It gives us another opportunity to do some math, too, right?" she said. "Now they're multiplying their top 1-minute scores to see how they match up to their 5-minute timed writing goals."

ASSESSING WRITING HOLISTICALLY

In addition to assessing the mechanics of writing related to spelling and fluency, there are also times when teachers want to evaluate the writing as a whole. This requires that they use an instrument that addresses both the content of the piece and the extent to which the writer conveyed the message with clarity and accuracy. This type of writing evaluation is referred to as a *holistic assessment*. The term *holistic* comes from the study of holism, a theory utilized in biology, anthropology, and physics that the universe can be correctly viewed only as systems of whole organisms, not as the sum of its parts. In the same fashion, holistic writing assessments measure the merits of a piece across several indicators. Most commonly, this is accomplished through the use of a rubric. Holistic writing rubrics are not confined to informal classroom assessments; indeed, they are widely used for large-scale state writing assessments at all school levels. Be sure to check your state, territorial, or provincial Department of Education website to view the holistic writing rubric used. These rubrics can be useful in gauging your students' progress on state accountability measures.

"I use the National Assessment Program for Literacy and Numeracy (NAPLAN) in my classroom so students can assess their own writing," said Year 5 teacher Edward Hurley. Students in Years 3, 5, 7, and 9 are assessed in the areas of reading, writing, language conventions, and numeracy. "I introduce them to a modified version of the marking criteria used by the state assessors," he said, "and teach them how to look for these in their own writing." He also said that he uses the posted anchor samples from a previous persuasive writing prompt asking Australian students whether it was cruel to keep animals in cages. "These anchor papers give me a good platform for talking about expectations of Year 5 writers," he noted.

Throughout the year, Mr. Hurley's writing instruction includes elements of writing, from use of conventions to structuring paragraphs to supporting arguments. "For the longer writing assignments, I ask students to score their own writing using a few of the marking criteria. "If I used all of them at once, it would be pretty overwhelming," he said. "But I do want them to be able to critique their work." Importantly, Mr. Hurley uses the same assessment rubric to score their writing. "Two things. First, it keeps me on track about where they are in relation to NAPLAN. But here's the second thing. If my score and the kid's score are very different, now we have something to talk about. I've got to get with that kid to find out what he is seeing and not seeing in his own writing. As the year progresses, I hope I am having fewer of those calibration discussions because they're getting better at analyzing their own writing."

Literacy Design Collaborative Student Work Rubrics

These rubrics have been designed and revised by a consortium of public educators and private business partners to develop instructional modules, curricula, and rubrics for addressing literacy standards. We have found the student work rubrics to be of value because they are developmentally aligned by grade bands, are individualized for argumentation and explanatory purposes, and can be applied to either written or oral work. They are organized according to seven scoring elements:

- **Focus,** in that the work addressed the prompt accurately and completely.

- **Controlling idea,** such that a claim or concept is maintained throughout.

- **Reading research (when applicable)** is used and the student makes direct links to it.

- **Development** of details that link to the focus and controlling idea.

- **Organizational structure** is apparent and suited to the task and purpose.

- **Conventions** of Standard English are evidenced.

- **Content understanding** is such that the student uses and understands the sources of information used.

These rubrics are vetted through a juried process and are frequently updated and improved. The rubrics are free and available at https://ldc .org/resources#Grades-K-12-Student-Work-Rubrics-3.0.

ASSESSING WRITING ATTITUDE AND MOTIVATION

As with reading, attitude and motivation in writing can greatly affect student performance. Consistent with the research on reading attitudes, student perceptions of writing decline through the elementary years (Graham, Berninger, & Fan, 2007). Therefore, a primary purpose for assessing attitude toward writing is to make adjustments to writing instructional practice that speak to student engagement.

Writing Attitude Survey

A survey similar to the Elementary Reading Attitude Survey is the Writing Attitude Survey (Kear, Coffman, McKenna, & Ambrosio, 2000). The 54 items on the survey use the same Garfield cartoon character format for gauging student responses to questions such as "How would you feel telling in writing why something happened?" (p. 16) and "How would you feel if your classmates read something you wrote?" (p. 21). Normed tables are available for Grades 1–12, giving teachers a comparison against same-aged peers. The Writing Attitude Survey can be found in Compendium 21.

The fourth graders in Alice Nguyen's class see themselves as writers, and that's not by accident. "I see myself as a writing teacher, first and foremost. I want them to see themselves as writers," she says. Ms. Nguyen begins each school year administering a number of different reading and writing assessments, and for her one of the most telling is the writing attitude survey. "Children who are resistant to writing and see it as a chore are going to limit themselves in their learning," she said. "It's a cascade effect, because the oral language development, the reading, all the things we teach, are most fully expressed though writing."

Based on their initial results, Ms. Nguyen begins planning writing opportunities that align to where her students are. "Some of them just see it

> Student perceptions of writing decline through the elementary years. Therefore, a primary purpose for assessing attitude toward writing is to make adjustments to writing instructional practice that speak to student engagement.

as laborious. They have a hard time getting their ideas down. So I have them audio-record their thoughts first, then play them back. It gives them a jumpstart, and they begin to realize how wise they are." She explains that other students don't see a purpose. "They become my list makers," she says. "I have them making all kinds of lists for the class, like 'Top Ten Reasons To Be On Time' or 'Top Ten Funniest Homework Excuses.' They have to survey their classmates, interview them, and compile the results."

Like Mr. Reynoso, who is concerned about his students' reading attitudes, Ms. Nguyen acknowledges that changing attitudes is difficult. "I want them to see the writing around them. Writing is a quiet and personal activity, and they don't see people around them writing so much. But I write. I like to write short stories and send them to magazines." Ms. Nguyen shares her writing, as well as the edits, acceptances, and rejections she receives. "I think lots of students believe that their teachers just know how to do stuff. It's so important that they see firsthand how we persist. Persistence is the key to writing. It's that stick-to-it attitude I want them to develop."

WHY ASSESS? KNOW YOUR IMPACT

Let's not forget why this chapter exists. Our purpose was not to simply catalog all the wonderful tools teachers can use to assess students. Assessment alone doesn't yield anything. A farmer can tell you that you can't fatten sheep by weighing them. It's what you *do* with the assessment data you have that determines whether children will continue to grow or not. Some will grow no matter what, and their accidental growth is not a gauge of your teaching prowess. Using assessment for the purpose of formative evaluation, in order to figure out what works, moves your teaching from the realm of chance to one of intentional design.

Key to student growth is time—time for teachers to talk and evaluate their own practice and its impact on student learning. First off, teachers need time to talk about what they want students to learn. This involves analyzing standards and addressing both academic and nonacademic expectations. And it involves sharing ideas for high-impact instruction. We teachers also need time to talk about assessment results with our colleagues, to get the support we need to make changes to our lessons, and, in turn, to strengthen our impact. In so doing, we all stand to learn a lot about effective approaches and to grow as professionals. These opportunities for collaboration are based on student data, and we have found that impact analysis facilitates the conversations that teachers have with one another.

CONCLUSION

There are any number of ways to assess students' literacy learning. This chapter has provided a few of them. Again, what's more important is what teachers do with the assessment information. All of the teachers profiled in this chapter, and in this book, used assessment information to determine their impact. They noted when their instruction worked and when it did not. And when the impact was less than desired, these teachers took action. They talked with their colleagues, reviewed their data, and made changes.

In addition to profiling teachers in this book, we described a number of strategies, actions, and routines that teachers can use to impact students' literacy learning. We hope readers do not simply adhere to these approaches, but rather use the data they collect to determine if students have learned. In many cases, hopefully more often than not, the approaches outlined in this book, for which there are sufficiently large effect sizes, will work to improve students' learning. But when they don't work for your students, in your grade, change it up and try something else. Never hold a strategy in higher esteem than students' learning. It's all, and always, about impacting students' literacy learning.

When this happens, students become their own teachers. They understand what they need and want to learn, seek feedback, understand that errors are opportunities to learn, engage in challenging tasks, and think about their thinking and their understanding. This will serve them well as they enter middle and high school classrooms, not to mention college and the workforce. As educators, we have chosen to be our own teachers for a long time. We seek out opportunities to learn and we should share that experience with our students.

COMPENDIUM
OF ASSESSMENTS

COMPENDIUM 1. EARLY CONCEPTS OF PRINT CHECKLIST

Name: _____   Teacher: _____

Grade Level: _____

Directions: Choose a picture book with large print and a variety of punctuation marks. Tell the child you will read the story but you will need some help. Note responses to the prompts in the right column.

Concepts About Print Prompts

Front of book	Hand book to child upside down. "Show me the front cover of the book."	
Title and author	"This book is called _____ and it is written by _____. Show me where that's written."	
Turns pages	"Show me how to open the book."	
Locates print	Turn to first page of story. "I'm going to read this to you. Show me where to begin reading." Correct response is pointing to a word on first page.	

Directionality on page	"Show me which way to read the words." Correct response indicates left to right.	
Return sweep	On a page with more than one line of print: "Which way do I go when I get to the end of the first line?"	
1:1 correspondence	"Point to the words while I read."	
Beginning and end of story	"Show me the beginning of the story." "Show me the end of the story."	
Period	Point to a period at the end of a sentence. "What does this mean?"	
Question mark	Point to a question mark at the end of a sentence. "What does this mean?"	
Directionality within words	Point to a word with at least three letters. "Show me the first letter in the word." "Show me the last letter in the word."	

Notes:

COMPENDIUM 2. YOPP-SINGER TEST OF PHONEME SEGMENTATION

Name: _____ Date: _____

Score (number correct): _____

Directions: Today we're going to play a word game. I'm going to say a word and I want you to break the word apart. You are going to tell me each sound in the word in order. For example, if I say "old," you should say "/o/-/l/-d/."

(Administrator: Be sure to say the sounds, not the letters, in the word.) Let's try a few together.

Practice items: *(Assist the child in segmenting these items as necessary.)* ride, go, man

Test items: *(Circle those items that the student correctly segments; incorrect responses may be recorded on the blank line following the item.)*

1. dog _____	12. lay _____
2. keep _____	13. race _____
3. fine _____	14. zoo _____
4. no _____	15. three _____
5. she _____	16. job _____
6. wave _____	17. in _____
7. grew _____	18. ice _____
8. that _____	19. at _____
9. red _____	20. top _____
10. me _____	21. by _____
11. sat _____	22. do _____

Source: Yopp, H. K. (1995). A test for assessing phonemic awareness in young children. *The Reading Teacher, 49,* 20–29. Used with permission. (The author, Hallie Kay Yopp, California State University, Fullerton, grants permission for this text to be reproduced. The author acknowledges the contribution of the late Harry Singer to the development of this test.)

 Available for download at **https://resources.corwin.com/VL-LiteracyK-5**

COMPENDIUM 3. DOLCH SIGHT WORD ASSESSMENT: LEVEL A

Name: _____   Teacher: _____

Directions: Present the student each Dolch sight word on an index card. Highlight or circle each correct response using the color code at the bottom of the page.

Dolch Sight Words: Level A

a	funny	look	see
and	go	make	the
away	help	me	three
big	hers	my	to
blue	I	not	two
can	in	one	up
come	is	play	we
down	it	red	yellow
find	jump	run	you
for	little	said	

Coding for sight words:

1st administration: red   (Date: _____)

2nd administration: blue   (Date: _____)

3rd administration: green   (Date: _____)

4th administration: yellow   (Date: _____)

COMPENDIUM 4. DOLCH SIGHT WORD ASSESSMENT: LEVEL B

Name: _____   Teacher: _____

Directions: Present the student each Dolch sight word on an index card. Highlight or circle each correct response using the color code at the bottom of the page.

Dolch Sight Words: Level B

all	four	out	this
am	get	please	too
are	good	pretty	under
at	has	ran	want
ate	he	ride	was
be	into	saw	well
black	like	say	went
brown	must	she	what
but	new	so	white
came	no	soon	who
did	now	that	will
do	on	there	with
eat	our	they	yes

Coding for sight words:

1st administration: red   (Date: _____)

2nd administration: blue   (Date: _____)

3rd administration: green   (Date: _____)

4th administration: yellow   (Date: _____)

COMPENDIUM 5. DOLCH SIGHT WORD ASSESSMENT: LEVEL C

Name: _____   Teacher: _____

Directions: Present the student each Dolch sight word on an index card. Highlight or circle each correct response using the color code at the bottom of the page.

Dolch Sight Words: Level C

after	from	let	some
again	give	live	stop
an	going	may	take
any	had	of	thank
as	has	old	them
ask	her	once	then
by	him	open	think
could	how	over	walk
every	just	put	where
fly	know	round	when

Coding for sight words:

1st administration: red   (Date: _____)

2nd administration: blue   (Date: _____)

3rd administration: green   (Date: _____)

4th administration: yellow   (Date: _____)

COMPENDIUM 6. DOLCH SIGHT WORD ASSESSMENT: LEVEL D

Name: _____   Teacher: _____

Directions: Present the student each Dolch sight word on an index card. Highlight or circle each correct response using the color code at the bottom of the page.

Dolch Sight Words: Level D

always	fast	pull	use
around	first	read	very
because	five	right	wash
been	found	sing	which
before	gave	sit	why
best	goes	sleep	wish
both	green	tell	work
buy	its	their	would
call	made	these	write
cold	many	those	your
does	off	upon	
don't	or	us	

Coding for sight words:

1st administration: red   (Date: _____)

2nd administration: blue   (Date: _____)

3rd administration: green   (Date: _____)

4th administration: yellow   (Date: _____)

Available for download at **https://resources.corwin.com/VL-LiteracyK-5**

COMPENDIUM 7. DOLCH SIGHT WORD ASSESSMENT: LEVEL E

Name: _____ Teacher: _____

Directions: Present the student each Dolch sight word on an index card. Highlight or circle each correct response using the color code at the bottom of the page.

Dolch Sight Words: Level E

about	fall	kind	seven
better	far	laugh	shall
bring	full	light	show
carry	got	long	six
clean	grow	much	small
cut	hold	myself	start
done	hot	never	ten
draw	hurt	only	today
drink	if	own	together
eight	keep	pick	try
			warm

Coding for sight words:

1st administration: red   (Date: _____)

2nd administration: blue   (Date: _____)

3rd administration: green   (Date: _____)

4th administration: yellow   (Date: _____)

COMPENDIUM 8. NARRATIVE STORY RETELLING RUBRIC

Name: _____   Teacher: _____

Title of book: _____

Who read the story?   ❑ Teacher   ❑ Student

	Proficient—3	Adequate—2	Needs Attention—1
Character	Main and supporting characters and their characteristics identified. Examples given to describe characters.	Most main and supporting characters identified. Characteristics are less descriptive.	Characters essential to the story are overlooked. Few or no examples or descriptions of characteristics offered.
Setting	Setting is identified and described in detail using vivid vocabulary.	Setting is identified and description is accurate. Some detail included.	Setting is either not identified or identified incorrectly.
Problem	Central problem of the story is identified. Character motivations or potential solutions included.	Central problem is identified. Character motivations or potential solutions are not included.	Central problem is not identified or is incorrectly identified.
Solution	Solution is identified. Retelling features connections to characteristics of characters. Student relates this to story's moral or theme.	Solution is identified but retelling does not include connection to moral or theme.	Solution is not identified or is incorrectly identified.
Plot	Sequence of story is told in correct order.	Sequence of story is told in nearly correct order, with one or two events out of sequence.	Sequence of story has three or more errors.

Script retelling in the box below, then score quality of the retelling.

	Character: _____
	Setting: _____
	Problem: _____
	Solution: _____
	Plot: _____
	TOTAL: _____

Available for download at **https://resources.corwin.com/VL-LiteracyK-5**

COMPENDIUM 9. INFORMATIONAL TEXT RETELLING RUBRIC

Name: _____ Teacher: _____

Title of book: _____

Who read the story?   ❏ Teacher   ❏ Student

	Proficient—3	Adequate—2	Needs Attention—1
Main Ideas	Main ideas are identified. Examples are given to illustrate these ideas.	Most main ideas identified. Examples are less descriptive.	Main ideas essential to the text are overlooked. Few or no examples or descriptions of main ideas offered.
Supporting Details	Supporting details are clearly connected to the main ideas.	Supporting details are identified but are not told in association with main ideas.	Few or no supporting details offered.
Sequence	Sequence of retelling is accurate and reflects the order used by the author.	Sequence is similar to order in book, with some instances of "doubling back" during retelling.	Sequence is difficult to discern.
Accuracy	Facts are relayed accurately.	Retelling is mostly accurate, with few errors.	Retelling is inaccurate.
Inferences	Student makes connections within text (e.g., meaning of title, usefulness of information).	Student makes few associations between pieces of information in text.	Student makes no associations within text.

Script retelling in the box below, then score quality of the retelling.

	Main Ideas: _____ Details: _____ Sequence: _____ Accuracy: _____ Inferences: _____ TOTAL: _____

COMPENDIUM 10. STUDENT FORM FOR LETTER IDENTIFICATION

O	W	E	X
S	A	G	D
H	K	P	J
C	N	U	V
Y	R	B	I
Q	L	F	M
Z	T		

o	w	e	x
s	a	g	d
h	k	p	j
c	n	u	v
y	r	b	i
q	l	f	m
z	t	a	g

Available for download at **https://resources.corwin.com/VL-LiteracyK-5**

COMPENDIUM 11. TEACHER RECORDING FORM FOR LETTER IDENTIFICATION

Name: _____ Date: _____

Teacher: _____

Letter	Correct	Incorrect	Letter	Correct	Incorrect
O			o		
W			w		
E			e		
X			x		
S			s		
A			a		
G			g		
D			d		
H			h		
K			k		
P			p		
J			j		
C			c		
N			n		
U			u		
V			v		
Y			y		
R			r		
B			b		
I			i		
Q			q		
L			l		
F			f		
M			m		
Z			z		
T			t		
			a		
			g		
Total uppercase	/26	/26	**Total lowercase**	/28	/28

Code for scoring: Correct = ✓

Incorrect = record student response

Available for download at **https://resources.corwin.com/VL-LiteracyK-5**

COMPENDIUM 12. CODING SHEET FOR MISCUE ANALYSIS

Responses and Miscues	Explanation	Coding	Example
Correct	Calls word correctly	✓	✓ ✓ ✓ ✓ ✓ The house is blue and white.
Substitution	Calls one word for another	horse ————— house	horse ✓ house ✓ ✓ ✓ The house is blue and white.
Omission	Skips a word	—— house	—— ✓ house ✓ ✓ ✓ The house is blue and white.
Insertion	Adds a word	big —	✓ **big** ✓ ✓ ✓ ✓ The house is blue and white.
Appeal	Asks for help	A ————— house	A ✓ house ✓ ✓ ✓ The house is blue and white.
Teacher told	Teacher tells word	TT ————— house	TT ✓ house ✓ ✓ ✓ The house is blue and white.
Rerun	Student repeats words, phrases, or entire sentence	◀— RR The house	RR ✓ ✓ ✓ ✓ ✓ The house is blue and white.
Self-correction	Reader corrects error on own	horse SC ————— house	horse SC ✓ house ✓ ✓ ✓ The house is blue and white.

Available for download at **https://resources.corwin.com/VL-LiteracyK-5**

COMPENDIUM 13. SAMPLE CLOZE PROCEDURE STUDENT FORM

Cloze Passage

Directions: Every fifth word has been deleted from this passage. Read the passage and write the words on a separate sheet of paper that best fit both the meaning and the structure of the sentence. You may read the passage more than once.

Alice's Adventures in Wonderland

By Lewis Carroll

Alice was beginning to get very tired of sitting by her sister on the bank, and of having nothing to do: once or twice she had peeped into the book her sister was reading, but it had no pictures or conversations in it, 'and what is the use of a book,' thought Alice 'without pictures or conversations?'

So she was considering _____ her own mind (as _____ as she could, for _____ hot day made her _____ very sleepy and stupid), _____ the pleasure of making _____ daisy-chain would be worth _____ trouble of getting up _____ picking the daisies, when _____ a White Rabbit with _____ eyes ran close by _____.

There was nothing so _____ remarkable in that; nor _____ Alice think it so _____ much out of the _____ to hear the Rabbit _____ to itself, 'Oh dear! _____ dear! I shall be _____ !' (when she thought it _____ afterwards, it occurred to _____ that she ought to _____ wondered at this, but _____ the time it all _____ quite natural); but when _____ Rabbit actually *took a* _____ *out of its waistcoat-pocket,* _____ looked at it, and _____ hurried on, Alice started _____ her feet, for it _____ across her mind that _____ had never before seen _ rabbit with either a _____, or a watch to _____ out of it, and _____ with curiosity, she ran _____ the field after it, _____ fortunately was just in _____ to see it pop _____ a large rabbit-hole under _____ hedge.

In another moment _____ went Alice after it, _____ once considering how in _____ world she was to _____ out again.

The rabbit-hole went straight on like a tunnel for some way, and then dipped suddenly down, so suddenly that Alice had not a moment to think about stopping herself before she found herself falling down a very deep well.

COMPENDIUM 14. SAMPLE CLOZE PROCEDURE ANSWER KEY

1. in	18. late	35. across
2. well	19. over	36. and
3. the	20. her	37. time
4. feel	21. have	38. down
5. whether	22. at	39. the
6. a	23. seemed	40. down
7. the	24. the	41. never
8. and	25. watch	42. the
9. suddenly	26. and	43. get
10. pink	27. then	
11. her	28. to	
12. very	29. flashed	
13. did	30. she	
14. very	31. a	
15. way	32. waistcoat-pocket	
16. say	33. take	
17. Oh	34. burning	

Available for download at **https://resources.corwin.com/VL-LiteracyK-5**

COMPENDIUM 15. METACOMPREHENSION STRATEGIES INDEX STUDENT FORM

Name:_____ Date:_____

Metacomprehension Strategy Index

Directions: Think about what kinds of things you can do to help you understand a story better before, during, and after you read it. Read each of the lists of four statements and decide which one of them would help you the most. Circle the letter of the statement you choose.

I. In each set of four, choose the one statement that tells a good thing to do to help you understand a story better *before* you read it.

1. Before I begin reading, it's a good idea to:
    A. See how many pages are in the story.
    B. Look up all of the big words in the dictionary.
    C. Make some guesses about what I think will happen in the story.
    D. Think about what has happened so far in the story.

2. Before I begin reading, it's a good idea to:
    A. Look at the pictures to see what the story is about.
    B. Decide how long it will take me to read the story.
    C. Sound out the words I don't know.
    D. Check to see if the story is making sense.

3. Before I begin reading, it's a good idea to:
    A. Ask someone to read the story to me.
    B. Read the title to see what the story is about.
    C. Check to see if most of the words have long or short vowels in them.
    D. Check to see if the pictures are in order and make sense.

4. Before I begin reading, it's a good idea to:
    A. Check to see that no pages are missing.
    B. Make a list of words I'm not sure about.
    C. Use the title and pictures to help me make guesses about what will happen in the story.
    D. Read the last sentence so I will know how the story ends.

5. Before I begin reading, it's a good idea to:
    A. Decide on why I am going to read the story.
    B. Use the difficult words to help me make guesses about what will happen in the story.
    C. Reread some parts to see if I can figure out what is happening if things aren't making sense.
    D. Ask for help with the difficult words.

6. Before I begin reading, it's a good idea to:
    A. Retell all of the main points that have happened so far.
    B. Ask myself questions that I would like to have answered in the story.
    C. Think about the meaning of the words, which have more than one meaning.
    D. Look through the story to find all of the words with three or more syllables.

7. Before I begin reading, it's a good idea to:
    A. Check to see if I have read this story before.
    B. Use my questions and guesses as a reason for reading the story.
    C. Make sure I can pronounce all of the words before I start.
    D. Think of a better title for the story.

8. Before I begin reading, it's a good idea to:
    A. Think of what I already know about the things I see in the pictures.
    B. See how many pages are in the story.
    C. Choose the best part of the story to read again.
    D. Read the story aloud to someone.

9. Before I begin reading, it's a good idea to:
   A. Practice reading the story out loud.
   B. Retell all of the main points to make sure I can remember the story.
   C. Think of what the people in the story might be like.
   D. Decide if I have enough time to read the story.

10. Before I begin reading, it's a good idea to:
    A. Check to see if I am understanding the story so far.
    B. Check to see if the words have more than one meaning.
    C. Think about where the story might be taking place.
    D. List all of the important details.

II. In each set of four, choose the one statement that tells a good thing to do to help you understand at story better *while* you are reading it.

11. While I am reading, it's a good idea to:
    A. Read the story very slowly so that I will not miss any important parts.
    B. Read the title to see what the story is about.
    C. Check to see if the pictures have anything missing.
    D. Check to see if the story is making sense by seeing if I can tell what's happened so far.

12. While I am reading, it's a good idea to:
    A. Stop to retell the main points to see if I am understanding what has happened so far.
    B. Read the story quickly so that I can find out what happened.
    C. Read only the beginning and the end of the story to find out what it is about.
    D. Skip the parts that are too difficult for me.

13. While I am reading, it's a good idea to:
    A. Look all of the big words up in the dictionary.
    B. Put the book away and find another one if things aren't making sense.

C. Keep thinking about the title and the pictures to help me decide what is going to happen next.
D. Keep track of how many pages I have left to read.

14. While I am reading, it's a good idea to:
    A. Keep track of how long it is taking me to read the story.
    B. Check to see if I can answer any of the questions I asked before I started reading.
    C. Read the title to see what the story is going to be about.
    D. Add the missing details to the pictures.

15. While I am reading, it's a good idea to:
    A. Have someone read the story aloud to me.
    B. Keep track of how many pages I have read.
    C. List the story's main character.
    D. Check to see if my guesses are right or wrong.

16. While I am reading, it's a good idea to:
    A. Check to see that the characters are real.
    B. Make a lot of guesses about what is going to happen next.
    C. Not look at the pictures because they might confuse me.
    D. Read the story aloud to someone.

17. While I am reading, it's a good idea to:
    A. Try to answer the questions I asked myself.
    B. Try not to confuse what I already know with what I am reading about.
    C. Read the story silently.
    D. Check to see if I am saying the new vocabulary words correctly.

18. While I am reading, it's a good idea to:
    A. Try to see if my guesses are going to be right or wrong.
    B. Reread to be sure I haven't missed any of the words.
    C. Decide on why I am reading the story.
    D. List what happened first, second, third, and so on.

19. While I am reading, it's a good idea to:
    A. See if I can recognize the new vocabulary words.
    B. Be careful not to skip any parts of the story.
    C. Check to see how many of the words I already know.
    D. Keep thinking of what I already know about the things and ideas in the story to help me decide what is going to happen.

20. While I am reading, it's a good idea to:
    A. Reread some parts or read ahead to see if I can figure out what is happening if things aren't making sense.
    B. Take my time reading so that I can be sure I understand what is happening.
    C. Change the ending so that it makes sense.
    D. Check to see if there are enough pictures to help make the story ideas clear.

III. In each set of four, choose the one statement that tells a good thing to do to help you understand a story better *after* you have read it.

21. After I've read a story it's a good idea to:
    A. Count how many pages I read with no mistakes.
    B. Check to see if there were enough pictures to go with the story to make it interesting.
    C. Check to see if I met my purpose for reading the story.
    D. Underline the causes and effects.

22. After I've read a story it's a good idea to:
    A. Underline the main idea.
    B. Retell the main points of the whole story so that I can check to see if I understood it.

C. Read the story again to be sure I said all of the words right.
D. Practice reading the story aloud.

23. After I've read a story it's a good idea to:
    A. Read the title and look over the story to see what it is about.
    B. Check to see if I skipped any of the vocabulary words.
    C. Think about what made me make good or bad predictions.
    D. Make a guess about what will happen next in the story.

24. After I've read a story it's a good idea to:
    A. Look up all of the big words in the dictionary.
    B. Read the best parts aloud.
    C. Have someone read the story aloud to me.
    D. Think about how the story was like things I already knew about before I started reading.

25. After I've read a story it's a good idea to:
    A. Think about how I would have acted if I were the main character in the story.
    B. Practice reading the story silently for practice of good reading.
    C. Look over the story title and pictures to see what will happen.
    D. Make a list of the things I understood the most.

Source: Adapted from Schmitt, M. C. (March 1990). A questionnaire to measure children's awareness of strategic reading processes. *The Reading Teacher, 43,* 454–461.

Available for download at **https://resources.corwin.com/VL-LiteracyK-5**

COMPENDIUM 16. METACOMPREHENSION STRATEGIES INDEX ANSWER KEY

Interpreting Results of the Metacomprehension Strategies Index

The MSI (Schmitt, 1990) is a measure of a student's use of strategies with narrative text. It may be read to the student or administered silently. The wording of the items can be changed for use with expository text. For example, you can replace the wording of #2 to read,

Before I begin reading, it's a good idea to:

    A. Look at the illustrations to see what the chapter will be about.

    B. Decide how long it will take for me to read the chapter.

    C. Sound out the words I don't know.

    D. Check to see if the information is making sense.

Answer Key: These answers represent the best answers; items may include strategies that are somewhat useful but not as efficient for the situation described.

1. C	6. B	11. D	16. B	21. C
2. A	7. B	12. A	17. A	22. B
3. B	8. A	13. C	18. A	23. C
4. C	9. C	14. B	19. D	24. D
5. A	10. C	15. D	20. A	25. A

Interpreting: The following item analysis is organized to more fully describe the types of metacomprehension strategies tested.

Strategies	Items
Predicting and Verifying Predicting and verifying the content of a story promotes active comprehension by giving readers a purpose to read (i.e., to verify predictions). Evaluating predictions and generating new ones as necessary enhances the constructive nature of the reading process.	1, 4, 13, 15, 16, 18, 23
Previewing Previewing the text facilitates comprehension by activating background knowledge and providing information for making predictions.	2, 3

Purpose Setting Reading with a purpose promotes active, strategic reading.	5, 7, 21
Self-Questioning Generating questions to be answered promotes active comprehension by giving readers a purpose for reading (i.e., to answer the questions).	6, 14, 17
Drawing From Background Knowledge Activating and incorporating information from background knowledge contributes to comprehension by helping readers make inferences and generate predictions.	8, 9, 10, 19, 24, 25
Summarizing and Applying Fix-Up Strategies Summarizing the content at various points in the story serves as a form of comprehension monitoring. Rereading or suspending judgment and reading on when comprehension breaks down represents strategic reading.	11, 12, 20, 22

Source: Adapted from Schmitt, M. B. (1990). A questionnaire to measure children's awareness of strategic reading processes. *The Reading Teacher, 43,* 454–461.

Available for download at **https://resources.corwin.com/VL-LiteracyK-5**

COMPENDIUM 17. ELEMENTARY READING ATTITUDE SURVEY

Directions for Use

The Elementary Reading Attitude Survey provides a quick indication of student attitudes toward reading. It consists of 20 items and can be administered to an entire classroom in about 10 minutes. Each item presents a brief, simply worded statement about reading, followed by four pictures of Garfield. Each pose is designed to depict a different emotional state, ranging from very positive to very negative.

Administration

Begin by telling students that you wish to find out how they feel about reading. Emphasize that this is *not* a test and that there are no "right" answers. Encourage sincerity.

Distribute the survey forms and, if you wish to monitor the attitudes of specific students, ask them to write their names in the space at the top. Hold up a copy of the survey so that the students can see the first page. Point to the picture of Garfield at the far left of the first item. Ask the students to look at this same picture on their own survey form. Discuss with them the mood Garfield seems to be in (very happy). Then move to the next picture and again discuss Garfield's mood (this lime, a *little* happy). In the same way, move to the third and fourth pictures and talk about Garfield's moods—a little upset and very upset. It is helpful to point out the position of Garfield's *mouth*, especially in the middle two figures.

Explain that together you will read some statements about reading and that the students should think about how they feel about each statement. They should then circle the picture of Garfield that is closest to their own feelings. (Emphasize that the students should respond according to their own feelings, not as Garfield might respond!) Read each item aloud slowly and distinctly; then read it a second time while students are thinking. Be sure to read the item *number* and to remind students of page numbers when new pages are reached.

Scoring

To score the survey, count four points for each leftmost (happiest) Garfield circled, three for each slightly smiling Garfield, two for each mildly upset Garfield, and one point for each very upset (rightmost) Garfield. Three scores for each student can be obtained: the total for the first 10 items, the total for the second 10, and a composite total. The first half of the survey relates to attitude toward recreational reading; the second half relates to attitude toward academic aspects of reading.

Interpretation

You can interpret scores in two ways. One is to note informally where the score falls in regard to the four nodes of the scale. A total score of 50, for example, would fall about midway on the scale, between the slightly happy and slightly upset figures, therefore indicating a relatively indifferent overall attitude toward reading. The other approach is more formal. It involves converting the raw scores into percentile ranks by means of the table in the Elementary Reading Attitude Survey Scoring Sheet. Be sure to use the norms for the right grade level and to note the column headings (Rec = recreational reading, Aca = academic reading, Tot = total score). If you wish to determine the average percentile rank for your class, average the raw scores first; then use the table to locate the percentile rank corresponding to the raw score mean. Percentile ranks cannot be averaged directly.

Elementary Reading Attitude Survey

School: _____   Grade: _____   Name: _____

Directions: Please circle the picture that describes how you feel when you read a book.

1. How do you feel when you read a book on a rainy Saturday?

2. How do you feel when you read a book in school during free time?

3. How do you feel about reading for fun at home?

4. How do you feel about getting a book for a present?

5. How do you feel about spending free time reading a book?

6. How do you feel about starting a new book?

7. How do you feel about reading during summer vacation?

8. How do you feel about reading instead of playing?

9. How do you feel about going to a bookstore?

10. How do you feel about reading different kinds of books?

11. How do you feel when a teacher asks you questions about what you read?

12. How do you feel about reading workbook pages and worksheets?

13. How do you feel about reading in school?

14. How do you feel about reading your school books?

15. How do you feel about learning from a book?

16. How do you feel when it's time for reading in class?

17. How do you feel about stories you read in reading class?

18. How do you feel when you read out loud in class?

19. How do you feel about using a dictionary?

20. How do you feel about taking a reading test?

Elementary Reading Attitude Survey Scoring Sheet

Student's name: _____

Teacher: _____

Grade: _____ Administration Date: _____

> *Scoring Guide*
>
> 4 points   Happiest Garfield
>
> 3 points   Slightly smiling Garfield
>
> 2 points   Mildly upset Garfield
>
> 1 point   Very upset Garfield

Recreational Reading	**Academic Reading**
1. _____	1. _____
2. _____	2. _____
3. _____	3. _____
4. _____	4. _____
5. _____	5. _____
6. _____	6. _____
7. _____	7. _____
8. _____	8. _____
9. _____	9. _____
10. _____	10. _____
Raw Score: _____	Raw Score: _____

Full-Scale Raw Score .... (Recreational + Academic): _____

Percentile Ranks: .... Recreational: [   ]

.... Academic: [   ]

.... Full Scale: [   ]

Source: McKenna, M. C., & Kear, D. (1990). Measuring attitude toward reading: A new tool for teachers. *The Reading Teacher, 43,* 626–639. Used with permission. (© PAWS, www.professorgarfield.org. Survey designed by Dennis J. Kear, Wichita State University.)

Available for download at **https://resources.corwin.com/VL-LiteracyK-5**

COMPENDIUM 18. DEVELOPMENTAL SPELLING ANALYSIS SCREENING INVENTORY

Directions: I am going to say some words that I want you to spell for me. Some of the words will be easy to spell, and some will be more difficult. When you don't know how to spell a word, just do the best you can. Each time, I will say the word, then use it in a sentence, and then I will say the word again.

1.	hen	The hen sat on her eggs.
2.	wish	The boy made a wish and blew out the candles.
3.	trap	A spider web is a trap for flies.
4.	jump	A kangaroo can jump high.
5.	brave	A brave dog scared the robbers.
6.	smile	A smile shows that you're happy.
7.	grain	One kind of grain is called wheat.
8.	crawl	The baby can crawl but not walk.
9.	clerk	The clerk sold some shoes to me.
10.	clutch	The clutch in the car needs fixing.
11.	palace	The king and queen live in a palace.
12.	observe	I like to observe birds at the feeder.
13.	shuffle	Please shuffle the cards before you deal.
14.	exciting	The adventure story I'm reading is very exciting.
15.	treason	The man was found guilty of treason.
16.	column	His picture was in the first column of the newspaper.
17.	variety	A grocery store has a wide variety of foods.
18.	extension	The workers need an extension ladder to reach the roof.
19.	competition	There was much competition between the two businesses.
20.	illiterate	An illiterate person is one who cannot read.

Stop when a child has spelled no words or 1 word correctly out of any set of five.

Source: Ganske, K. (2000). *Word journeys: Assessment-guided phonics, spelling, and vocabulary instruction.* New York: Guilford. Reprinted with permission of Guilford Press.

 Available for download at **https://resources.corwin.com/VL-LiteracyK-5**

COMPENDIUM 19. DEVELOPMENTAL SPELLING ANALYSIS SCREENING INVENTORY PREDICTION CHART

Letter Name (LN)—Students learn about beginning sounds, blends (bl, sl, etc.), word families, and short-vowel sounds. This is the stage in which students are usually taught to read.

Within Word (WW)—Students spell most short-vowel sounds correctly, and they learn about long-vowel sounds and patterns in one-syllable words. In this stage, students can read and spell many words correctly because of their automatic knowledge of letter sounds and short-vowel patterns.

Syllable Juncture (SJ)—Students learn about the conventions of joining syllables in words with two or more syllables. Students are expected to spell many words of more than one syllable. Students consider spelling patterns where syllables meet and at meaning units such as affixes (prefixes and suffixes).

Derivational Constancy (DC)—Students learn that meaning as well as sound and pattern are important in the spelling of the English language. This last stage in the developmental model continues through adulthood.

Inventory Score	Predicted Stage(s)	Inventory Score	Predicted Stage(s)
20	DC	10	WW/SJ
19	DC	9	WW
18	DC	8	WW
17	DC	7	WW
16	SJ/DC	6	LN/WW
15	SJ/DC	5	LN/WW
14	SJ	4	LN
13	SJ	3	LN
12	SJ	2	LN
11	WW/SJ	1	LN*
		0	LN*
			* Children who achieve a score of 0 or 1 may or may not be letter name spellers.

Source: Ganske, K. (2000). *Word journeys: Assessment-guided phonics, spelling, and vocabulary instruction.* New York: Guilford. Reprinted with permission of Guilford Press.

 Available for download at **https://resources.corwin.com/VL-LiteracyK-5**

COMPENDIUM 20. CLASS RECORD OF WRITING FLUENCY

Teacher Name: _____   Grade: _____

Name	Date				Date				Date				Date			
	TW	TS	EPS	MSL	TW	TS	EPS	MSL	TW	TS	EPS	MSL	TW	TS	EPS	MSL

TW = Total words written

TS = Total sentences written

EPS = Average number of errors per sentence (TS ÷ # of errors)

MSL = Mean sentence length (TW ÷ TS)

COMPENDIUM 21. WRITING ATTITUDE SURVEY

Directions for Use

The Writing Attitude Survey provides a quick indication of student attitudes toward writing. It consists of 28 items and can be administered to an entire classroom in about 20 minutes. Each item presents a brief, simply worded statement about writing, followed by four pictures of Garfield. Each pose is designed to depict a different emotional state, ranging from very positive to very negative.

Administration

Begin by telling students that you wish to find out how they feel about writing. Emphasize that this is not a test and that there are no right answers. Encourage sincerity.

Distribute the survey forms and, if you wish to monitor the attitudes of specific students, ask them to write their names in the space at the top. Hold up a copy of the survey so that the students can see the first page. Point to the picture of Garfield at the far left of the first item. Ask the students to look at the same picture on their own survey form. Discuss with them the mood Garfield seems to be in (very happy). Then move to the next picture and again discuss Garfield's mood (this time, somewhat happy). In the same way, move to the third and fourth pictures and talk about Garfield's moods—somewhat upset and very upset.

Explain that the survey contains some statements about writing and that the students should think about how they feel about each statement. They should then circle the picture of Garfield that is closest to their own feelings. (Emphasize that the students should respond according to their own feelings, not as Garfield might respond!) In the first and second grades read each item aloud slowly and distinctly, then read it a second time while students are thinking. Be sure to read the item number and to remind students of page numbers when new pages are reached.

In Grades 3 and above, monitor students while they are completing this survey. It is not necessary for the teacher to read the items aloud to students, unless the teacher feels it is necessary for newer or struggling readers.

Teachers should review the items prior to the administration of the survey to identify any words students may need defined to eliminate misunderstanding during completion of the instrument.

Scoring

To score the survey, count four points for each leftmost (very happy) Garfield circled, three points for the next Garfield to the right (somewhat happy), two points for the next Garfield to the right (somewhat upset), and one point for the rightmost Garfield (very upset). The individual scores for each question should be totaled to reach a raw score.

Interpretation

The scores should first be recorded on the scoring sheet. The scores can be interpreted in two ways. An informal approach would be to look at where the raw score falls related to the total possible points of 112. If the raw score is approximately 70, the score would fall midway between the somewhat happy and somewhat upset Garfields, indicating the student has an indifferent attitude toward writing. The formal approach involves converting the raw score to a percentile rank by using the table in the Writing Attitude Survey Scoring Sheet. The raw score should be found on the left-hand side of the table and matched to the percentile rank in the appropriate grade-level column.

Writing Attitude Survey

School: _____   Grade: _____   Name: _____

1. How would you feeling writing a letter to the author of a book you read?

2. How would you feel if you wrote about something you have heard of or seen?

3. How would you feel writing a letter to a store asking about something you might buy there?

4. How would you feel telling in writing why something happened?

5. How would you feel writing to someone to change their opinion?

6. How would you feel keeping a diary?

7. How would you feel writing poetry for fun?

8. How would you feel writing a letter stating your opinion about a topic?

9. How would you feel if you were an author who writes books?

10. How would you feel if you had a job as a writer for a newspaper or magazine?

11. How would you feel about becoming an even better writer than you already are?

12. How would you feel about writing a story instead of doing homework?

13. How would you feel about writing a story instead of watching TV?

14. How would you feel writing about something you did in science?

15. How would you feel writing about something you did in social studies?

16. How would you feel if you could write more in school?

17. How would you feel about writing down the important things your teachers says about a new topic?

18. How would you feel writing a long story or report at school?

19. How would you feel writing answers to questions in science or social studies?

20. How would you feel if your teacher asked you to go back and change some of your writing?

21. How would you feel if your classmates talked to you about making your writing better?

22. How would you feel writing an advertisement for something people can buy?

23. How would you feel keeping a journal for class?

24. How would you feel writing about things that have happened in your life?

25. How would you feel writing about something from another person's point of view?

26. How would you feel about checking your writing to make sure the words you have written are spelled correctly?

27. How would you feel if your classmates read something you wrote?

28. How would you feel if you didn't write as much in school?

Writing Attitude Survey Scoring Sheet

Student name: _____

Teacher: _____

Grade: _____ Administration Date: _____

Scoring Guide

4 points	Very happy Garfield
3 points	Somewhat happy Garfield
2 points	Somewhat upset Garfield
1 point	Very upset Garfield

Item Scores

1.	_____	15.	_____
2.	_____	16.	_____
3.	_____	17.	_____
4.	_____	18.	_____
5.	_____	19.	_____
6.	_____	20.	_____
7.	_____	21.	_____
8.	_____	22.	_____
9.	_____	23.	_____
10.	_____	24.	_____
11.	_____	25.	_____
12.	_____	26.	_____
13.	_____	27.	_____
14.	_____	28.	_____

Full-Scale Raw Score: _____

Percentile Rank: _____

Source: Kear, D. J., Coffman, G. A., McKenna, M. C., & Ambrosio, A. L. (2000). Measuring attitude toward writing: A new tool for teachers. *The Reading Teacher, 54*, 10–23. Used with permission. (© PAWS, www.professorgarfield.org. Survey designed by Dennis J. Kear, Wichita State University.)

 Available for download at **https://resources.corwin.com/VL-LiteracyK-5**

APPENDIX: EFFECT SIZES

Rank	Influence	ES
1	Self-reported grades/student expectations	1.44
2	Piagetian programs	1.28
*3	Response to intervention	1.07
*4	Teacher credibility	0.90
5	Providing formative evaluation	0.90
6	Micro-teaching	0.88
*7	Classroom discussion	0.82
8	Comprehensive interventions for students who are learning disabled	0.77
9	Teacher clarity	0.75
10	Feedback	0.75
11	Reciprocal teaching	0.74
12	Teacher–student relationships	0.72
13	Spaced versus mass practice	0.71
14	Metacognitive strategies	0.69
15	Acceleration	0.68
16	Classroom behavioral	0.68
17	Vocabulary programs	0.67
18	Repeated reading programs	0.67
19	Creativity programs on achievement	0.65
20	Prior achievement	0.65
21	Self-verbalization and self-questioning	0.64
22	Study skills	0.63
23	Teaching strategies	0.62
24	Problem-solving teaching	0.61
25	Not labeling students	0.61
26	Comprehension programs	0.60
27	Concept mapping	0.60
28	Cooperative versus individualistic learning	0.59
29	Direct instruction	0.59
30	Tactile stimulation programs	0.58
31	Mastery learning	0.58
32	Worked examples	0.57

(Continued)

Rank	Influence	ES
33	Visual perception programs	0.55
34	Peer tutoring	0.55
35	Cooperative versus competitive learning	0.54
36	Phonics instruction	0.54
*37	Student-centered teaching	0.54
38	Classroom cohesion	0.53
39	Pre-term birth weight	0.53
40	Keller's Master Learning	0.53
41	Peer influences	0.53
42	Classroom management	0.52
43	Outdoor/adventure programs	0.52
44	Home environment	0.52
45	Socio-economic status	0.52
46	Interactive video methods	0.52
47	Professional development	0.51
48	Goals	0.50
49	Play programs	0.50
50	Second/third chance programs	0.50
51	Parental involvement	0.49
52	Small group learning	0.49
53	Questioning	0.48
54	Concentration/persistence/engagement	0.48
55	School effects	0.48
56	Motivation	0.48
57	Student ratings of quality of teaching	0.48
58	Early interventions	0.47
59	Self-concept	0.47
60	Preschool programs	0.45
61	Writing programs	0.44
62	Expectations	0.43
63	School size	0.43
64	Science programs	0.42
65	Cooperative learning	0.42

Rank	Influence	ES
66	Exposure to reading	0.42
67	Behavioral organizers/adjunct questions	0.41
68	Mathematics programs	0.40
69	Reducing anxiety	0.40
70	Social skills programs	0.39
71	Integrated curricula programs	0.39
72	Enrichment	0.39
73	Principals/school leaders	0.39
74	Career interventions	0.38
75	Time on task	0.38
*76	Psychotherapy programs	0.38
77	Computer-assisted instruction	0.37
78	Adjunct aids	0.37
79	Bilingual programs	0.37
80	Drama/arts programs	0.35
81	Creativity related to achievement	0.35
82	Attitude to mathematics/science	0.35
83	Frequent/effects of testing	0.34
84	Decreasing disruptive behavior	0.34
*85	Various teaching on creativity	0.34
86	Simulations	0.33
87	Inductive teaching	0.33
88	Ethnicity	0.32
89	Teacher effects	0.32
90	Drugs	0.32
91	Inquiry-based teaching	0.31
*92	Systems accountability	0.31
93	Ability grouping for gifted students	0.30
94	Homework	0.29
95	Home visiting	0.29
96	Exercise/relaxation	0.28
97	Desegregation	0.28

(Continued)

Rank	Influence	ES
98	Teaching test-taking	0.27
99	Use of calculators	0.27
*100	Volunteer tutors	0.26
101	Lack of illness	0.25
102	Mainstreaming	0.24
103	Values/moral education programs	0.24
104	Competitive versus individualistic learning	0.24
105	Programmed instruction	0.23
106	Summer school	0.23
107	Finances	0.23
108	Religious schools	0.23
109	Individualized instruction	0.22
110	Visual/audio-visual methods	0.22
111	Comprehensive teaching reforms	0.22
*112	Teacher verbal ability	0.22
113	Class size	0.21
114	Charter schools	0.20
115	Aptitude/treatment interactions	0.19
116	Extra-curricular programs	0.19
117	Learning hierarchies	0.19
118	Co-/team teaching	0.19
119	Personality	0.18
120	Within-class grouping	0.18
121	Special college programs	0.18
122	Family structure	0.18
*123	School counseling effects	0.18
124	Web-based learning	0.18
125	Matching learning styles	0.17
126	Teacher immediacy	0.16
127	Home-school programs	0.16
128	Problem-based learning	0.15
129	Sentence-combining programs	0.15

Rank	Influence	ES
130	Mentoring	0.15
131	Ability grouping	0.12
132	Diet	0.12
133	Gender	0.12
134	Teacher education	0.12
135	Distance education	0.11
136	Teacher subject matter knowledge	0.09
*137	Changing school calendar/timetable	0.09
138	Out-of-school curricular experiences	0.09
139	Perceptual motor programs	0.08
140	Whole language	0.06
*141	Diversity of students	0.05
142	College halls of residence	0.05
143	Multi-grade/age classes	0.04
144	Student control over learning	0.04
145	Open versus traditional learning spaces	0.01
146	Summer vacation	−0.02
147	Welfare policies	−0.12
148	Retention	−0.13
149	Television	−0.18
150	Mobility	−0.34

Source: Adapted from Hattie (2012). Reproduced with permission.

*Represents an effect that has been added to the original list since the publication of *Visible Learning: A Synthesis of Over 800 Meta-Analyses Relating to Achievement* (Hattie, 2009).

Note: Effect size for collective teacher efficacy published separately in Hattie (2015), The Applicability of Visible Learning to Higher Education, *Scholarship of Teaching and Learning in Psychology*, 1(1), 79–91. In-chapter references to effect sizes for identifying similarities and differences, note-taking, organizing and transforming notes, positive behavior, summarizing, transforming and organizing conceptual knowledge, and wide reading are not listed here and are based on the ongoing synthesis of learning strategies research.

REFERENCES

Adams, G. L., & Engelmann, S. (1996). *Research on direct instruction: 20 years beyond DISTAR.* Seattle, WA: Educational Achievement Systems.

Ainsworth, L. (2014). *Unwrapping the standards: A simple process to make standards manageable.* New York: Houghton Mifflin Harcourt.

Alexander, A. (2008). *Towards dialogic teaching: Rethinking classroom talk* (4th ed.). York, England: Dialogos.

American Educational Research Association (AERA), Knowledge Forum. (2016). *Research fact sheet: Counter-intuitive findings from the science of learning.* Retrieved from http://www.aera.net/Portals/38/docs/Annual_Meeting/2016%20Annual%20 Meeting/2016%20Knowledge%20Forum/Chi.pdf

American Psychological Association, Coalition for Psychology in Schools and Education. (2015). *Top 20 principles from psychology for preK–12 teaching and learning.* Retrieved from http://www.apa.org/ed/schools/cpse/top-twenty -principles.pdf

Anderson, N. J. (2002). *The role of metacognition in second language teaching and learning.* Retrieved from http://www.cal.org/resources/digest/0110anderson .html

Anderson, R. C., Wilson, P. T., & Fielding, L. G. (1988). Growth in reading and how children spend their time outside of school. *Reading Research Quarterly, 23,* 285–303.

Applebee, A. N., Langer, J. A., Nystrand, M., & Gamoran, A. (2003). Discussion-based approaches to developing understanding: Classroom instruction and student performance in middle and high school English. *American Educational Research Journal, 40,* 685–730.

Arrasmith, D., & Smith, K. (2001). The TRAITS of an effective reader. *Journal of School Improvement, 2*(1), 15–19.

Ashton-Warner, S. (1965). *Teacher.* New York: Simon & Schuster.

Bandura, A. (1997). *Self-efficacy: The exercise of control.* New York: Freeman.

Beckham-Hungler, D, & Williams, C. (2003). Teaching words that students misspell: Spelling instruction and young children's writing. *Language Arts, 80,* 299–309.

Betts, E. A. (1946). *Foundations of reading instruction.* New York: American Book Company.

Biggs, J., & Collis, K. (1982). *Evaluating the quality of learning: The SOLO taxonomy.* New York: Academic Press.

Blyth, C. (2009). *The art of conversation: A guided tour of a neglected pleasure.* New York: Gotham Books.

Bransford, J. D., Brown, A. L., & Cocking, R. R. (Eds.). (2000). *How people learn: Brain, mind, experience, and school.* Washington, DC: National Academy Press.

Caughlan, S., Juzwik, M. M., Borsheim-Black, C., Kelly, S., & Fine, J. G. (2013). English teacher candidates developing dialogically organized instructional practices. *Research in the Teaching of English, 47*(3), 212–246.

Cazden, C. B. (1988). *Classroom discourse: The language of teaching and learning.* Portsmouth, NH: Heinemann.

Clark, A. M., Anderson, R. C., Kuo, L., Kim, I. H., Archodidou, A., & Nguyen-Jahiel, K. (2003). Collaborative reasoning: Expanding ways for children to talk and think in school. *Educational Psychology Review, 15*(2), 181–198.

Clarke, S., Timperley, H., & Hattie J. (2003). *Unlocking formative assessment: Practical strategies for enhancing students' learning in the primary and intermediate classroom* (NZ Ed.). Auckland: Hodder Moa Beckett.

Clay, M. M. (1979). *Concepts about print tests: Sand and stones.* Portsmouth, NH: Heinemann.

Clay, M. M. (2003). Child development. In J. Flood, D. Lapp, J. R. Squire, & J. M. Jensen (Eds.), *Handbook of research in teaching the English language arts* (2nd ed.) (pp. 46–52). Mahwah, NJ: Erlbaum.

Connor, C., Phillips, B., Kaschak, M., Apel, K., Kim, Y., . . . & Lonigan, C. (2014). Comprehension tools for teachers: Reading for understanding from prekindergarten through fourth grade. *Educational Psychology Review, 26*(3), 379–401.

Csikszentmihalyi, M. (1990). *Flow: The psychology of optimal experience.* New York: Harper and Row.

Daiute, C., & Dalton, B. (1993). Collaboration between children learning to write: Can novices be masters? *Cognition and Instruction, 10*, 281–333.

Daniels, H. (2002). *Literature circles: Voice and choice in book clubs and reading groups* (2nd ed.). York, ME: Stenhouse.

Daniels, H. (2006). What's the next big thing with literature circles? *Voices from the Middle, 13*(4), 10–15.

Davey, B. (1983). Think aloud: Modeling the cognitive processes of reading comprehension. *Journal of Reading, 27*(1), 44–47.

Dolch, E. W. (1948). *Problems in reading.* Champaign, IL: Garrard.

DuFour, R., DuFour, R., & Eaker, R. (2008). *Professional learning communities at work: New insights for best practices.* Bloomington, IN: Solution Tree.

Duke, N. (2000). 3.6 minutes per day: The scarcity of informational texts in first grade. *Reading Research Quarterly, 35*(2), 202–224.

Durkin, D. (1978/79). What classroom observations reveal about reading comprehension instruction. *Reading Research Quarterly, 14*, 481–533.

Durkin, D. (1981). Schools don't teach comprehension. *Educational Leadership, 37*, 453–454.

Elliot, A., & Harackiewicz, J. (1994). Goal setting, achievement orientation, and intrinsic motivation: A meditational analysis. *Journal of Personality and Social Psychology, 66*(5), 968–980.

Fearn, L., & Farnan, N. (2001). *Interactions: Teaching writing and the language arts.* Boston: Houghton Mifflin.

Fendick, F. (1990). *The correlation between teacher clarity of communication and student achievement gain: A meta-analysis.* Unpublished doctoral dissertation, University of Florida, Gainesville.

Fisher, D., & Frey, N. (2008). Homework and the gradual release of responsibility: Making "responsibility" possible. *English Journal, 98*(2), 40–45.

Fisher, D., & Frey, N. (2012). Close reading in elementary school. *The Reading Teacher, 66*(3), 179–188.

Fisher, D., & Frey, N. (2014a). Closely reading informational texts in the primary grades. *The Reading Teacher, 68*, 222–227.

Fisher, D., & Frey, N. (2014b). *Text-dependent questions, grades K–5: Pathways to close and critical reading.* Thousand Oaks, CA: Corwin.

Fisher, D., Frey, N., Anderson, H., & Thayre, M. (2015). *Text-dependent questions: Pathways to close and critical reading, grades K–5.* Thousand Oaks, CA: Corwin.

Fisher, D., Frey, N., & Hattie, J. (2016). *Visible learning for literacy: Implementing the practices that work best to accelerate student learning.* Thousand Oaks, CA: Corwin.

Fisher, D., Frey, N., & Lapp, D. (2009). *In a reading state of mind: Brain research, teacher modeling, and comprehension instruction.* Newark, DE: International Reading Association.

Fountas, I. C., & Pinnell, G. S. (2001). *Guiding readers and writers grades 3–6: Teaching comprehension, genre, and content literacy.* Portsmouth, NH: Heinemann.

Ganske, K. (1999). The developmental spelling analysis: A measure of orthographic knowledge. *Educational Assessment, 6*(1), 41–70.

Ganske, K. (2000). *Word journeys: Assessment-guided phonics, spelling, and vocabulary instruction.* New York: Guilford.

Gibbs, V., & Proctor, S. (1977). Reading together: An experiment with the neurological-impress method. *Contemporary Education, 48*, 156–157.

Ginsburg-Block, M., Rohrbeck, C., & Fantuzzo, J. (2006). A meta-analytic review of social, self-concept, and behavioral outcomes of peer-assisted learning. *Journal of Educational Psychology, 98*(4), 732–749.

Ginsburg-Block, M., Rohrbeck, C., Lavigne, N., & Fantuzzo, J. (2008). Peer assisted learning: An academic strategy for enhancing motivation among diverse students. In A. E. Gottfried & C. Hudley (Eds.), *Academic motivation and the culture of school in childhood and adolescence* (pp. 247–273). New York: Oxford University Press.

Goddard, R. D., Hoy, W. K., & Hoy, A. W. (2000). Collective teacher efficacy: Its meaning, measure, and impact on student achievement. *American Educational Research Journal, 37*, 479–507.

Goodman, L. (2001). A tool for learning: Vocabulary self-awareness. In C. Blanchfield (Ed.), *Creative vocabulary: Strategies for teaching vocabulary in grades K–12* (p. 46). Fresno, CA: San Joaquin Valley Writing Project.

Goodman, Y. M., & Burke, C. L. (1972). *Reading miscue inventory manual: Procedure for diagnosis and evaluation.* New York: Macmillan.

Graham, S., Berninger, V., & Fan, W. (2007). The structural relationship between writing attitude and writing achievement in first and third grade students. *Contemporary Educational Psychology, 32*(3), 516–536.

Gray, W. S. (1925). Reading activities in school and society. In G. M. Whipple (Ed.), *The twenty-fourth yearbook of the National Society for the Study of Education, Part I* (pp. 1–18). Bloomington, IL: Public School Publishing.

Halliday, M. A. K. (1975). *Learning how to mean: Explorations in the development of language.* London: Edward Arnold.

Hansen, J. (2001). *When writers read.* Portsmouth, NH: Heinemann.

Harste, J. C. (1994). Literacy as curricular conversations about knowledge, inquiry, and morality. In R. B. Ruddell, M. R. Ruddell, & H. Singer (Eds.), *Theoretical models and processes of reading* (4th ed., pp. 1220–1242). Newark, DE: International Reading Association.

Hasbrouck, J., & Tindal, G. A. (2006). Oral reading fluency norms: A valuable assessment tool for reading teachers. *Reading Teacher, 59*(7), 636–644.

Hattie, J. (2009). *Visible learning: A synthesis of over 800 meta-analyses relating to achievement.* New York: Routledge.

Hattie, J. (2012). *Visible learning for teachers: Maximizing impact on learning.* New York: Routledge.

Hattie, J., & Donoghue, G. (2016). Learning strategies: A synthesis and conceptual model. *Nature: Science of Learning, 1.* doi:10.1038/npjscilearn.2016.13

Hattie, J., & Timperley, H. (2007). The power of feedback. *Review of Educational Research, 77*(1), 81–112.

Hattie, J. (n. d.). *Visible Learning, tomorrow's schools, the mindsets that make the difference in education* [PowerPoint presentation]. Visible Learning Laboratories, University of Auckland, New Zealand. Retrieved from http://docplayer .net/4137828-Visible-learning-that-make-the-difference-in-education -john-hattie-visible-learning-laboratories-university-of-auckland.html

Head, M. H., & Readence, J. E. (1986). Anticipation guides: Meaning through prediction. In E. K. Dishner, T. W. Bean, J. E. Readence, & D. W. Moore (Eds.), *Reading in the content areas* (2nd ed., pp. 229–234). Dubuque, IA: Kendall-Hunt.

Heckelman, R. G. (1986). N. I. M. revisited. *Academic Therapy, 21,* 411–420.

Henderson, E. H. (1990). *Teaching spelling* (2nd ed.). Boston: Houghton Mifflin.

Henk, W. A. (1983). Adapting the NIM to improve comprehension. *Academic Therapy, 19,* 97–101.

Henk, W. A., & Selders, M. L. (1984). Test of synonymic scoring of cloze passages. *The Reading Teacher, 38,* 282–287.

Herbel-Eisenmann, B. A., & Breyfogle, M. L. (2005). Questioning our patterns of questioning. *Mathematics Teaching in the Middle School, 10*(9), 484–489.

Houser, K. (n. d.). *Tracking my progress: Fluency.* Retrieved from http://www .mshouser.com/instructional-coaching/tracking-my-progress-fluency

Hudson, R. F., Lane, H. B., & Pullen, P. C. (2005). Reading fluency assessment and instruction: What, why, and how? *Reading Teacher, 58*(8), 702–714.

Hunter, M. (1982). *Mastery teaching.* El Segundo, CA: TIP Publications.

Iacoboni, M., Molnar-Szakacs, I., Gallese, V., Buccino, G., Mazziotta, J. C., & Rizzolatti, G. (2005). Grasping the intentions of others with one's own mirror neuron system. *PLoS Biology, 3*(3), e79.

Jeong, J., Gaffney, J. S., & Choi, J. (2010). Availability and use of informational texts in second-, third-, and fourth-grade classrooms. *Research in the Teaching of English, 44*(4), 435–456.

Joos, M. (1961). *The five clocks.* New York: Harcourt, Brace & World.

Kane, T. J., & Staiger, D. O. (2012). *Gathering feedback for teaching: Combining high-quality observations with student surveys and achievement gains.* Seattle, WA: Bill & Melinda Gates Foundation.

Kear, D. J., Coffman, G. A., McKenna, M. C., & Ambrosio, A. (2000). Measuring attitude toward writing: A new tool for teachers. *Reading Teacher, 54*(1), 10–23.

Knight, J. (2014). *Focus on teaching: Using video for high-impact instruction.* Thousand Oaks, CA: Corwin.

Kush, J. C., & Watkins, M. W. (1996). Long-term stability of children's attitudes toward reading. *Journal of Educational Research, 89,* 315–319.

Lai, M., Wilson, A., McNaughton, S., & Hsiao, S. (2014). Improving achievement in secondary schools: Impact of a literacy project on reading comprehension and secondary school qualifications. *Reading Research Quarterly, 49*(3), 305–334.

Lamott, A. (1995). *Bird by bird: Some instructions on writing and life.* New York: Anchor Books.

Locke, E. A., & Latham, G. P. (1990) *A theory of goal setting and task performance.* Englewood Cliffs, NJ: Prentice-Hall.

Marita, S. M. (1965). *A comparative study of beginning reading achievement under three classroom organizational patterns--modified individualized, three-to-five groups, and whole-class language-experience* (Report No. CRP-2659). Milwaukee, WI: Marquette University. (ERIC Document Reproduction Service No. ED003477)

Martinez, M., Roser, N. L., & Strecker, S. (1998). "I never thought I could be a star": A Readers Theatre ticket to fluency. *The Reading Teacher, 52,* 326–334.

McCarrier, A., Pinnell, G. S., & Fountas, I. C. (2000). *Interactive writing: How language and literacy come together, K–2.* Portsmouth, NH: Heinemann.

McKenna, M. C., & Kear, D. (1990). Measuring attitude toward reading: A new tool for teachers. *The Reading Teacher, 43,* 626–639.

Meece, J. L., Anderman, E. M., & Anderman L. H. (2006). Classroom goal structure, student motivation, and academic achievement. *Annual Review of Psychology, 57,* 487–503.

Michaels, S., O'Connor, M. C., Hall, M. W., & Resnick, L. B. (2010). *Accountable talk® sourcebook: For classroom conversation that works* (v.3.1). University of Pittsburgh Institute for Learning. Retrieved from http://ifl.lrdc.pitt.eduhttp://ifl.lrdc.pitt.edu

Murphy, P. K., Wilkinson, I. A. G., Soter, A. O., Hennessey, M. N., & Alexander, J. F. (2009). Examining the effects of classroom discussion on students' high-level comprehension of text: A meta-analysis. *Journal of Educational Psychology, 101,* 740–764.

Nation, K., & Hulme, C. (1997). Phonemic segmentation, not onset rime segmentation, predicts early reading and spelling skills. *Reading Research Quarterly, 32,* 154–167.

National Institute of Child Health and Human Development. (2000). *Report of the National Reading Panel. Teaching children to read: An evidence-based assessment of the scientific research literature on reading and its implications for reading instruction* (NIH Publication No. 00–4769). Washington, DC: US Government Printing Office.

Palincsar, A. S., & Brown, A. L. (1986). Interactive teaching to promote independent learning from text. *The Reading Teacher, 39,* 771–777.

Paris, S. G. (2005). Reinterpreting the development of reading skills. *Reading Research Quarterly, 40*(2), 184–202.

Paris, S. G., Wasik, B. A., & Turner, J. C. (1991). The development of strategic readers. In R. Barr, M. L. Kamil, P. Mosenthal, & P. D. Pearson (Eds.), *Handbook of reading research* (vol. 2, pp. 609–640). New York: Longman.

Parker, W. (2010). Listening to strangers: Classroom discussion in democratic education. *Teachers College Record, 112*(11), 2815–2832.

Pearson, P. D., & Johnson, D. D. (1978). *Teaching reading comprehension.* New York: Holt, Rinehart and Winston.

Pew Research Center. (2013). E-reading rises as device ownership jumps. Retrieved from http://www.pewinternet.org/files/old-media//Files/Reports/2014/PIP_E-reading _011614.pdfhttp://www.pewinternet.org/files/old-media//Files/Reports/2014/ PIP_E-reading_011614.pdf

Piaget, J. (1952). *The origins of intelligence in children.* New York: W. W. Norton.

Purkey, W. W. (1992). An introduction to invitational theory. *Journal of Invitational Theory and Practice, 1*(1), 5–15.

Raphael, T. E. (1986). Teaching learners question-answer relationships, revisited. *The Reading Teacher, 39,* 516–522.

Rasinski, T. V. (2003). Fluency is fundamental. *Instructor, 113*(4), 16–20.

Rasinski, T. V. (2010). *The fluent reader: Oral reading strategies for building word recognition, fluency, and comprehension* (2nd ed.). New York: Scholastic.

Rizzolatti, G., & Craighero, L. (2004). The mirror-neuron system. *Annual Review of Neuroscience 27*(1), 169–192.

Ross, P., & Gibson, S. A. (2010). Exploring a conceptual framework for expert noticing during literacy instruction. *Literacy Research & Instruction, 49*(2), 175–193.

Rowe, M. B. (1986). Wait time: Slowing down may be a way of speeding up! *Journal of Teacher Education, 37*, 43–50.

Schmitt, M. C. (1990). A questionnaire to measure children's awareness of strategic reading processes. *Reading Teacher, 43*, 454–461.

Schroth, M. L. (1992). The effects of delay of feedback on a delayed concept formation transfer task. *Contemporary Educational Psychology 17*(1), 78–82.

Stanovich, K. E. (1986). Matthew effects in reading: Some consequences of individual differences in the acquisition of literacy. *Reading Research Quarterly, 21*, 360–406.

Templeton, S., & Morris, D. (1999). Questions teachers ask about spelling. *Reading Research Quarterly, 34*, 102–112.

Topping, K. (2001). *Peer assisted learning*. Brookline, MA: Brookline Books.

Tyler, B., & Chard, D. (2000). Using readers theatre to foster fluency in struggling readers: A twist on the repeated reading strategy. *Reading & Writing Quarterly, 16*, 163–168.

Vygotsky, L. S. (1962). *Thought and language*. Cambridge, MA: MIT Press.

Vygotsky, L. S. (1978). *Mind and society: The development of higher psychological processes*. Cambridge, MA: Harvard University Press.

Wenger, E. (1998). *Communities of practice*. Cambridge, UK: University of Cambridge Press.

Wilkinson, I. A. G., & Nelson, K. (2013). Role of discussion in reading comprehension In J. Hattie & E. M. Anderson (Eds.), *International guide to student achievement* (pp. 299–302). New York: Routledge.

Worthy, J., & Broaddus, K. (2001/2002). Fluency beyond the primary grades: From group performance to silent, independent reading. *The Reading Teacher, 55*, 334–343.

Wylie, R. E., & Durrell, D. D. (1970). Teaching vowels through phonograms. *Elementary English, 47*, 787–791.

Yopp, H. K. (1995). A test for assessing phonemic awareness in young children. *The Reading Teacher, 49*, 20–29.

Zhang, X., Anderson, R. C., Morris, J., Miller, B., Nguyen-Jahiel, K. T., . . . & Hsu, J. Y. (2016). Improving children's competence as decision makers. *American Educational Research Journal, 53*(1), 194–223.

CHILDREN'S LITERATURE CITED

Applegate, K. (2012). *The one and only Ivan*. New York: Harper.

Asch, F. (2014). *Moonbear's shadow*. New York: Aladdin.

Avi. (2003). *Crispin: The cross of lead*. New York: Hyperion.

Carroll, L. (2008). *Alice in wonderland*. Hoboken, NJ: Brandywine Press. [Original work published 1865]

Cushman, K. (1995). *Catherine, called Birdy*. New York: Clarion.

Dahl, R. (1988). *Matilda*. New York: Penguin Books

De Angeli, M. (1990). *The door in the wall*. New York: Yearling.

de la Peña, M. (2015). *Last stop on Market Street*. New York: Putnam.

Deedy, C. A. (2014). *Martina the beautiful coackroach: A Cuban folktale*. Atlanta, GA: Peachtree.

DeGross, M. (1994). *Donavan's word jar*. New York: Trophy.

Harman, R. (2005). *The water cycle: Evaporation, condensation, and erosion*. Portsmouth, NH: Heinemann.

Karlins, M. (1998). *Music over Manhattan*. New York: Doubleday.

L'Engle, M. (1962). *A wrinkle in time*. New York: Farrar, Strauss, and Giroux

Osborne, M. P. (2003). *High tide in Hawaii: Magic Treehouse #28*. New York: Random House.

Pallota, J., & Bolster, R. (2014). *Who would win?* [Book series]. New York: Scholastic.

Papunya School. (2001). *Papunya School book of country and history*. Sydney, AUS: Allen & Unwin.

Paulsen, G. (1987). *Hatchet*. New York: Viking Penguin.

Randell, B. (1995). *Baby bear's present*. Boston, MA: Rigby.

Rattini, K. B. (2014). *Seed to plant*. Washington, DC: National Geographic Society.

Rohmer, H. (1999). *Honoring our ancestors: Stories and pictures by fourteen artists*. San Francisco, CA: Children's Book Press.

Schwartz, D. (2004). *How much is a million?* New York: HarperCollins.

Scieszka, J. (1996). *The true story of the three little pigs*. New York: Puffin Books.

Scieszka, J., & Smith, L. (1992). *The stinky cheese man and other fairly stupid tales*. New York: Viking.

Silverstein, S. (1964). *The giving tree*. New York: Harper & Row.

Swinburne, S. R. (1999). *Guess whose shadow?* Honesdale, PA: Boyds Mills Press.

Weatherford, C. B. (2015). *Voice of freedom: Fannie Lou Hamer*. Somerville, MA: Candlewick.

Wick, W. (1997). *A drop of water*. New York: Scholastic.

INDEX

A SAGE Publishing Company

Helping educators make the greatest impact

CORWIN HAS ONE MISSION: to enhance education through intentional professional learning.

We build long-term relationships with our authors, educators, clients, and associations who partner with us to develop and continuously improve the best evidence-based practices that establish and support lifelong learning.

BECAUSE ALL TEACHERS ARE LEADERS

Douglas Fisher, Nancy Frey, John Hattie

Renowned literacy experts Douglas Fisher and Nancy Frey work with John Hattie to apply his groundbreaking research to literacy practices. These practices are "visible" because their purpose is clear, they are implemented at the right moment in a student's learning—surface, deep, and transfer—and their effect is tangible.

Douglas Fisher, Nancy Frey, John Hattie, Marisol Thayre

These companions to *Visible Learning for Literacy* show you how to use learning intentions, success criteria, formative assessment, and feedback to achieve profound instructional clarity. Make this the year you feel more assured about delivering sustained, comprehensive experiences that bring your students further, faster.

John Hattie, Douglas Fisher, Nancy Frey

All students can demonstrate more than a year's worth of mathematics learning for a year spent in school. In *Visible Learning for Mathematics*, six acclaimed educators show how you can design powerful, precision teaching by using the right strategy at each phase of the learning cycle—surface, deep, and transfer.

Also by Douglas Fisher & Nancy Frey

To order your copies, visit www.corwin.com/literacy

Use the Right Literacy Approach at the Right Time and Accelerate Student Learning

Discover the literacy practices that **ensure students demonstrate more than a year's worth of growth for every year spent in school.** Bring Douglas Fisher, Nancy Frey, or a member of their collaborative to your school or district for any of the following workshops.

INTRODUCTORY WORKSHOP

This workshop covers Visible Learning research; its connections to surface, deep, and transfer learning as it relates to literacy; the best literacy strategies to use in each stage of learning; and the tools for measuring your impact on student learning.

DETERMINING IMPACT

Participants will explore the importance of the effect sizes of different high-impact literacy approaches, and how to calculate your own effect size for classes and individual students. This workshop will also review effective components of successful response to intervention (RTI).

SURFACE LEARNING

Surface learning isn't superficial. A strong foundation of surface learning sets the stage for deeper learning. Participants will walk through different literacy approaches and participate in exercises that promote surface learning.

DEEP LEARNING

This workshop focuses on practical approaches for deep learning using Visible Learning research as a guide. Participants will walk through different approaches and participate in the exercises that promote deeper learning.

TRANSFER LEARNING

Participants will explore the importance of transfer learning, the paths that transfer learning can take, and the conditions needed for transfer. This workshop will also review strategies for teaching students to organize and transform conceptual knowledge.

RESPONSE TO INTERVENTION

With an effect size of 1.07, a successful RTI effort has great impact on students. Using examples and guides from *Visible Learning for Literacy*, participants will review successful approaches including screening, quality core instruction, progress monitoring, and supplemental and intensive intervention.

Who Should Attend:

- Principals
- Staff Development Directors
- Literacy/Reading Coaches
- English/Reading Department Chairs
- Reading Teacher/Specialists
- English Teachers
- Classroom Teachers

Learning Outcomes:

- Discover how to **build successful relationships with students,** critical to long-term student gains
- Understand **learning intentions and success criteria** and why they are so critical to student growth
- Explore the **three phases of learning—surface, deep, and transfer**
- Examine **key literacy strategies** that work best at each phase of learning and provide **built-in lessons and exercises**
- Discover how to use effect size and other assessment tools to **measure student learning**

To learn more about booking one or more of these workshops, please contact Corwin at 1-800-233-9936

DOUGLAS FISHER

NANCY FREY

MPACT
Making Literacy
Learning Visible

visible learning^{plus}

3 Ways to Get Started

1. Understand Your Baseline

School Capability Analysis

How does your school measure against the five strands of Visible Learning? Certified consultants will conduct a half-day site visit to collect and analyze baseline capability data to determine your school's readiness for Visible Learning^{plus}. A full written report is provided.

The Foundation Series

Begin your Visible Learning^{plus} journey by building your team's foundational knowledge of the Visible Learning research. Teachers and school leaders will receive tools for gathering evidence of effective practice and create a plan for making learning visible for all students.

2. Build Foundational Knowledge

Collaborative Impact Program

The Collaborative Impact program is our gold standard for sustainable reform, as it aligns system leaders, school leaders, and teachers with a proven process to build capacity for change over 3-5 years, with measurable results.

3. Drive Whole-System Reform

Seminars
Training
Consulting

**Contact your account manager at (800) 831-6640
or visit www.corwin.com/visiblelearning**